DO QUALITY DIFFERENTLY

The Playbook for Creating More Success in Biopharma (or any) Manufacturing

Clifford Berry and Amy D. Wilson, *Ph.D.*

February 2023

Cover Design & Illustrations by Amazing Studios Inc.,
www.amazingstudiosinc.com
Edited by Denise Willson, BEOP Inc., www.beop.ca
Interior Formatting & Design by Sanserofin Studio, www.sanserofin.com

ISBN 979-8-218-12324-6 (paperback)
ISBN 979-8-218-12326-0 (ebook)

Printed in the U.S.A.

This book is dedicated to daring innovators, respected early adopters,
and the people who will benefit.

Contents

Before enlightenment: Chop wood, carry water.
After enlightenment: Chop wood, carry water.
– A Traditional Zen Thought

Foreword

When Cliff and Amy told me they were thinking about writing a book about human and organizational performance in biopharmaceutical manufacturing to serve their work community, I was pretty excited to hear the news. I was always worried these ideas would be pigeonholed to the safety community. The world only gets better when we apply the knowledge of human and organizational performance to bigger and bigger problems. And Cliff and Amy know a lot about the challenges the biopharmaceutical manufacturing industry has faced over the last several years.

This playbook will help begin the discussion on how to think about using the fundamental ideas of human performance to challenge operational, shall we say, opportunities. Just the effort to translate these ideas into a more effective message for the biopharmaceutical manufacturing industry is a great idea. It takes nerve and skill to do what Cliff and Amy have done on the following pages, and they did it with skill and agility.

Humans In Biopharmaceutical Manufacturing
Humans are the most important part of the success that this industry creates

i

over and over in doing this important work. The adaptive skills workers bring to this complex and detailed industry allow success to be snatched from the jaws of failure on an almost routine basis. And they do so daily in a highly regulated and highly disciplined manufacturing context. These workers are the secret sauce that makes this industry a success.

Humans are also the least reliable part of the manufacturing process. When failure happens, it is fairly easy to see where a person or team failed to do the necessary things to make a batch succeed. People are fallible; they make mistakes and misinterpret signals all the time. In many ways, industry workers are the weakest links in the manufacturing model.

How can these two ideas coexist?

The answer is: "Quite well, thank you."

This book will help you and your company build a case for understanding the need for change in how we have traditionally seen workers within our manufacturing systems. This shift in thinking can dramatically alter an organization's approach to operations. The movement towards building processes and procedures that understand the adaptive quality of the workforce to create operational success will gift your organization with an entirely new set of questions to ask and answers to discover.

Cliff and Amy have taken their years of experience understanding high-risk system performance and applied what they've learned to similar but different problems. This book will lead you to discover an entirely new set of questions that will reveal more helpful answers.

Enjoy the ride.

Todd Conklin

Todd Conklin spent almost thirty years at Los Alamos National Laboratory as a Senior Advisor for Organizational and Safety Culture. He has since retired from that organization and now works as a human performance consultant to executive groups and work teams. Todd holds a Ph.D. in organizational behavior. He has written several books, including *Pre-Accident Investigations*, *The 5 Principles of Human Performance*, and *Do Safety Differently*. Todd is the host of the Pre-Accident Investigations Podcast, an ongoing discussion about doing safety differently.

Introduction

Jens Rasmussen, a highly influential cognitive science, human factors, and safety science researcher, wisely stated, "When entering a study of human performance in real-life tasks, one rapidly finds oneself 'rushing in where angels fear to tread'. It turns out to be a truly interdisciplinary study for which an acceptable frame of reference has not yet been established, and interaction between rather general hypothesis, tests, methods, and detailed analysis is necessary." This quote was universally true in 1970. Now, in 2022 when this book was written, there are acceptable frames of reference available. Yet those acceptable frames of reference have not been adopted by the biopharmaceutical industry and its regulators.

Why is this a problem? Because we are not, as an industry, learning the right things from our failures. And we are not learning the right things from our successes, or even learning from our successes at all.

According to the New York Times, in April of 2021, a biopharma manufacturing plant discarded five lots of the AstraZeneca vaccine for COVID-19 due to manufacturing issues. Each lot was the equivalent of two to three million doses. That same biopharma plant determined it was necessary to destroy up to fifteen million doses of the Johnson & Johnson COVID-19 vaccine due to related issues. The news story included statements attributed to plant employees and reports. *Errors were not investigated to determine the root cause. Mistakes were not investigated adequately. Investigations were terminated without sufficient cause.*

The article told the story of an imperfect system and operational failure—a story we can all relate to. Business performance led to product quality failure that damaged the company's reputation and further stained the industry. Millions of dollars in company revenue were lost, and up to thirty million people were left waiting for a COVID-19 vaccine. To put that into perspective, the entire population of Canada is a bit over thirty-seven million people, and almost two hundred countries have a population lower than thirty million. This was a quality failure on a massive scale.

We *must* learn the right lessons from our failures and successes.

The lessons in this book were learned while integrating human and organizational performance principles and practices at multiple biopharmaceutical companies, eight manufacturing sites, and eleven factories. Our combined experience in improving operations and manufacturing performance across multiple industrial sectors spans over forty years. Our real-time experiences with frontline workers, support staff, and leaders helped to create the learning within these pages. We understand the problems manufacturing facilities and their employees face and are confident this book will help you address many of the issues you and your plant struggle with today.

While numerous articles and books helped develop our fluency, this book is different in that it provides helpful *how-to* guidance regarding applying that fluency to a biopharmaceutical manufacturing workplace. *Do Quality Differently* is a playbook for what happens at the *blue line*[1]. A playbook for what needs to be done to better learn from and improve what happens at the blue line. A playbook that describes the local workplace factors and system and organizational factors that heavily influence product quality and overall performance outcomes.

The purpose of this book is to provide biopharmaceutical leaders, practitioners, and regulators with a reference for change—and why change is absolutely necessary to improve the likelihood of manufacturing good quality

---

1 Blue line is a contemporary human factors and system safety term that refers to the reality of how work is actually done and acknowledges the necessity of worker adaptation in managing risk and creating success.

products for patients. W. Edwards Deming defined good quality as a predictable degree of uniformity and dependability with a quality standard suited to the customer. This includes meeting defined regulatory requirements in the biopharmaceutical industry.

While written in plain language using biopharmaceutical industry terminology and based on a wide range of industry experiences, the guidance provided is transferable to any industry where there are risks of harm to what an organization values in their operations. Harm to what an organization values, aka assets, may be falls from heights and electrocutions that are life-changing or fatal for electrical lineworkers, lost and discarded batches of drug product in biopharma manufacturing that are needed by patients, a medication administered in a healthcare setting that results in the death of a patient, or a nuclear reactor tripping off-line during a severe weather event. Any company or manufacturing facility could use the guidance provided in this book to reduce or eliminate recurring production failures. Regardless of the industry, undesired outcomes are still undesired outcomes, and they are influenced by latent conditions that are the result of decisions made by organizations and leaders that create the context of work and system weaknesses.

What are some examples of those latent conditions in biopharmaceutical manufacturing? What about that ten-digit material number that lacks chunking[2], and where the first three and last three characters are always the same? Consider the inconsistent use of red and green as a coding technique to indicate the status of a pump, valve, or breaker—locally or on a control console. Then there is the clumsily worded automation prompt leading to an irreversible step that, when answered incorrectly, dumps the product down

---

2 Chunking is when a long string of characters is broken up into smaller strings or chunks by inserting spaces or dashes as delimiters. For examples of chunking, look at the account number on one of your credit cards or the phone number in your email signature.

the drain. Or a crew staffing change that scatters knowledgeable performers of critical unit operations. These conditions, which are oftentimes recognized in retrospect after a failure, are almost always present during successful operations for months to years before a significant mishap.

The industry has hit a dead end on improving the current situation. Perhaps the industry's continued dedication to standard engineering and quality management techniques is unfit to address complex systems. Management at every biopharmaceutical manufacturing plant today, including the plant noted in the New York Times article, likely believes proper systems are already in place and working well. A state of control does exist. There are assurances to gauge reliability and product quality. Yet batches continue to be lost, drug shortages loom, and the public's distrust grows. Instead of rehashing old ways, we need to look to the new.

The fact that you are reading this book likely means you are considering thinking differently about operational success and failure. You are curious about how systems work to manage risk, and you are open to trying something new.

This book is the perfect place to start.

While your sentiment may not currently be shared with others in your workplace, including key leaders and influential colleagues, we encourage you to move forward. This is not unusual. There is the area manager that shares that they generally agree that people want to do a good job, but in their department that is not the case with all workers. We all know a Continuous Improvement practitioner who will argue that all the organization needs is increased rigor of Lean Six Sigma efforts. And of course, we have all met the department director who complains that, if people would just follow the procedures we give them, then all adverse events would be prevented. The good news is that you won't need to convince everyone to move your organization to a tipping point of improved performance. In fact, you need as little as 25 percent to incite change[3]. This book will help you adjust systems to improve operational performance so that even resisters might agree to participate. Most will become converts and advocates based on the results that will follow.

The information presented in the following chapters is intended to match the typical steps necessary to create the change that supports a human and organizational performance integration journey. Making these changes within an organization is not easy. While small changes will happen quickly, it takes years to shift the performance of an entire organization. We'll teach you why it's best to be patient yet relentless. You'll learn why and how to contest misguided opinions suggesting people are a hazard to systems. You'll understand industry bias and ways to overcome groupthink. We will show you when to meet people where they are, the best ways to gather support, and how to keep your chin up when the backsliding occurs.

Loaded with examples, each chapter tackles relatable manufacturing problems and solutions. Our work in the biopharmaceutical industry, aka biopharma, has become more complex. Contemporary human factors and system safety thinking originating from the safety domain can be applied to biopharma manufacturing—improving performance by enhancing the robustness and resilience of operations. We require new ways of thinking when approaching system improvement, and this book will help shape how you see people, technology, and work.

Do Quality Differently makes essential human and organizational performance information accessible to everyone within the biopharmaceutical manufacturing community and beyond. It also serves as a bridge to the original

---

3 A 2018 study from Pennsylvania State University found that when the size of a minority committed to social change reached just one-quarter of the group, it was consistently able to establish a new norm in the larger group, a finding with implications for behavior in the workplace, online, and in our communities.

writings of the highly regarded authors whose work we have referenced and employ in our explanations.

Be ready to celebrate the small wins. Positive change affects workers, leaders, organizations, and of course, patients. And when the big wins come, you'll feel a sense of accomplishment. Other companies and regulators will take notice of the improvements to your organization's performance and culture, and that curiosity will spark broader change. Be the catalyst for change. *Do Quality Differently*.

More information can be found at www.doqualitydifferently.com.

Understanding 'Human Error'

While *Do Quality Differently* can drive change within the industry, the transformation must start somewhere—you. And your perspective regarding *human error* is vital to understanding how and why industry change is necessary.

Production losses are not a new issue. Neither is blaming manufacturing problems on staff closest to where the problem became visible. A 2019 report by the U.S. Food & Drug Administration (FDA) revealed that between 2013 and 2017, over 150 much-needed drugs went into shortage, and 62 percent of the shortages were caused by manufacturing problems. The report states that *mature quality management* is needed to improve current performance. This purportedly includes elements such as *vigilant attention to upgrading facilities and equipment, training that promotes superior performance, increased understanding of the product and manufacturing process, and statistical-based monitoring of manufacturing processes and laboratories.*

The FDA also suggests a *reduction in human error can lead to a system that prevents problems before they occur.* But what does this mean? If human error is reduced, system performance will improve? Or does it mean there will be fewer human errors if systems are improved? The statement reads as if the authors lack requisite knowledge to provide guidance on this thing called human error.

There are many definitions of human error. What all these definitions have in common is that human error is a label assigned to an action or assessment that has a negative consequence or fails to achieve a desired outcome. Stopping there by accepting such definitions ignores the system design and complexity that sets the stage for the undesired outcome.

The FDA Report on drug shortages provides guidance from a perspective that may actually be the origin of the problems. The focus areas that are being proposed as the solution are also creating and reinforcing the conditions that are influencing current performance. Yes, better facilities, better training, and better monitoring are always desirable, but perhaps other very necessary factors are missing or must be adjusted. Perhaps there is an additional focus that must exist within biopharma.

Consider how the European Commission uses the term human error in *The Rules Governing Medicinal Products in the European Union.* "Where human error is suspected or identified as the cause, this should be justified having taken care to ensure that process, procedural, or system-based errors or problems have not been overlooked, if present." Like the FDA, the European Commission does not understand that *error* is an *outcome*, a symptom of deeper system issues—organizational, technological, or both. If we truly have not overlooked process, procedural, or system we would not conclude that human error is the cause of undesired outcomes.

In failing to reject human error as a cause of mishaps, the regulators of biopharma are failing to adopt systems thinking[4] perspectives and methods, which leads to missing opportunities to improve the capacity and controls of systems to better handle disturbances and performance variability. This

---

4 According to McNab et al, system thinking involves exploring the characteristics of components within a system, such as work tasks and technology, and how they interconnect to improve understanding of how outcomes emerge from these interactions.

focus on human error by the biopharma regulators and those companies that it regulates de-emphasizes the organization's role in system design and distracts from the real work that must be done to create more operational success for patients.

As one reads the 124 pages of *Drug Shortages: Root Causes and Potential Solutions*, it must be noted the terms *human factors*[5] and *system safety*[6] are never mentioned. The International Ergonomics Society defines human factors (ergonomics) as the scientific discipline concerned with the understanding of interactions among humans and other elements of a system and the profession that applies theory, principles, data, and methods to design for human well-being and overall system performance.

In relation to medical devices, the FDA has defined human factors as the study of how people use technology, involving the interaction of human abilities, expectations, and limitations within work environments and system designs. The FDA medical device definition would be substantially appropriate if applied to biopharmaceutical manufacturing. But it isn't. Proper regulatory recognition and application of human factors in biopharmaceutical manufacturing is necessary to create more operational success.

The FDA report is incomplete. When reviewing the references cited, you will not find mention of books like *Behind Human Error*, *The Field Guide for Understanding 'Human Error'*, or any other text on human factors and system safety. The FDA report also fails to mention practices used by a growing number of biopharmaceutical manufacturing plants that manage risk differently—factories where quality deviation investigations do not assign human

---

5   In the biopharmaceutical industry, the term human factor(s) is often misused as a synonym for human error. The term should always be used in reference to work processes and technology being designed to fit people.

6   System safety is the forward-looking identification and control of hazards to acceptable levels to prevent mishaps.

error as a cause. Plants where reporting risks and near misses occur below the threshold of quality deviation. Regional manufacturing units where the right lessons are learned from failure and success. Companies where mistakes are not used against workers like demerit points from a department of motor vehicles. These factories boast leaders willing to learn about operational challenges from the experts who perform the work, rather than to find fault and badger with advice on their behaviors. They understand work context drives behaviors, systems create outcomes, and *human error is not a cause.*

In order to achieve less severe and less frequent operational upsets, human factors and system safety must extend to a macro-level focus that includes work context, and the interactions within the elements of the broader sociotechnical system. A holistic view that includes system inputs and outputs, and the recognition that success and failure are emergent properties of mostly well-functioning complex systems.

Operational risk can and should be managed differently within the biopharmaceutical industry if we are to improve quality. When people talk and work together in a way that manages risk more effectively, everyone wins. Unit operations are executed smoothly, and everyone involved is better prepared to respond to surprises. Teams learn from challenges and failures. Rework rates, discards, deviations, and undesired outcomes are measurably lowered. Outcomes improve while costs decrease, resulting in improved quality. Operational performance is changed.

You *can* manage operational risk better and thereby improve quality. Human and organizational performance gives you a way to do this.

Human and organizational performance is a holistic application of human factors and system safety that improves the management of risk in operations. Human and organizational performance was established based upon concepts originating from human factors and system safety, as well as organizational psychology and organizational development, driven by the practical need of workers, leaders and organizations to better manage risk present in systems. There is no definitive definition for human and organizational performance in the biopharmaceutical industry—or any other industry. There is no college major or accepted accreditation authority, and human and organizational performance practitioners may be educated and trained as industrial engineers, ergonomists, human factors engineers, organizational psychologists, or even sociologists. They may be professionals who specialize in continuous improvement, quality control, safety, or engineering. They include scientists and technicians. What all these people have in common is a passion to learn about everyday work to help organizations and people create more operational success through enhancing system robustness and resilience. Robustness makes a system more likely to withstand risk from known failure modes, while resilience helps a system extend performance when challenges force operations to the system boundaries.

According to David Woods, founder of resilience engineering as an approach to safety in complex systems, reliability is a record of the past, and focusing on reliability assumes the future will be the same as the past. And it never is. This is because there are finite resources and things in our world are always changing. To adapt to situations where resources become limited and change occurs, robustness and resilience is essential. While robustness and resilience are nouns, think of resilience as a verb—it is something that a system does, not has.

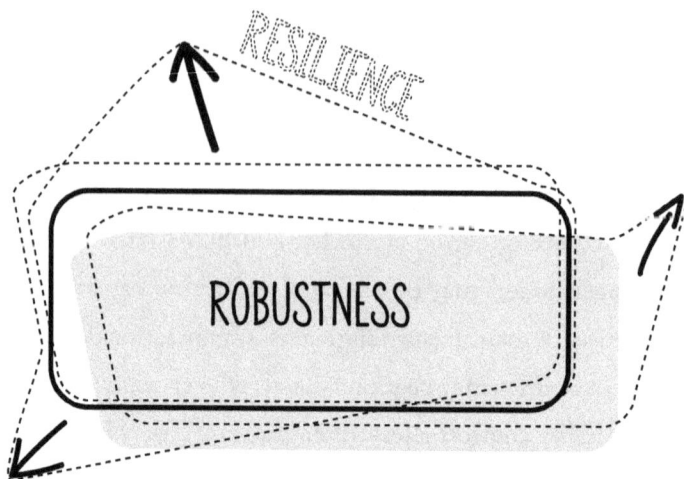

Illustration of Robustness versus Resilience.

Human and organizational performance was once called *human performance*[7] by the U.S. commercial nuclear industry. In the 1990s, the Institute of Nuclear Power Operations (INPO) established a human performance fundamentals training course to address a human performance recommendation from the Special Review Committee[8]. The number of equipment-related problems within the commercial nuclear power industry declined, and suddenly personnel and organizational performance factors became apparent. This training course was offered to thousands of nuclear industry workers across do zens of companies, and the training content became part of a nuclear plant evaluation criteria used by INPO.

A significant amount of the content in INPO's human performance

7 Human performance, or human and organizational performance, was born of concepts that originated in cognitive system engineering from the 1970s. Cognitive system engineering then evolved over thirty to forty years into what is now known as new view, safety differently, Safety-II, and resilience engineering; all of which share common ideas, concepts, and practices. Human and organizational performance has matured as it stayed connected to the offshoots of cognitive systems engineering.

8 The Special Review Committee on human performance was established to examine ways to create a working environment that enhanced human performance at nuclear plants.

fundamentals training course was influenced by the work of Dr. James Reason—primarily his books titled *Human Error* and *Managing the Risks of Organizational Accidents*. Dr. Reason's books were also heavily referenced within healthcare following the 1999 report called *To Err is Human: Building a Safer Health System*, which received widespread attention from the U.S. media. The INPO training materials were also influenced by authors such as Hollnagel, Woods, Rasmussen, Vaughn, Kletz, Deming, Wickens, Weick, Sutcliffe, Turner, Pidgeon, Hopkins, Senge, Gilbert, Norman, and Schein. In 2001, the training materials were consolidated into the *Human Performance Fundamentals Desk Reference* by INPO's National Academy of Training.

While it is difficult to locate the *Human Performance Fundamentals Desk Reference* outside of the U.S. commercial nuclear power industry, the Department of Energy's *Human Performance Improvement Handbook* is easily found using an internet search engine or from well-intentioned consultants. Like the *Human Performance Fundamentals Desk Reference*, this document synthesizes many resources that may be helpful to the beginner interested in human and organizational performance. But be aware. It also includes information and listed resources that are no longer contemporary guidance—details that may limit progress or cause unintentional harm to an organization. The world has continued to change since it was written as well as the scientific mosaic of human factors and system safety. Use it with caution and skepticism. Use it as a doorway to more contemporary perspectives of human factors and system safety.

The *Human Performance Improvement Handbook* is now mostly a historical artifact from an idyllic period where management attention and resources in both the commercial nuclear power industry and the Department of Energy helped pioneer new approaches to improve operational performance. This was a golden age of trying to think differently about operations, organizations, and performance. And while there was good progress made during this time and a clear change in how leaders in nuclear talked about human error and operational failure in the abstract, there was less progress in how many leaders responded and learned. Transformational progress was hampered by the limitations of the written guidance material and the shared underlying assumptions of the people in the nuclear industry. And human error was still believed to be a cause of operational failures.

Organizations that use the Department of Energy's *Human Performance Improvement Handbook* are bound to repeat the mistakes and limited success experienced by the U.S. commercial nuclear industry and the Department of Energy in the first decade of the 21st century. Instead, consider using the reference as you might a twenty-year-old encyclopedia.

A group of biopharmaceutical manufacturers working collectively through the organization BioPhorum came upon the work of the U.S. commercial nuclear industry in 2012. Representatives from over a dozen companies met to address the growing concerns of industry regulators and their organizations. Human error was the most assigned cause of quality deviations, and retraining was the common corrective action. Even today, it is not uncommon for a biopharmaceutical manufacturing plant to claim human error causes over 50 percent of its hundreds of quality deviations each year. A subset of those deviations leads to millions of dollars in lost product, rework, and delayed batch releases.

The group of biopharmaceutical manufacturing representatives that met in 2012 agreed to collaborate on efforts they framed as *Human Error Reduction.* Much of their learning that year (and in the following years) was based on the U.S. commercial nuclear industry and their informal relationship with INPO. Because of this, this group's published writings and training materials closely resembled the decades-old concepts espoused by INPO.

After all, what industry would not want to replicate the transformation that had taken place in the U.S. commercial nuclear industry since the Three Mile Island[9] accident occurred in 1979? The reliability of U.S. commercial nuclear reactors had improved by almost 100 percent, as measured by the industry's capacity factor[10] metric, moving from 48 percent in 1971 to 90 percent in 2010. One of the metrics the U.S. nuclear industry was most proud of was its industrial safety accident rate, which improved from 0.38 industrial accidents per 200,000 worker hours in 1997 to 0.09 in 2010. As a visitor to a nuclear power plant's training simulator control room, you'd witness a crew of licensed operators who execute emergency operating procedures to simulated plant events with precision, professionalism, and admirable teamwork as part of their frequent continuing training. Who wouldn't want that level of excellence in their workplace? It is reasonable to feel some amount of professional awe and operational envy.

Yet, there are pitfalls in attempting to replicate the recipe used by the nuclear industry. The nuclear industry transformation was not solely due to the text of their *Human Performance Fundamentals Desk Reference*. And there are stark differences between nuclear power plant operations and biopharmaceutical plant operations. In basic terms, the nuclear industry's economics, regulatory environment, organizational workforce composition, training, and workplace design are quite different than those within the biopharmaceutical industry. These differences were not adequately recognized by the team of

---

9 The Three Mile Island reactor near Middletown, Pa. partially melted down on March 28th, 1979. This was the most serious accident in U.S. commercial nuclear power plant operating history, although its small radioactive releases had no detectable health effects on plant workers or the public. Its aftermath brought about sweeping changes involving emergency response planning, reactor operator training, human factors engineering, radiation protection, and many other areas of nuclear power plant operations.

10 Capacity factor is the measure of how often a power plant runs for a specific period of time. It's expressed as a percentage and calculated by dividing the actual unit electricity output by the maximum possible output.

biopharmaceutical representatives seeking to learn from the nuclear industry or the INPO representatives who took extreme pride in being world-class.

These differences would play an important role in the application and effectiveness of the nuclear industry's so-called *Human Performance Program* when bolting it onto biopharma as a formal *Human Error Reduction Program*. The results said it all. Many biopharmaceutical companies that attempted to directly apply the nuclear playbook without appropriate regard for workplace and organizational differences saw no results, uneven results, or performance that was not sustained over time.

During this period, a small number of biopharmaceutical companies chose a different approach. Leaders changed how they thought about human fallibility, and accepted error as normal. They recognized that blame fixes nothing, and accountability was not a synonym for discipline. These leaders had a new understanding that work context drives behavior and systems create outcomes. Systems were recognized as complex and imperfect, always running in a degraded mode. Leaders in these organizations learned that hindsight bias prevented learning during quality investigations. Most importantly, these leaders understood that operational learning is vital and how their response to failure set the tone for that learning.

How did this new thinking by leaders make a difference? Take quality investigations for example. A unique approach was taken by deviation investigators at this small number of companies and plants that proved far more effective in learning about work within complex systems. This approach involved learning about work from the perspective of the worker. Deviation investigators went to where the work occurred and asked manufacturing associates to demonstrate how work was performed successfully in the past and listened to their stories. Manufacturing associates performed operations or walked deviation investigators through production steps while describing the factors that could increase the risk of failure. They openly discussed why detailed parts of the procedure could not always be done as prescribed, and options to improve the risk within operations. For those companies, changes were made to improve systems robustness and resilience, and the performance results were quite positive.

How will your company change for the better?

Start by shifting your mindset to move your organization from the typical biopharma approach where the behavior of people is a fixation treated as a cause of failure, which leads to no improvement in performance. The focus must be on the whole system, which includes people, and the interrelationships of the other parts that comprise the system. That system focus must be present during design, work execution, and when learning from both success and failure.

Thinking differently leads to new ideas and actions. *To Do Quality Differently*, endurance will be required. Past damage done to the people and the organization will need to be overcome and new trust built. Naysayers and defenders of the status quo will need to be convinced or outlasted. In time, the performance results will speak independently.

The chapters within this book provide practical guidance to move your organization away from the typical biopharmaceutical approach leading to ongoing production problems. Applying what you learn from *Do Quality Differently* will create more operational success in your organization.

We'll show you the way.

Your Blue Line

Take some time to consider your current situation. What do you wish was different, and how do you suspect human and organizational performance will help your factory or company? You recognize you don't have all the answers and are open to learning. Consider how Zen Master Ryutan poured a scholar a cup of tea and kept pouring as the cup overflowed onto the table. "Before you can learn," he said, "you'll have to empty your cup." Stated less metaphorically:

It's hard to learn if you think you already know.

What will change? How will things be different if you had a time machine to jump forward one or two years? Jot your answer down on a piece of paper or within the margins of this page. Maybe include today's date to timestamp your prediction, so you can refer back to the future you envisioned as you progressed through these chapters. Perhaps, by the end of this book, you will amend your initial thinking with a more informed and complete vision.

So, how do you develop an understanding of your situation? First, change your perspective. Empty your cup. Ensure you are open to seeing and learning how to bring about change. You must acknowledge the biases in your viewpoint to see what is shaping your organization's current performance. Only then will you be prepared to take the next step.

It can be difficult to fully understand a situation when you've been part of it for an extended period of time. The contextual details can blur together, and that mess gives the appearance of a problem with no points of leverage aside from what has already been tried. Don't fret. New points of leverage are indeed there. To see them, you must develop a new understanding of the situation. As with William Ely Hill's drawing below, there is always more than one way to see something. Do you see an old woman looking down or a young woman turning her head? Now think of your company or plant. Might there be different perspectives of work?

My Wife and My Mother-In-Law by cartoonist William. Ely Hill, 1915.

Work As Done refers to how a task is actually performed by the people who do the work. This is the *blue line*. *Work As Imagined* refers to the various assumptions people who do not perform the work have about how the work should be done. This is referred to as the black line. The first documented reference to these two perspectives of work is believed to have originated from the field of ergonomics in the mid-twentieth century. Perhaps the first visualization of two different trajectories of work perspectives first appeared in Dekker's *The Field Guide to Understanding 'Human Error'*, where the author explained the concept of *drift into failure*. Dekker suggested the variance from the norm is driven by success in cost, time, and efficiency improvements. Another version of the visual appears in Conklin's *Pre-Accident Investigations: An Introduction to Organizational Safety*. The gap between Work As Imagined and Work As Done is referred to by Conklin as Operational Safety Learning. While these books focus primarily on industrial safety, the concepts are directly applicable to quality in biopharmaceutical manufacturing.

Work carried out in any organization includes Work As Imagined and Work As Done. In the illustration that follows, Work As Imagined is depicted as a thick, straight black line representing work from the perspective of written procedures and those who design them. Work As Done is presented as a thin curvy line depicting the adaptations needed to create success at varying distances from the straight black line. The dashed line that runs below is Risk. In biopharmaceutical manufacturing, Risk may represent any source of product harm impacting identity, strength, quality, purity, or potency.

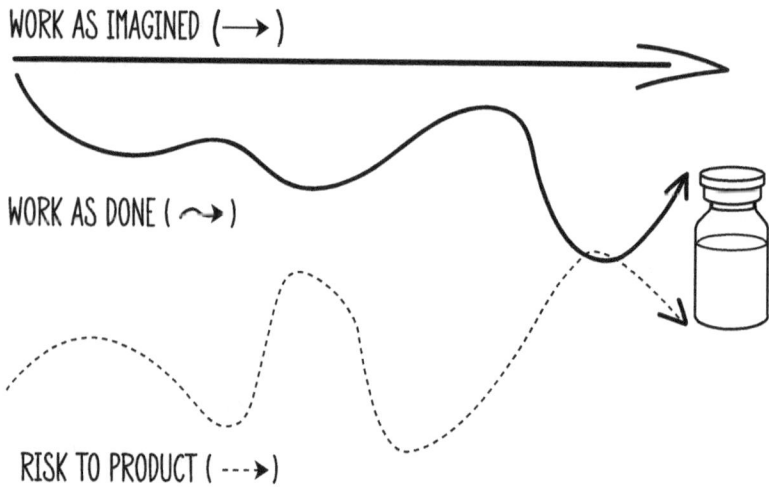

WORK AS IMAGINED (→)

WORK AS DONE (↝)

RISK TO PRODUCT (⇢)

Adapted from Figure 4.3, *Pre-Accident Investigations: An Introduction to Organizational Safety* by Todd Conklin, published by Taylor & Francis Group: CRC Press, 2012.

How does your organization talk about and measure the blue line?

Understanding an organization's blue line can begin with understanding how your organization tells stories about the occurrences reported at the blue line. A convenient place to hear such stories is daily tier[11] or huddle meetings. During meeting conversations about a failure or near miss, is the term *operator error* or *human error* used to describe what happened? Is the phrase *should have* used to explain what a person involved with a failure did not do? Do the meeting attendees believe failure would have been averted if the worker had behaved differently? Is there a metric to count the days since the last deviation? Does the metric track the days since the last so-called human error

---

11 Tier meetings are short duration meetings where daily operations are discussed, often used in organizations where Lean manufacturing principles and practices have been introduced. These meetings are organized by various levels of the organizational hierarchy, and information and requests are moved upwards from the factory floor to area management to senior management. Then information and support move downwards.

deviation? Does the organization use the term *avoidable deviation* as a sly synonym for human error deviation? Is there a metric that counts deviations occurring each month, with a target number of deviations to differentiate desirable performance from undesirable performance?

Unfortunately, everything described in the previous paragraph is commonly found at most biopharmaceutical manufacturing sites. There is a fixation on error, or human error, and a strong bias by people who manage or design work. This bias includes the perspective that Work As Imagined is correct and complete in describing work. It's not, but the industry heavily emphasizes compliance with the (thick) black line, and approval from the FDA and other applicable regulators is necessary to get products to patients. Deficiencies are exacerbated by the need to show regulators that systems are functioning well and procedures are being followed.

This compliance mentality supports a *just follow the rules* mindset and tends to stunt discussion that might reveal areas in which the organization may not be managing risk as well as they believe or hope. Old ideas and beliefs, described as old views or old view thinking by Sidney Dekker in *The Field Guide to Understanding 'Human Error'*, are also a problem. Beliefs like *humans are the cause of most failures*, or *the system is safe; people are the hazard* halt further inquiry. If you insist that reliable performance can only be made by protecting the system from people, you'll never search beyond these limitations. These old ideas and beliefs are counterproductive to creating success.

How does your organization learn about past performance?

In biopharmaceutical manufacturing, most operational performance learning is done through quality deviation investigations of failures. Industrial safety investigations also provide valuable insight into how an organization learns.

Take a look through your company's cause codes, the ones investigators select within your deviation management system. Are there cause codes that blame people, noted as *human error, worker violation,* or *procedure not followed?* These cause codes and accompanying metrics say more about the organization and its systems than the people involved in the failures. The use of these codes is nothing more than organizationally sanctioned blaming. When the organization or investigators settle on what happened as the cause rather than how or why it happened, the learning stops.

Consider looking at deviations investigated without an assigned corrective action. Actions identified as a result of an investigation are often referred to as CAPA in the biopharmaceutical industry, an acronym for Corrective Action/Preventive Action. If low-impact or low-level deviation investigations frequently conclude with causes blaming workers and no CAPA, no learning is taking place. Nothing will drive change to prevent future recurrences. Why is this important? Consider that a typical low-impact deviation may take upwards of twenty-five work hours to close, and a factory may have thirty or more low-impact deviations a month. That is potentially seven hundred and fifty hours of labor per month wasted or used ineffectively. Doing so damages the morale of the people involved in the process while fixing nothing.

Now review the assigned CAPA for a sample of low, medium, and high-impact deviations. What percentage of those CAPA provide awareness training? How many add notes or updates to procedures? Which include adding witness steps? These CAPA are largely person-focused and will have a negligible positive influence on future performance. In fact, these CAPA may worsen future performance by creating clutter and adding complexity.

What analysis methods are used during investigations?

The analysis methods used during investigations provide insight into how the organization thinks about systems[12]. When digging into the details of investigations, you may find your organization primarily uses the 5 Whys or Ishikawa 6M Fishbone diagrams as their analysis methods. The use of the 5 Whys technique may indicate the organization believes work is simple and linear, which is almost never the case. Use of Ishikawa 6M Fishbone diagrams creates the impression of thoroughness and formality, while investigators actually use brainstorming and a *guess-and-check* form of analysis rather than going to where the work occurs to learn about how it's done.

How an organization's investigators analyze failure may perpetuate imperfect systems that deliver undesirable results, wasting hundreds of hours of labor per month while damaging morale.

The conversations that take place during and after an investigation will offer additional insight. Ask an investigator to allow you to sit in on discussions with people involved in a failure. You will likely hear them volunteering to accept the blame for the failure and promise to do better next time. This self-blame has been learned. Organizations have taught employees to take responsibility, even when unjustified. But self-blaming most often short-circuits valuable learning. After all, if we already accept that humans are the cause of failures, what more is there to learn? Worse than self-blame is silence, when the people involved in a failure don't offer candid thoughts or detailed context about the event or their work because they have learned their role in an investigation is to accept that they are the cause.

Does your organization publicly or secretly track error counts of workers? Are these counts used in annual performance reviews? Is there a formal written

---

12 System is a generic and broad term used to describe an interconnected set of elements that is coherently organized in a way that achieves something. Systems can be large, like all of the work in an entire business unit, or systems can be small, such as the combination of equipment, documentation, automation, and people that are required to perform a unit operation.

process on how to issue a warning letter to workers as part of a deviation investigation? When a contractor is involved in a quality failure or near miss, is that person escorted off the site before the investigation? Rather than ask people in the organization if workers are comfortable speaking up to report problems or if there is adequate psychological safety[13] for operational learning, consider being present during an investigation to bear witness to the reality of the current state. Using the analogy of a confined space, you only know if the atmosphere is safe by sampling the air, not by asking other people if they think it is safe.

What do I look for within my organization or manufacturing facility?
Observe the blue line in action for yourself. Go to where work occurs to learn about what is really happening. This is essential to developing an understanding of the situation. Watch everyday work, sometimes referred to as normal work by *new view* quality and safety practitioners. Observe unit operations, as well as pre-use and post-use activities. Watch the setup and breakdown of processes. Be present for an hour or more to allow the people doing the work to almost forget you are there so they can relax and focus. You want to witness the work they normally do when you are not present. Remember, the organization and the industry have taught workers to put on a show when visitors arrive at their workplace. When the visitors leave, the real Work As Done begins again. How have the organization and industry trained workers to hide or alter Work As Done from visitors in their workplace? Well, skip back a few pages in this book. The training of workers results from biopharmaceutical leaders with a strong compliance mindset, a belief that people are

---

13 Amy Edmondson defines psychological safety as a shared belief that the team is safe for interpersonal risk taking. Psychological safety means an absence of interpersonal fear, where people are able to speak up with work relevant content.

the cause of failures, and the thinking that our systems are nearly perfect. When leaders do not think change is needed or wanted, employees will follow.

Watch everyday work on the manufacturing floor. Are people working quickly, or are they working at an even and unrushed pace? Are there distractions and interruptions to the workflow? Are employees staying in their roles as *performer* and *witness*[14], or is there unplanned role-swapping taking place? Is switch-tasking happening, where people switch rapidly between monitoring and executing more than one activity? Are people talking aloud to share step completion, system status, and parameter changes? Or, are people working silently, with little or no communication, creating siloes of system status recognition and risk awareness? Is the work being discussed in terms of risk? Is a supervisor present to provide support when the work risk is high?

Take a look at the documentation for the work you are observing. Do the procedures, work instructions, and batch records[15] match the workflow, or do workers have to jump back and forth between steps and sections? Is there one action per step or multiple actions within each step? Are there multiple informational or cautionary notes associated with each step? If so, are the notes located before or after the associated step? Do the notes communicate actions that, if not performed, will result in the work activity failing? Does the batch record or procedure include information that supports risk awareness on the part of the user? Was the batch record designed with the engagement of the end-users from the manufacturing floor? Do procedures contain specific

---

14 Varied terms are used within biopharma to refer to expectations of witnessing or verifying actions. We use the term witness specifically to refer to actions that require a person to be present and witness the step at the time of performance.

15 Batch records in biopharma manufacturing are the primary documentation that capture real time performance of production activities. Batch records are a key part of what is used to confirm that all expected and required actions have been completed within parameters to produce product that meets specifications.

equipment and valve numbers? Or are generic character strings such as XXX used so the same documentation can be used across multiple pieces of equipment or areas? Do most steps require a witness, or are witness steps used only for process variables that impact a critical quality attribute? Where the batch record design collects multiple process parameters with one corresponding performer and witness signature, does the workflow allow for Good Data and Documentation Practices (GDDP) and data integrity? How many procedures, batch records, forms, logbooks, and human-machine interfaces (HMI) are required to perform this unit operation?

While in the area, observing work, look at the design of the work environment and automation. Are the labels and tags on valves and equipment logical and concise, or are they designed using an illogical string of more than five characters without spaces or dashes for chunking? Is similar equipment close to each other, creating opportunities for mix-ups? Is color coding used to group systems and related devices, or does everything look similar regardless of function and relationships? Are devices within reach, without the need for step stools or ladders? Are there emergency shutoff switches in the work area, and are they visible and accessible?

Are HMI display screens crowded with data and images, possibly creating a dazzle camouflage[16] effect? Are alarms locked, stale, or chattering? Is there audible alarm functionality, and is the volume turned up to be heard throughout the workspace? Is there stack light functionality for HMI alarms or equipment status, and is that stack light visible from a distance? Are workers required to manually record data that is also recorded through automated systems? Are automation prompts generic and not aligned with other instructions? When

---

16 Dazzle camouflage originated in World War I where startling stripes, swirls, and irregular abstract shapes were painted onto ships. Dazzle camouflage was intended to confuse the enemy rather than hide an object from the enemy.

multiple sources of work guidance and record-keeping exist, is it clear at each point in time what the driving instruction is?

The work environment design and the tools provided to workers are vital for success. Anything less than optimal sets your staff up for failure.

Chapter Summary

So, now you have a better understanding of your organization's situation. As stated in the book, *Behind Human Error,* your problem is not a human error problem or a problem with erratic, unreliable operators. Human error is a *symptom.* The fact that humans are fallible offers little leverage to improve performance if we ignore the work context. Rather, the problem you have is organizational, involving complexity and technology. The goal is to adjust systems—work processes, technology, documentation, and their interrelationships so they help create operational success. When optimal, these will reduce the frequency and severity of failure—and human error.

While the concepts covered in this chapter may seem overwhelming, you have already identified leverage points by beginning to understand your blue line. "How do I fix all of this?" you may be asking. The answer is patience, strong leadership, and thinking differently. The details are in the chapters to come.

A Sponsor is Born

The headlines read *human error* caused the contamination of Moderna COVID-19 vaccines. The news stories reported that the incorrect setup of the stopper star wheel[17] on a vial filling line led to metal particle contaminants in some of the vials in three of five sequential batches. Three of the five batches were shipped outside the country where the vials were filled, where they were to be used to vaccinate people. Two months later, the drug authority of the country that received the vaccines suspended the use of the contaminated batches, which amounted to 1.63 million doses.

An investigation was performed at the biopharmaceutical manufacturing site where the vials were filled. The report stated that the problem stemmed from the friction of two pieces of 316L stainless steel installed in the stoppering station of the filling line. The problem occurred due to the incorrect setup of the equipment during a manufacturing line changeover. The incorrect assembly was cited as human error specific to visually misjudging a required 1mm gap. This visual assessment was intended to be performed with the naked eye, without using a jig, tools, or instruments.

---

17   A star wheel is a wheel with notches formed on the outer periphery that engage a vial and move it along a circular path to the next station.

A paragraph within the report provides insight into how the organization thinks about the management of risk during the setup of the fill line: "The two pieces of the stoppering station are the star wheel and a lateral part of the star wheel called the stopper feeding device. These two elements feed and deliver the stoppers to the vials. There is a required gap of 1mm between the star wheel and the stopper feeding device and the regulation of that gap is conducted visually. A proper alignment relies on the capability, qualification, and experience of the person performing the setup."

This incident was a significant failure that could have harmed numerous people. The manufacturing organization that filled the vials had a system that relied upon the capability, qualification, and experience of a single fallible human to visually ensure a required 1mm gap existed between two parts in their machine. Think about this. The system was totally dependent on one person being perfect in order to prevent metal contaminants from entering vials of product that would be used to treat millions of human beings.

The investigation report pays very little attention to the fact that their system failed to detect the metal particles in the vials. Their vial inspection process, manual visual inspection or automated visual inspection, is not mentioned in the report.

The headline proclaiming human error was the cause of recalling 1.63 million vaccine doses was ridiculous, and the opportunity to learn was potentially lost the minute no one looked past human error.

This type of significant event could shake an organization, which may lead a senior leader to recognize that a different way to manage risk is necessary. Such a senior leader might then become your sponsor to initiate change.

A Sponsor for Change

A sponsor is a leader with the ability to gather support for change within an organization. Sometimes referred to as a *change sponsor*, this person has access to resources, funding, and other leaders. A sponsor will initiate change and champion new ideas, setting an example for others to follow. A sponsor takes the reins by gathering the right talent, directing the project scope, participating in vital decisions, and setting clear timelines and expectations. With the support of an executive team or leaders, projects meant to improve operations not only take flight but soar, even when faced with setbacks or resistance to change caused by fear and uncertainty.

Sponsors are Born from Fundamental Surprises in Operational Failures

According to Zvi Lanir, an expert in coping with disruptive change in social, economic and strategic domains, a fundamental surprise is a sudden revelation of the incompatibility of self-perception with environmental reality. Robert Wears and L. Kendall Webb, leading experts in patient safety and emergency medicine, associate a fundamental surprise with failure that refutes basic beliefs, cannot be anticipated, challenges mental models that produced past success, and requires model revision and changes that will reverberate throughout an organization. An often-cited example describes a situational surprise as buying a lottery ticket and winning the lottery, while a fundamental surprise is not buying a lottery ticket and winning the lottery. In biopharmaceutical manufacturing, the lack of understanding the context of work and the reality of brittle[18] systems can certainly create that feeling of winning the undesirable event lottery without buying a ticket.

Fundamental surprise in regard to operational failure is often denied by people as a result of Cartesian anxiety. The fear of letting go of what was a

---

18 As defined by David Woods, a founder of resilience engineering as an approach to safety in complex systems, the performance of a brittle system rapidly falls off or collapses when events push it beyond its boundaries for handling changing disturbances and variations.

body of stable knowledge in exchange for the chaos of the unknown leads to redefining incidents as situational surprises to maintain a sense of control and comfort. Consciously or unconsciously, a decision is made that the failure is not a fundamental problem that requires new thinking. The failure is considered a one-off event that the ordinarily stable and effective system would magically correct.

Sometimes people will force fit the fundamental surprise into the category of a situational surprise. A situational surprise is an event that was unexpected but explainable and compatible with ideas generally already held about how things work or fail. The differences between situational and fundamental surprises are described in the table below.

SITUATIONAL SURPRISE	FUNDAMENTAL SURPRISE
A lack of individual pieces of information	An inadequate perceptual outlook
Missing information is readily recognized	Missing information is misidentified
Recovery is quick and easy	Recovery takes time
Occurs frequently	Occurs rarely but inevitably

Table comparing situational surprise to fundamental surprise, adapted from *Airpower's Response to Fundamental Surprise*, a Monograph by D. Elgersma, 2018, School of Advanced Military Studies US Army Command and General Staff College Fort Leavenworth, KS.

People typically dislike the feeling of a fundamental surprise since it requires altering one's worldview and their view of their place in the world. Biases take over the mind. Causes with easy-to-explain status quo fixes are assigned. This mindset remains until a leader experiences multiple failures that are all treated as situational surprises—generating an initial pang of fundamental surprise the leader struggles to believe. This is followed by the creeping realization of a pattern in system conditions and results and the pattern of their own personal responses to the events, shaking the leader to the core.

Sadly, it often takes those repeats, where the so-called root causes and conventional corrective actions have failed, to weaken a leader's confidence in their operational management practices. The world they thought they understood so well suddenly comes crashing down upon them as they hear the news of the critical repeat failure. Only then the search for new mental models and solutions can begin. This type of scenario may be best characterized as a cumulative fundamental realization.

Consider high-frequency, low-severity incidents that include data recording errors, calculation errors, missed performer or witness signatures, missed samples, missed steps in written guidance, and improperly executed steps. While most of these failures result in hours of rework, some lead to material discards, and a small number lead to partial or full batch losses. During these years of repeated failures, there are dozens of meetings attempting to explain red metrics and a handful of well-intentioned, resource-wasting projects. Task forces meant to be transformational create little improvement and no sustainable performance change. The wasted efforts often include lengthy deviation investigation checklists falsely described as the gold standard, doubling down on DMAIC[19], more martial arts-inspired improvement belts, and increased quality assurance staff on manufacturing floors looking for compliance violations. *Right the First Time and Speak Up* posters are hung on walls across the site. Thousands of hours are spent in meetings discussing

---

19 DMAIC is a continuous improvement acronym for Define, Measure, Analyze, Improve, and Control. DMAIC is a data driven improvement cycle used for improving business processes.

mindsets and behaviors while omitting people's motivations influenced by workplace factors that bridge mindsets to behaviors[20].

In this sponsor-creating scenario, living among the bleak failures and years of busted improvement attempts creates a cumulative fundamental realization from a thousand cuts[21]. Continuing as before is suddenly recognized as irrational. A sponsor is born.

Alternative Paths to Creating A Sponsor

What if you, as a leader, or your organization, don't experience a fundamental surprise or cumulative fundamental realization that makes a sponsor? Buying and sharing copies of this book could spur change and encourage a sponsor to take the initiative. Explaining how the ideas noted in these pages can guide your organization in building a plan for this year's must-win initiative could help. Start a grassroots human and organizational performance community or a book club that concentrates on publications introducing new concepts. Invite like-minded colleagues, especially those who could be a sponsor, to join. Begin with this book, then read Dekker's *Field Guide to 'Human Error' Investigations* and Conklin's *The 5 Principles of Human Performance*. Use the resources on www.doqualitydifferently.com to spark interest and generate dialogue. Sprinkle in discussions of recent instances of discards and batch losses to make the concepts explained in the readings applicable to your situation, and a sponsor may step forward.

---

20 For example, a person can have a mindset such as quality is a priority, but when faced with a job deadline, a lack of support, confusing HMI prompts, or ostracism for slowing down work to better manage the risks, these workplace factors influence or motivate behavior that may not align with their mindset. Thus, focusing on mindset alone, which may not need to be changed, may be insufficient to influence behavior as desired.

21 Lingchi, or death by a thousand cuts, was a form of torture and execution practiced in China where a knife was used to remove portions of the body over an extended period of time, eventually resulting in death. The phrase in modern times has come to mean a situation where many small undesirable things are happening, none of which are significantly impactful in themselves, but which add up to a slow change in thinking or a significant outcome.

When attempting to create a sponsor through reading and discussing human and organizational performance principles and practices, be mindful of being *client-oriented* rather than *innovation-oriented*. As described by Everett Rogers in his book, *Diffusion of Innovations*, putting yourself in the client's shoes better ensures your message is persuasive. As Rogers explains, "An important factor with the adoption rate of an innovation is its compatibility with the values, beliefs, and past experiences of individuals in the social system."

If you have watched the movie *Wolf of Wall Street*, you saw the difference between a client-orientated sales pitch and an innovation-orientated pitch, demonstrated in the *sell me this pen* scenes. Your messaging cannot be about selling a fancy pen or the awesomeness of human and organizational performance principles and practices. Instead, address your client's beliefs and values, and deal with a pain or need they are experiencing. Your messaging must address a problem your potential sponsor is interested in solving.

A sponsor is essential to the effective integration of human and organizational performance. Remember, a sponsor is someone who champions change and helps remove obstacles that might harm its overall success. The sponsor provides credibility and resources and is key to recurring communications activities that explain the why and what to the organization. This change in operational thinking will be viewed as high-risk because it will seem foreign and counterintuitive to most people in the organization. For this reason, the sponsor must be a senior site leader or a senior executive if the integration will be implemented at multiple sites.

The sponsor will need to resist the pressure to do what has been done in the past. Avoid recipes that follow the status quo. As Karl Weick, an expert on organizational behavior and sensemaking, says, simply pushing harder within the old boundaries will not suffice. The sponsor must think differently. That is not to say that a biopharmaceutical manufacturing organization would abandon Lean Six Sigma or current ideas about Quality Culture. That prospect today is unthinkable. Rather, the sponsor needs a strategy that can coexist and enhance existing continuous improvement and quality practices.

A Sponsor's First Steps

Once there is a sponsor—a willing leader to drive change—the first steps in the process can be defined. Marry the ideas gained from the learnings outlined in chapter one and two with the sponsor's ideas about what needs to be different, and a problem or opportunity statement can be created. This statement becomes the foundation for your organization's strategy. Your strategy will define what the organization is doing today and what the organization will now do differently in the future. A good strategy relates to a current challenge. It must identify the problem or problems, the challenges to overcome, and provide a design to create change. As Richard Rumelt explains it in his book *Good Strategy, Bad Strategy*, a good strategy has three parts: a diagnosis, a guiding policy, and coherent action.

Suppose your organization has recurring batch losses all pointing to human error—this is the challenge, the problem. Your diagnosis will likely include that the organization must learn more effectively from failure. Your guiding policy will be based on the specific operational learning practices you want to change or integrate. As for the coherent action, there are three ideal options that you or your sponsor should consider:

1. Investigations will no longer identify human error as a cause.

2. Investigations will include workplace context that explains how the assessments and actions of people made sense at the time.

3. Leaders will respond to undesired outcomes in a manner that respects people, demonstrates empathy, and uses systems-focused language.

Your Sponsor As Storyteller

Storytelling will be an important part of how the sponsor drives people out of their comfort zone and beyond the status quo. The story that must be developed by the sponsor and repeatedly told to small and large audiences in hallways, meetings, and over coffee is the story of the operational surprise—the fundamental surprise—that forced their awakening.

The story, told in the words of the sponsor, will unite the problem and strategy with emotions. It should describe a situation all or most can relate to. There should be intrigue and wonder and a change in expectations and reality. The story should create urgency—listeners must realize that a change is required if the organization is to continue existing. Communicate the need for patience by including information about small-scale changes that will take place over a period of time. To lead people, the sponsor must have a just cause. That just cause is the why that inspires others. And what cause is more just than improving operational performance to better serve *everyone*?

Here's an example of a genuine and effective sponsor story:

"We had a deviation during centrifuge operations where product was sent to drain. It was reported as operator error. Since I was learning about human and organizational performance, I knew to go to the floor to learn more. I talked to the people involved. I found there were two critical activities occurring at the same time, over a shift exchange. The team continued to perform end-of-shift activities like closing out logbooks and documentation review while leaving a small number of people to oversee operations. It was clear that part of the problem was how we run the facility. We could address this with greater impact if we don't stop at operator error."

Your Sponsor's New Vocabulary

There will need to be new vocabulary shared between the sponsor's fundamental surprise story and the compelling vision. Use the term *risk management* instead of error prevention. Start asking *how* versus why during conversations following failures and big successes. Explain to others that human error[22] is an attribution and a what—not an adequate explanation for failure. Consider defining the improvement goal as more opportunities for operational success instead of deviation reduction. Encourage systems thinking instead of finding component-level root causes. And adjust the workplace systems rather than fixating on the behavior of people. According to Karl Weick, changing vocabulary is important because what we say determines how we think. Some people make the mistake of believing it is the reverse.

The following table provides examples of words and terms the sponsor might consider using and explanations for why the change in vocabulary could be beneficial:

WHEN TALKING ABOUT	DON'T SAY	INSTEAD	REASON
Failure	Human error	Use words that describe the undesired outcome. Examples include batch loss, over-pressurization, and contamination	Human error assigns blame to people and ignores the work context and system weaknesses.
Learning about failure	Why	How	Why will lead to a story that is contextually thin and linear. How will lead to a context-rich explanation that is focused on the system.

22 Describing human error as an attribution, a judgement of a behavior based on an outcome, can be traced back to the 1983 NATO Conference on human error. Internationally recognized specialist in the fields of resilience engineering and system safety Erik Hollnagel stated that human error characterizes the outcome of an action rather than the cause.

WHEN TALKING ABOUT	DON'T SAY	INSTEAD	REASON
The mistakes made by people	Human factors	Error is normal	Human factors is about how the workplace is designed to help people be successful—it is not a label for human fallibility.
The workplace	Best practices	Human factors	Organizations are different, so what works well in one workplace may not work well elsewhere. Consider what is being measured to compare performance as well as what is being sacrificed when labeling something as a best practice.
Explanations of current performance	True root cause	Performance conditions, context, workplace factors, or organizational factors	In success and failure, there are almost always multiple contributors.
Explanation of the failure	Smoking gun	Failure mode or its failure mechanism	A smoking gun implies incriminating evidence of a crime. Look for the initiating condition to a failure, which can be used as a starting point for finding systems and organizational factors that allowed the condition to exist and the undesired outcome to be as severe as it was.

This table of suggested vocabulary enables organizations to integrate human and organizational performance principles and practices.

Distill a Compelling Vision

In addition to the sponsor's fundamental surprise story, a compelling vision must be crafted into an elevator pitch. This is a two-minute (or less) explanation of what the organization's future will look like.

Here is an example that includes concepts meant to connect the fundamental surprise story to the vision:

"We create operational success by applying systems thinking to our many successes and occasional failures. We will devise an individual and collective understanding of how people interact with the workplace, processes, and each other—as part of a system that must manage risk to protect our product from harm. Our new understanding of systems and risks will change how we see and use equipment, perform workplace design, and create processes to better serve everyone involved."

More than one elevator pitch may be needed to meet the needs of a specific audience.

Here's another example, written for colleagues working on the manufacturing floor:

"We will create operational success by learning about work from you, the experts who perform the work. By watching you work and listening to your needs, we will improve our systems to protect you and our product from harm. Our new understanding of systems and risks will change how we see and use equipment, perform workplace design, and create processes to better serve everyone involved."

Beyond the Sponsor

While the sponsor initiates change, they cannot do it alone. The sponsor must select someone to help with human and organizational performance integration. That person must be, or needs to become, an expert in human factors and system safety. The lead will develop additional practitioners and be a resource for leaders and staff on all human and organizational performance matters.

While finding an outside-the-box thinker can be difficult, there are criteria the sponsor can apply to find the best candidate. Look for someone who has read *new view* or *safety differently* books and academic papers. This person might have connections with human factors and system safety thought leaders outside and inside the biopharmaceutical industry. Maybe they attend human and organizational performance workshops not associated with how the biopharmaceutical industry currently thinks about human error. It's a status quo red flag when conferences and workshops use the term human error in their title.

The sponsor's right hand might have an advanced degree in industrial engineering, human factors, ergonomics, or organizational psychology. This person would understand change management principles and has had success with past organizational changes. They have a rapport with senior management and manufacturing associates and enjoy leaving the office or conference rooms to watch work being performed for the purpose of learning. While this candidate might come from another department, such as manufacturing, operational excellence, engineering, health and safety, or another function, they demonstrate respect and industrial empathy for the frontline staff whose work impacts the quality of the product.

Having experience in biopharmaceutical manufacturing is a big benefit, but adding someone from outside the industry can also prove successful. People with unique experiences often offer a new perspective. Such individuals may be found in industries like petroleum and gas, commercial nuclear electric generation, and high-hazard manufacturing. Past solutions will need to be modified to meet your biopharmaceutical organization's unique technical and cultural situation, but new solutions are born through thinking differently, collaboration, and operational learning.

Chapter Summary

While it usually takes a fundamental surprise to birth a sponsor, there are other ways a leader can be inspired to initiate change. A strong sponsor needs a person who can lead the integration of human and organizational performance principles and practices into their operations. This is where the magic begins.

How to Get Started

A sponsor has chosen you to lead the human and organizational performance integration effort, and you may now need to convince others to support the change journey. There is very little chance that your request for support to begin this human and organizational performance transformation will result in a parade to celebrate the epiphany contained within the PowerPoint slides of your proposal. Nor will you be carried out of the conference room on the meeting attendee's shoulders at the conclusion of your presentation as the song *L'arena* by Ennio Morricone plays—the ultimate accolade for slayers of human error deviations. Rather, there may be fear and disbelief.

The Iron Law of Bureaucracy[23] and learning anxiety[24] will most likely need to be overcome through existing rituals and norms, which might include plans described within rigid project templates that require tiny fonts to fit big

---

23 According to Jerry Pournelle's Iron Law of Bureaucracy, in any bureaucracy, the people devoted to the benefit of the bureaucracy itself always gain control, and those dedicated to the goals the bureaucracy is supposed to accomplish have less and less influence, and are sometimes eliminated entirely.

24 According to Edgar Schein, learning anxiety is the feeling that if we allow ourselves to enter a learning or change process or if we admit to ourselves and others that something is wrong or imperfect, we will lose our effectiveness, our self-esteem, and maybe even our identity.

ideas into limited page space. The more your proposal looks and reads like the proposals of others, the more likely it will be embraced. Yet, your proposal will need to include key differences in order for it to have the necessary impact. One of those differences is how you measure progress.

You will likely be met with the demand for a roadmap of your intended journey[25] in addition to a project charter[26]. You will surely be asked to justify the effort by presenting a return on investment, also known as an ROI. The ROI is management speak for *show me the money*.

Though an ROI was probably not needed to justify the creation of the current processes and culture that is delivering disappointing results, it is typically a requirement for anything new or different.

Asking for an ROI before fully implementing human and organizational performance changes is similar to asking for an ROI before beginning yoga or meditation. It's difficult to accurately predict the monetary value of avoided illness and unhappiness over the lifetime of a person that is full of change, surprises, and entropy. But since the yoga analogy will not likely sway decision-makers, let's look at how an ROI will help convince others to support your human and organizational performance integration plan.

Measuring Success

There is an investment in resources—time, effort, and energy—for any

---

25 Journey and roadmap are common terms likely used by your stakeholders. We believe the terminology suggested by Erik Hollnagel, terms such as voyage and nautical chart, are more applicable since there is no regularly travelled known road to implementing human and organizational performance. However, in this case, we use the language of stakeholders.

26 A project charter typically includes the project requirements, the business needs, a summary schedule, assumptions and constraints.

endeavor. Before committing, many will ask, "What is my return on investment?" They will demand you prove the benefits outweigh the costs.

Providing proof can be difficult when human and organizational performance focuses largely on the business of prevention—building robust and resilient systems that fail less often and less severely. Human and organizational performance is akin to an insurance policy, like deciding whether to purchase auto and fire insurance in the game of LIFE (pre-1991 versions). You may never land on a gameboard space where the insurance saves you money. But if you do, the loss can cost you the game.

There are several different approaches to handle this situation.

First, whatever you do, *do not* link human and organizational performance success with a straight reduction in deviation numbers. Though, in theory, this should happen and might be believed to be a good indicator, too many factors influence the overall number of deviations—problems outside the direct influence of human and organizational performance. Examples include: changes in staffing and voluntary turnover, changes in deviation severity leveling guidance, changes in the rate of product changeovers, changes in business strategies that take new products straight to process performance qualification (PPQ), supply chain constraints that increase the frequency of production schedule changes, and maybe even a global pandemic. When those situations do happen, engage people in conversations about how much worse it would have been if we did not improve capacity and controls with human and organizational performance.

So, what do you do instead? Use the existing metric of Percent Human Error Deviations—with a twist. Human error should never be the cause identified at the end of deviation investigations, so flip that metric on its head. In every instance where an investigation ended with human error as the cause, consider it an instance where the organization failed to learn and improve. Investigations should be conducted to encourage improvement, not place blame. Be sure to change the metric's name to match its new intent.

Another impactful measure is batch loss recurrence. If you can prevent one batch loss each year, the monetary savings would be the cost of that batch, which could typically be on the order of two to twenty million dollars, depending on the product and where in the manufacturing process the loss occurred. This measure may not be as easy to create as it sounds, but not because opportunities do not exist. Rather, it is likely that your organization has a very narrow definition of recurrence driven by an unspoken desire to create a Looking Good Index (LGI)[27]. Instead of letting the organization and the current data define recurrence, you will need to review instances of past batch losses and identify recurring ones using a broader definition of the failure occurring at the same step or the same part of the unit operation. Do not rely on the same cause as the recurrence identifier because the cause is subjective. You already know that your organization is not doing operational learning well since there is an unacceptable rate of batch losses. The situation is a bit of a paradox.

In his book, *The Field Guide to Understanding 'Human Error'*, Sidney Dekker explains the choice of causes as, "This choosing can be driven more by socio-political and organizational pressures than by mere evidence found in the rubble. The cause is not something you find. The cause is something you construct. How you construct it and from what evidence depends on where you look, what you look for, who you talk to, what you have seen before, and likely on who you work for."

A corrective action preventive action (CAPA) strength metric could be used to explain why the integration of human and organizational performance is necessary, in addition to providing a measure to show improvement. But

---

27 Sidney Dekker describes a Looking Good Index as a negative outcome of bureaucracy where metrics are manipulated to obscure poor performance.

chances are, your organization does not use a CAPA strength metric and might argue that CAPA Effectiveness is the same thing. It certainly is not the same thing. CAPA strength is forward-looking and objective, while CAPA Effectiveness is retrospective and subjective. For CAPA strength, use a rubric similar to that in the table below to score every CAPA created from an investigation. Higher CAPA strength will likely improve system performance and prevent a negative recurrence. Organizations with higher human and organizational performance maturity will have better CAPA strength scoring.

CAPA STRENGTH SCORE	CAPA DESCRIPTION
1. Administrative	Little to no system change. Includes awareness, communications, and retraining
2. Duplication	More people watching the operation, adding a witness step, adding a note to documentation
3. Problem Detection & Recovery	Making it easier to detect a problem so severity is reduced, making complexity visible: alarms, warning signals, in-process testing
4. Hazard / Risk Reduction	Simplifying a work process, or the redesign of work: ergonomics, workflow, cognitive load reduction, standardization, and human factoring of documentation
5. Hazard / Risk Elimination	Engineered solution to remove or greatly reduce negative recurrence: safety devices and guarding, forcing functions, interlocks, automation where necessary, work redesign or sequence change that removes risk, mistake proofing, etc.

The CAPA strength metric is an example of a new way of thinking about business processes. Adopting a CAPA strength metric will create data and enable you to develop helpful metrics that do not already exist within your organization. Essentially, by building new metrics, your organization can measure new processes and outcomes, aligning with what you are trying to accomplish. For example, if you want to drive work observations and identify problematic workplace factors or system factors during those observations, then use a measure that tracks how many observations are performed and the percentage of time workplace factors and system factors are observed as adequate or better.

Suppose you have an open reporting system where anybody can submit reports of near misses and risks below the threshold of a quality deviation. In that case, you can monitor the health of that process by tracking the backlog and how many reported issues were resolved with solutions implemented. For advice and common pitfalls to avoid with metrics, we recommend the book *The Tyranny of Metrics* by Jerry Z. Muller.

A maturity model used to perform periodic assessments is an effective approach to show the progress toward a desired end state. One such maturity model we have applied successfully is the *Human Performance Assessment (HPA)*, available through membership in BioPhorum[28]. Maturity models are not new; they are available across nearly every type of organizational capability. Since maturity models are generally tied to a number, such as *we are a five out of ten*, a maturity model can also provide you with a quantifiable way to describe your journey and ROI.

Result Expectations of Leaders

Your organization will embark on a human and organizational performance journey because the leaders want something to get better—like human error or deviation reduction. Human and organizational performance, therefore,

---

28 BioPhorum is a global collaboration of biopharmaceutical industry leaders. BioPhorum's purpose as stated on their website is "To solve pertinent pre-competitive industry challenges, improve operational best practices, and engage with key industry stakeholders." More information can be found at https://www.biophorum.com/.

becomes an intervention that needs to deliver. It must lead to a positive change. At the outset people will want to show a reduced count of errors to demonstrate effectiveness. As explained by Dekker and others, counting errors is meaningless at best and counterproductive at worst. Such counts typically lack statistical significance due to the small sample size and treating all errors as the same. This is worse than counting apples and oranges because the context leading to the action or assessment labeled as error is ignored. It's more like counting anvils and ostriches. But you still need to show the efforts are helping, so how do you do this?

In addition to establishing a roadmap and measures that are meaningful to what you are trying to change, we suggest you create a human and organizational performance *community* in your organization. Establishing Communities of Practice (CoPs) is a great way to provide an opportunity for the organization to self-select participation in learning and engaging in human and organizational performance concepts and practices. Communities also provide a great vehicle for sharing case studies, which serve two purposes. Case studies demonstrate the results your organization seeks. They also role model effective human and organizational performance integration for a broader audience.

Another way to expand awareness for value and overall results is through a network of experts in specific human and organizational performance practices. This could mean establishing a certification program to denote individuals with the demonstrated knowledge and skill to coach others in practices like a pre-job brief.[29] Having a network is a result in and of itself. Networks demonstrate a built-in organizational capability to grow and mature in human and organizational performance practices.

---

29 A pre-job brief is a conversation among people who will be performing a work activity. This includes a discussion about risks associated with the work, and how risks will be managed. Pre-job briefs are covered in more detail in chapter twelve.

Leverage good stories and communication pathways. You may struggle to accurately quantify the overall impact of your changes. Still, you can certainly tell the story of the specific batch saved with a pre-job brief, the positive changes made in a work process because of a work observation, or the open report that led to a high-risk failure situation being addressed proactively. The more stories you tell, the more you influence a positive narrative, which will go a long way to sway opinion.

Result Expectations of Frontline Workers

Frontline workers may not have a label to describe how they experience work every day. Yet they intrinsically know when they are working around and adapting to imperfect processes and systems. They make adjustments to complete the work design and create success every day. Frontline workers generally won't be difficult to convert to human and organizational performance practices. In fact, they will likely breathe a sigh of relief. Most frontline workers are pleased when organizations finally see what they experience. Frontline workers want the organization to be successful. They want physical and psychological safety and financial security. They do not want to be blamed for mistakes largely out of their control.

So, the first expectation of your frontline workers will be that your human and organizational performance integration will work.

Yes, you will face those who don't want change. Some won't want to discuss or plan for risk. A few might not like sharing the details of their work activity. Some may feel uncomfortable using new, non-technical risk management practices during task execution—even when it leads to positive control[30]. In these cases, we recommend utilizing Gilbert's Behavior Engineering Model

---

30 Positive control is when all that happens is as intended, and nothing else happens.

(explained in more detail later in this chapter) to overcome obstacles and drive change.

Generally, frontline workers will be supportive. Look for opportunities to provide increased responsibility and visibility to those who take the initiative regarding new human and organizational performance practices. Recognize their efforts publicly. Have supporters speak at Community of Practice events. Provide feedback to management about the great work they are doing. In other words, encourage frontline workers to participate in change. Make them feel valued for their efforts.

Another key expectation of frontline workers—possibly critical to the sustained success of change—is that their leaders effectively manage individual performance. This is an expectation frontline workers have whether or not the organization is integrating human and organizational performance practices. In the biopharmaceutical industry, quality deviations are often a primary trigger to use performance management[31]. This is at best incomplete, and is generally wrong. People in healthy and effective organizations value regular feedback—appreciation, evaluation, and coaching.

The regular practice of setting and reinforcing performance expectations day in and day out becomes elevated. Where in the past every worker mistake visible to those outside the immediate team led to punishment by managers, with the new emphasis of improving system weaknesses one needs to ensure all performance management does not come to a stop.

You might hear phrases like, "That's a get out of jail free card," and, "People are just not held accountable anymore." Statements like these simply

---

31 Performance management is an ongoing process of communication between a supervisor and an employee that occurs throughout the year, in support of accomplishing the strategic objectives of the organization. The communication process includes clarifying expectations, setting objectives, identifying goals, providing feedback, and reviewing results.

reflect that those individuals who cannot effectively meet the expectations of their roles are not effectively managed by their leaders. Or that managers are not effective in establishing clear expectations. It may even mean that the context of work at the sharp-end[32] is error-prone and not designed for success. As the lead, you will need to help managers understand what drives or stands in the way of the performance they expect.

Altering individual performance management practices is probably not something you should tackle as a human and organizational performance practitioner. Instead, we recommend you educate yourself regarding individual performance management practices and initiate dialog in your organization. Talk to managers about how human and organizational performance is distinguished from individual performance management. Discuss how learning context when things go wrong is not to absolve individuals of responsibility but to address organizational factors and workplace design so similar situations are less likely to happen again. Distinguish between *individuals* who struggle to meet expectations others meet and *instances* in which something goes wrong.

Similar to the thinking of Jens Rasmussen, if people's behavior does not make sense to you, then that says something about you; about the perspective that you have taken. Not about them and their performance. You must learn about the work at hand to understand the Work As Done.

Build Your Team

Most human and organizational performance integrations in the biopharmaceutical industry begin as a single-site initiative—mostly because large

---

32 Sharp-end is a way of saying that the person is 'in touch' and appreciates the actualities of the work. It is roughly equivalent to the British and Australian idiom "at the coalface", which refers to the workplace of an underground mine worker where coal is being cut from the rock, and these workers being directly involved with the core of the business.

corporations have entrenched thinking that is difficult to change. A site with fewer people and a brave sponsor is a great place to start. For the lead of a human and organizational performance integration, full-time or close to full-time hours will be required.

The type of people needed depends on the plan. Here is a list of potential expertise to consider:

Adult Learning & Development Expertise – a person able to identify training needs, develop effective content, and help others present that content well.

Manufacturing Leadership – a person who understands the manufacturing process, has worked on the manufacturing floor, has the respect of colleagues, and has led a manufacturing team with positive results.

Quality Investigation Expertise – someone who has performed or approved quality investigations, understands the process and appreciates the goal conflicts of batch release on time, inspection readiness, compliance, quality systems, and effective operational learning.

Some organizations hire an outside human and organizational performance expert or consultant. Such an expert could be used to develop the skills and knowledge of in-house human resources, help create and deliver training, diagnose problems, and suggest solutions. An outside perspective can lend credibility to a human and organizational performance plan, easing the minds of stakeholders. When selecting a consultant, avoid those who use the term *human error* frequently as part of their vocabulary or try to sell a branded one-size-fits-all program. You want a consultant who has the experience of living with the results of their solutions. Effective consultants learn about the unique needs of their clients through humble consulting[33]

---

33 Humble Consulting is the title of a book by Edgar Schein in which he describes how consultants can be more effective and helpful by working with clients in a more personal way, with authentic openness, curiosity, and humility.

and propose focused adaptive moves that adjust performance and yield new diagnostic information.

With the successful single-site integration of human and organizational performance practices, other sites will notice, ask questions, and want to implement changes within their manufacturing facility. These sites will hope fully ask for assistance and take advantage of the learning to date, rather than take a competitive position that delays progress, competes for resources, and creates confusion. At some point, global leaders should realize that something good is happening. They will want to know more. In this case, the resource model would probably shift from site-specific to distributed, and a network lead would be assigned to ensure alignment, while resources at the site would be responsible for local implementation.

A network lead is most successful when they are from an existing network in the company that has acquired knowledge and experience during a human and organizational performance integration. An experienced network lead is motivated to create positive change, not preserve the status quo.

Building Fluency

A human and organizational performance plan must include building the necessary fluency to enable the organization to adopt new practices and processes. This fluency building is most often accomplished with training sessions and fostering engagement. A structure for the fluency-building part of your plan might include the following:

STEP	ACTIVITY	SUGGESTED FACILITATOR
1.	Socialize applicable new concepts with the site leadership team	Lead and expert consultant
2.	Conduct middle-management engagement sessions	Lead and expert consultant
3.	Train business unit resources to be able to teach content	Lead and expert consultant
4.	Conduct first-line supervisor engagement sessions	Business unit resources
5.	Conduct workforce training based on needs	Business unit resources

Coexistence With Existing Practices

Every organization has its unique flavor of various practices and programs. These likely include versions of Operational Excellence, Production Systems, Digital Strategies, Visions and Destinations, Quality Culture statements and training, Safety Programs, and Business Process Management programs. Integrating human and organizational performance means just that—you are integrating practices and principles into what is already there in your organization.

The question is then how to best fit human and organizational performance into your organization. Which of these programs have full leadership alignment and support? Align with those. Which of these programs are not well supported? Be different from those. Which programs are emerging and have good synergy with what you are trying to do? Join forces with them.

Of the many programs you may have in your organization, the two areas we recommend paying close attention to are: Operational Excellence (i.e., Lean Six Sigma) and Industrial Safety programs. The latter is because the majority of human and organizational performance research and experience comes from contemporary safety management. There is a high degree of likelihood your plan will partner well with the safety efforts within your organization. It has been our experience that regulatory bodies for worker safety have been more receptive to human and organizational performance practices than health authorities, which makes it easier to try new practices.

We note in future chapters some of the traditionally accepted approaches under Lean Six Sigma that need to be rethought, including *going to gemba*[34] and the 5 Whys and 6M Fishbone as approaches to all problem-solving. How you do this will depend on the degree to which these existing practices are ingrained in your organization. Regardless, look for like-minded individuals who see how a different approach could help. Work with others to set an example and be a role model. If individuals have influence, they will be a strong lever to drive subsequent pull for change while coexisting with existing programs and practices.

Human and Organizational Performance Principles

One of your organization's first and most important steps is establishing a set of guiding principles for human and organizational performance. These principles will become the plan's foundation and develop the values that inspire new organizational norms. The principles will help people align to new ways of thinking and working that must occur for change to happen. They will also guide the organization to identify where the focus is needed.

Principles are fundamental truths or propositions that serve as the foundation for a system of belief and reasoning. As such, the entire organization will need to become familiar with established human and organizational

---

34 Gemba is a Japanese word for the actual place, and when used as part of Lean it refers to the place where the actual work is done.

performance principles. From the Aristotelian principle of human motivation[35] to John Stuart Mill's Harm Principle[36], principles represent significant truths and provide people with an understanding of how the world works. Human and organizational performance principles will help people understand how the integration of human factors and system safety into operations works.

Organizations often resist creating more principles or values in addition to those that already exist for the corporation or for continuous improvement. People may claim it will create confusion. But these principles are specific to human factors and system safety and are essential to the success of this important journey. These principles will not conflict with corporate principles. If a set of human and organizational performance principles are not adopted and clearly communicated, your integration effort will likely fail.

Todd Conklin provides a very good set of human and organizational performance principles that work well in any industry, including biopharmaceutical manufacturing, in his book, *The 5 Principles of Human Performance*. Since there is no reason to reinvent the wheel, here are his main principles:

1. People Make Mistakes

   People are fallible, and even the most proficient humans will make mistakes. Error is normal and not a choice.

   An example of this principle adopted: Leaders are not surprised when a person makes a mistake during their work.

---

35 Human beings enjoy the exercise of their realized capacities (their innate or trained abilities), and this enjoyment increases the more the capacity is realized, or the greater its complexity.

36 The Harm Principle originates from the book, On Liberty, written by John Stuart Mill. The subject passage reads "The only purpose for which power can be rightfully exercised over any member of a civilized community, against his will, is to prevent harm to others. His own good, either physical or moral, is not sufficient warrant."

2. Blame Fixes Nothing

   Blaming people for failure ignores the fact that error is a symptom of trouble within the system.

   An example of this principle adopted: Leaders use systems-based language when describing failures and do not attribute judgment to failures when they occur.

3. Learning and Improving is Vital

   Failure is a feature of learning. Every failure is an opportunity to improve future performance if we choose to learn. We learn from both success and failure.

   An example of this principle adopted: People describe a purpose of an investigation as learning, and CAPA are considered investments in future improved performance.

4. Context Drives Behavior

   The actions and assessments of people make sense to them at the time of performance. Workplace local factors are the main drivers of behavior, and our systems drive outcomes.

   An example of this principle adopted: Leaders spend time watching work to learn about the context of work.

5. How You Respond to Failure Matters

   You have two choices; getting better or getting even. Leaders shape how the organization learns by their response to failure.

   An example of this principle adopted: Leaders demonstrate empathy for people involved with an undesired outcome and provide support to understand how the system created the results.

PEOPLE MAKE MISTAKES

LEARNING AND IMPROVING IS VITAL

BLAME FIXES NOTHING

HOW YOU RESPOND TO FAILURE MATTERS

CONTEXT DRIVES BEHAVIOR

Illustration of the five principles of human and organizational performance.

If you believe your situation to be unique and in need of additional principles, keep your list as short and simple as possible. Examples of additional principles that might be necessary for your organization include *People Want to Do a Good Job, Systems are Complex and Imperfect, and Safeguards Save Batches.*

Change Models

Since human and organizational performance is not standard or expected in the biopharmaceutical industry, pretty much everything you do will require change. Much of this chapter is oriented toward helping you identify where applying change will likely be successful and where applying change may not. We encourage you to start with areas likely to succeed.

So how do you go about creating the change you desire? There are a lot of good approaches and models to drive organizational change and behavior change. There are two primary models upon which we rely: Schein's Model of Organizational Culture (for thinking about organizational change) and Gilbert's Behavior Engineering Model (for individual or more specific behavior change influenced by systems).

In the book *Organizational Culture and Leadership*, Schein outlines six primary cultural embedding mechanisms, captured in the following table:

MECHANISM	WHY THIS IS IMPORTANT
What leaders pay attention to, measure, and control on a regular basis	• One of the most powerful embedding mechanisms • Can be anything leaders notice or question • May include casual comments • Consistency is important, not intensity
How leaders react to critical incidents and organizational crises	• Creates new organizational norms, values, and working procedures • Reveals important underlying assumptions • Heightened emotions increase the intensity of learning • Also consider what leadership considers a crisis
Observed criteria by which leaders allocate scarce resources	• Best described as *putting your money where your mouth is* • Includes the actual resource allocation process—top down versus bottom up
Deliberate role modeling, teaching, and coaching	• A leader's visible behavior communicates values and assumptions • Accomplished formally or informally • Informal messages are the more powerful teaching and coaching mechanism
Observed criteria by which leaders allocated rewards and status	• Includes promotions, appraisal ratings, and punishments • What really happens is important, not what is espoused or preached • Promotion and reward systems must be consistent with underlying assumptions • Judged over the long term
Observed criteria by which leaders recruit, select, promote, retire, and excommunicate organizational members	• Subtle yet potent method to embed and perpetuate cultural assumptions • Often operates unconsciously in organizations • Founders and leaders may hire those who resemble their desired style, assumptions, values, and beliefs

Table of Primary Cultural Embedding Mechanisms adapted from Exhibit 13.1,
How Leaders Embed Their Beliefs, Values, and Assumptions,
in *Organizational Culture and Leadership*, Third Edition,
by Edgar H. Schein, published by Jossey-Bass, A Wiley Imprint, 2004.

When driving organizational change, change you want a large number of people to adopt, cultural embedding mechanisms provide key areas of focus for you as the agent of change. Human and organizational performance integration requires working directly with leaders and workers at all levels of your organization, and coaching and supporting them to enable changes specified in your plan. Their actions will, in turn, influence the rest of the organization.

Two of the mechanisms we emphasize in human and organizational performance implementations are how leaders respond to crises and coaching through deliberate role modeling. How leaders respond has a ripple effect on an organization. Leader response is so fundamental to human and organizational performance, Todd Conklin lists it as one of the five principles: *How you respond to failure matters.*

A primary area of focus for role modeling and coaching is work observations. Leaders must be present where work is performed. They must participate in a way that engages workers in conversations about operational risks to success in their work. A good leader demonstrates humility in learning about how work is done, aka Work As Done. While a leader is present and engaging with workers, this also provides an opportunity for them to reinforce and ask about general human and organizational performance practices. This then supports another one of the cultural embedding mechanisms: *What leaders pay attention to.*

When trying to drive a specific or focused change, develop your action plan using Gilbert's Behavior Engineering Model, captured in the following summary table[37]:

---

37 There are multiple adaptations of the original Behavior Engineering Model developed by Gilbert. We present an adaptation developed by Tony Muschara. Additional references include Training Ain't Performance by Harold D. Stolovich and Carl Binder's Six Boxes.

TASK AND ENVIRONMENTAL FACTORS	1. EXPECTATIONS AND FEEDBACK	2. TOOLS, RESOURCES, AND JOB SITE CONDITIONS	3. INCENTIVES AND DISINCENTIVES
Factors *external* to the person doing the job	Job-specific requirements, standards, guidance, reinforcement, coaching, correction, and feedback	Job-related instruments, supplies, aids, and means for accomplishing work. External workplace conditions influencing actions and choices	An environment of rewards and sanctions explicitly and implicitly intended and unintended, associated with the job
HUMAN AND INDIVIDUAL FACTORS	**4. KNOWLEDGE AND SKILLS**	**5. CAPACITY AND READINESS**	**6. PERSONAL MOTIVES AND PREFERENCES**
Factors *internal* to the person doing the job	A person's competence and understanding of the technology, fundamentals, systems, and construction, including abilities, level of proficiency, and expertise	A person's physical, mental, and emotional factors influencing their ability to perform the job, including human factors	A person's attitudes, motives, anticipations, and preferences related to their needs for security, achievement, affiliation, and control

Table of Gilbert's Behavior Engineering Model adapted from Table 3.2, Local Factors Categories in *Risk-Based Thinking*, Third Edition by Tony Muschara, published by Routledge Taylor & Francis Group, 2018.

This Behavior Engineering Model points to system changes that *must* occur to sustain changes in the workplace. Hence, the term *engineering*. This model would influence behavior changes in situations such as pre-job briefs where they are not being done, starting to use three-part communication as part of operational work, or reviewing shift documentation before shift-end where this is not a standard. We provide a guide for this approach in Appendix D.

This model recognizes and outlines the multiple areas that influence what people do and don't do. It is not enough to simply tell someone to do something. You also need to ensure the expectation is understood as intended. You need to provide feedback when performance does and does not meet expectations.

You need to identify and provide the necessary tools and resources for people to meet the expectation—likely more, depending on expectations and the extent of action it will take to reinforce and monitor in real time.

Gilbert's model can also apply to broad organizational changes similar to Schein's mechanisms. We would suggest you try it out first on well-defined changes. Once you are comfortable, you could consider applying the same approach to organizational-level changes.

Do Not Push

Even though your organization overall may be supportive of human and organizational performance practices, you will still encounter areas that will not be ready or fully onboard. Even with a high-level sponsor or good cross-functional support, there will be functions, levels, or groups in the organization that will not open their doors to you. Do not break the door down and force your way in. Leave your invitation at their door. Keep bringing gift baskets. Be a role model and make suggestions, but recognize you cannot change something or someone who will not even open the door to you. You have limited resources and will be much better off focusing those resources on opportunities rather than trying to get in where the door is constantly closed in your face—or where you are occasionally invited in but without any real outcome. Being deliberate about keeping strong resistors away from early change efforts will limit the mischief and damage they can cause.

Though we urge against breaking the door down, perform what we call a risk assessment for these areas. How will their lack of support impact the overall integration plan? As an example, we did not conduct a risk assessment in one case, and five years into implementation, due to changes in organizational circumstances, the nonsupporting group was able to undo changes we considered complete. In hindsight, it is difficult to know whether or not such a risk assessment could have helped. However, we may have identified ways to modify approaches or tactics to lead to a different outcome.

Start in areas where the pain is the greatest and leadership is open to being helped. You will spend less effort and achieve greater results.

Chapter Summary

You now have all of the pieces you need to get started. You've satisfied your organization's need to understand the return on investment. You have measures that will help you evaluate success along the way and an idea of the resources you can apply to the effort. You've ensured your plan is based on human and organizational performance principles while considering your organization's current practices, programs, and cultural messaging. Your plan incorporates ideas from helpful change models and focuses on areas with the greatest expected need and willingness to participate. Connect with your sponsor to align the strategy and plan, build your team, and get started.

CHAPTER FIVE

Complex Systems Demand
Thinking Differently

The force of the crash was comparable to that of a family-sized automobile colliding with a similar-sized object at ninety miles per hour. All sixteen people on the rollercoaster suffered injuries, and four were hospitalized. Vicky Bath, age 19, and Leah Washington, age 17, both sitting in the front row, required leg amputations as a result of the horrific accident. The train they occupied with the other passengers hit a stalled empty train on June 2, 2015, on the popular rollercoaster ride known as The Smiler at the Alton Towers theme park in Staffordshire, England. A Daily Mail headline proclaimed, "Alton Towers Smiler ride crash caused by human error." The article reported that the theme park owner had completed an investigation of the incident and concluded that the incident was the result of human error culminating in the manual override of the ride safety control system without the appropriate protocols being followed.

Much of the information that follows about the incident was taken from the Health & Safety Executive Factual Report of The Smiler Ride Incident. The Smiler was manufactured by German manufacturer Gerstlauer and the ride was opened in May 2013. It is a multi-loop steel rollercoaster with fourteen inversions, otherwise known as loops. The Smiler can have up to five trains in operation. Each train has four rows of four seats, allowing sixteen passengers per train. The ride duration is two minutes and forty-five seconds along a track length of 3,840 feet. The highest drop is ninety-eight feet with a maximum ride g-force of four point five.

The Smiler uses a block zone system where several trains can be in operation at the same time. The ride's programmable logic controller (PLC) provides an automatic fail-safe control system that ensures the trains are kept separate to prevent collisions. The entire track is sectioned into blocks that have braking capabilities and sensors at the entry and exit points of each block. Entry and exit point sensors are under the control of the ride's PLC, which ensures that only one train can occupy a block at any given time. The track is divided into five block sections, allowing a maximum of four trains to run on the track simultaneously, with the fifth train loading at the station. The ride also has trim brakes at strategic points on the track to reduce a train's speed if it travels too fast.

The Smiler has a control panel, or human-machine interface (HMI), used by the ride operator. The HMI includes a visual display of the track layout, blocks, and ride status. Twenty-five CCTV cameras monitor various locations of the track. The camera images are displayed on two fifty-inch screens mounted above the ride control panel, and two fifteen-inch LCD screens positioned on top of a wall-mounted cabinet nearby. The CCTV images on the smaller screens are very small, and little detail can be seen by the ride operator standing at the control panel.

The PLC alerts the ride operator when trains can be dispatched from the loading station. In *normal* mode, once a train has been dispatched from the loading station, it will automatically advance from block to block under the PLC's control and monitoring system until it returns to the loading station. Should a train attempt to enter a block that the PLC has registered as occupied, the control systems will automatically initiate a block stop that halts the trains behind the occupied block.

Four trains were in operation that day. At 1:06 p.m., the sixteen people who would later become accident victims were loaded onto a train. At 1:08 p.m., a fault was generated on the ride control panel when the start button in the loading station was pressed too long. Two mechanical engineers were called to resolve the fault, and the sixteen people were unloaded from the train and returned to the queue on the station platform.

One of the mechanical engineers prepared to add the fifth train because the park had become busier with more customers. While that activity was happening, the ride was put into *maintenance* mode by two electrical engineers. They cleared the minor fault by acknowledging the message. At 1:20 p.m., the fifth train was added by the two mechanical engineers. The electrical engineers were not aware of the fifth train.

At 1:29 p.m., an empty train was sent around the ride to ensure the track was operational. This was the procedure after a cleared fault. But the empty train stopped just short of Lift No. 2, having failed to engage at that lift, and stalled in Block No. 3. As a result of the stalled train, Block No. 3 showed as occupied by the PLC. Three engineers made their way to the stuck train, and one electrical engineer went to the ride's control room. The three engineers arrived at the bottom of Lift No. 2 at 1:35 p.m. They pushed the empty train until it visibly engaged with Lift No. 2. The three engineers returned to the control room at 1:38 p.m. The empty train arrived at the loading station at 1:40 p.m.

All five trains were now at the station, and all were empty of passengers. Just after 1:40 p.m., Train No. 3, at the front of the queue, is sent out empty to round the track. It climbs Lift No. 1 and goes into the first gravity section of the track, Block No. 3. One minute later, it stalls in the Cobra Loop. It hangs upside down at the apex for twenty seconds before it slips backward, pendulums at the bottom of the loop, and comes to rest. No engineer sees this.

At 1:41 p.m., the sixteen passengers were reloaded onto Train No. 4, and the train set off around the ride. Another block stop fault was registered at 1:42 p.m. The fault was recorded in the Park Operations Breakdown Checklist. So was the believed location of all five trains: *Four vehicles at ground level and one vehicle at the top of the lift.* One of the engineers proceeded to the bottom of Lift No. 2, where a remote-control panel is used to perform a block reset. The engineer returns to the control room at 1:49 p.m.

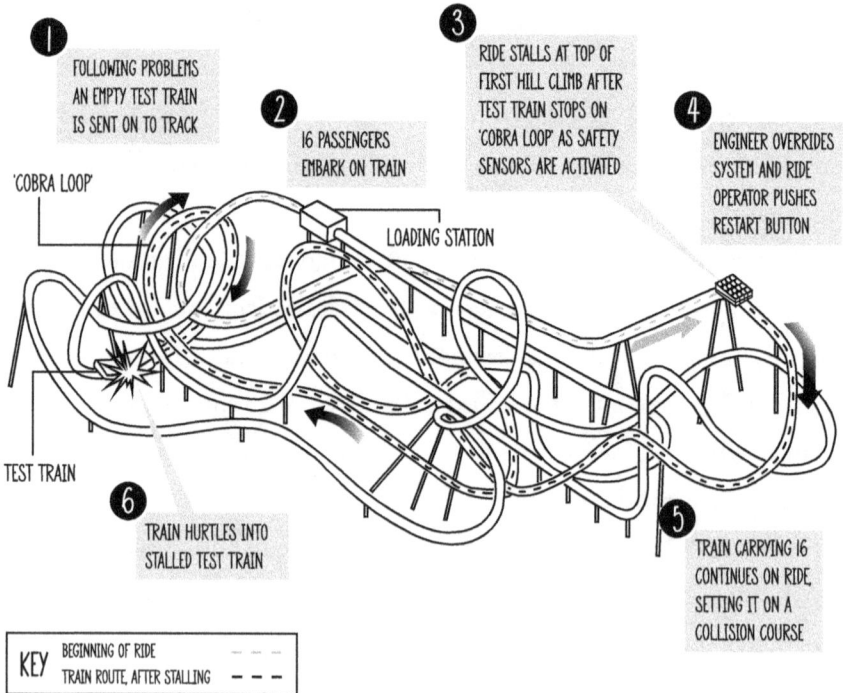

An illustration of The Smiler at Alton Towers theme park
and a simplified sequence of the events.

The electrical engineers in the control room mistakenly believed the stalled empty train was a phantom train caused by a hangover glitch from the previous fault on the ride. They thought the empty train sent at 1:29 p.m. had returned to the loading station. Because of this, as was the common practice, they conducted a manual reset of the occupied block to clear the stalled train from the PLC system. The engineer performing the trackside reset had not observed the stalled empty train, nor was it spotted on the CCTV images in the control room[38].

In order to reset the ride from *maintenance* to *normal,* the system was switched to EVAC (*evacuation*) mode, where the ride's control system returns all trains to the station beginning with the furthest train and working backward. At 1:50 p.m., having agreed to ignore the occupied status of Block No. 3, EVAC mode was initiated, sending Train No. 4—carrying sixteen passengers—back to the loading station. Twenty-six seconds later, they crashed into the back of the empty train at the bottom of the Cobra Loop.

The Health & Safety Executive Factual Report of The Smiler Ride Incident contains additional information relevant to the accident. A notable environmental condition on the day of the accident was that The Smiler was operated in forty-six-mile-per-hour winds, which exceeded the ride manufacturer's guideline of thirty-three miles per hour. A notable organizational factor was that management had set targets for ride downtime with employee monetary bonuses linked to achieving acceptably low levels. Staff was encouraged to keep rides operational.

---

38 Readers may question how four engineers failed to see the stalled train from trackside and on the CCTV. In Scott Snook's book Friendly Fire he shares writings by Karl Weick that help to explain an F-15 pilot's misidentification of two friendly helicopters as enemy combatants, which may have relevance for The Smiler Incident. In the words of Karl Weick, as quoted by Scott Snook, "In matters of sensemaking, believing is seeing." The four engineers believed that four trains were at the loading station even though there were actually three, one train was on Lift No.1, and a hangover glitch was registering as a phantom train at Block No. 3. So this is what they saw.

[Chapter 5]

System Complexity

While there are no rollercoasters at biopharmaceutical manufacturing sites, there are important similarities between The Smiler rollercoaster and biopharmaceutical operations. Both are systems—complex systems.

A *system* is an interconnected set of elements coherently organized to achieve something. A system consists of elements, interconnections, and a function or purpose. The elements of a biopharmaceutical manufacturing system could be grouped to include people, technology, and work. The *people* include manufacturing associates, quality control analysts, supervisors, scientists, engineers, and senior leaders. The *technology* is machinery like bioreactors, chromatography columns, and automation control systems. The *work* could be inoculation or chromatography operations. What is considered to be in the system versus out of the system depends on the goal. As Donella Meadows, an environmental scientist and one of the world's foremost systems analysts, explains, "It's a great art to remember that boundaries are of our own making, and that they can and should be reconsidered for each new discussion, problem, or purpose."

Another similarity between The Smiler operations and biopharmaceutical operations is the complexity that lives at the intersection of people, technology, and work. Complexity means there is no simple relationship between what an individual system element does and what the system as a whole will do—especially when the system includes some amount of adaptation or problem-solving to achieve its goals in new and different situations. As technology progresses, businesses look to improve their productivity by leveraging new technology. As technology is added to systems, interdependencies are created, more interconnections appear, and complexity grows. Even when a technological advancement improves product safety or lessens people's workload, the Law of Stretched Systems[39] explains how the increased safety margin and capacity are whittled away to create higher productivity.

Another contributor to complexity is the performance variability of humans who adapt to make up for the always-present gaps in systems design. System design flaws feed complexity and can include factors beyond the physical nature of a missing fail-safe or a clunky interface. The failings of a system also include the inability to compensate for risks not recognized from external variability or internal variability created from organizational factors such as goal conflicts and resource limitations. Today's complex system failures are sudden and unexpected due to their brittle[40] nature, tightly coupled[41] and operated at the margin—like a lost batch or two rollercoaster trains colliding.

The inexorable complexity of our biopharmaceutical systems leads to more and different problems, forcing organizations to solve issues beyond the thinking of simpler times. The human mind is comfortable with straight lines and Newtonian explanations of cause and effect. Messiness, variability, and emergent system behaviors are misunderstood by many, and organizations push for simple, quick fixes. It is essential to think differently to address uniquely complex systems problems.

---

39 The Law of Stretched Systems is described in the book Joint Cognitive Systems: Patterns In Cognitive Systems Engineering by David Woods and Erik Hollnagel. The Law of Stretched Systems notes how every system is stretched to operate at its capacity, and as soon as it is improved, that improvement will be exploited to achieve new intensity and tempo.

40 David Woods describes three ways that brittleness, or a lack of necessary graceful extensibility, may exist in systems as decompensation, working at cross-purposes, and getting stuck in outdated approaches. In the case of The Smiler accident, the organization certainly fell victim to working at cross-purposes and getting stuck in outdated approaches.

41 Perrow's approach to risk management recognizes the concept of coupling, which is the amount of slack, buffer, or give between two or more parts within a system. Tightly coupled systems have tight links between parts of the system that create a quick response to perturbations, where the response can lead to failure. Loosely coupled systems have fewer or less tight links between parts and therefore are able to absorb perturbations without destabilization that might lead to failure.

[Chapter 5]

When The 5 Whys Don't Work

One well-known problem-solving methodology that continues to be wrongly espoused as an effective and simple approach to any problem is the 5 Whys. Consider Taiichi Ohno's well-known problem-solving example from the book *Toyota Production System: Beyond Large-Scale Production*:

1. Why did the machine stop?
   There was an overload, and the fuse blew.

2. Why was there an overload?
   The bearing was not sufficiently lubricated.

3. Why was it not lubricated sufficiently?
   The lubrication pump was not pumping sufficiently.

4. Why was it not pumping sufficiently?
   The shaft of the pump was worn and rattling.

5. Why was the shaft worn out?
   There was no strainer attached, and metal scrap got in.

Giving Ohno the benefit of the doubt, this 5 Whys example is more about getting beyond symptoms and surface-level issues to identify conditions that are considered causal. He goes a bit too far by stating that this method is "The scientific basis of the Toyota system." In coordination with imitative senior leaders, the cult-like nature of some in the Lean Six Sigma community has made this simplistic problem-solving method mandatory in many industries. Unfortunately, Ohno's example has become a foundation for problem-solving in the biopharmaceutical manufacturing industry. This enshrines first-order problem-solving, while ignoring the necessity of second-order problem-solving.

5 Whys continues to be applied within biopharmaceutical plants to try and understand how complex systems fail. Yet, the example used by Ohno is not indicative of a complex system—it is a moderately complicated machine, somewhere between a toaster and an intercontinental ballistic missile, but closer to a toaster[42]. Reductionist thinking[43] and component-level failure analysis are not helpful in learning about complex system incidents like The Smiler accident or most biopharmaceutical quality failures involving people doing work. Component-level analysis misses how a complex system behaves and ignores the interconnections between elements. While humans are an element of a complex system, reductionist component level analysis frequently ends with the human identified as the so-called root cause or malfunctioning part. Human error—again.

The lack of appropriate system thinking will also frequently lead to a single so-called root cause, ignoring the likelihood of what Woods and Cook describe as *multiple contributors, each necessary but only jointly sufficient,* present in a complex system.

Systems Thinking Requires Different Perspectives

Effective systems thinking requires different perspectives to identify helpful points of leverage within a complex system. Interdependencies must be recognized, as well as to what degree coupling is loose or tight. People tasked with operational learning must *think about their thinking* and recognize the mental

---

42 Complicated systems can be reduced to components; they are solvable and deterministic. Complex systems have emergent properties and behavior that make them non-deterministic or non-solvable.

43 Reductionist thinking is the idea that something can be broken down into smaller parts that can thus be used to describe the system as a whole.

model being applied to the problem. There must be an understanding of the system boundaries and the ability to change these boundaries by adding or subtracting elements to aid problem-solving. Thinking in systems requires going wide, up, and out—avoiding what might be a learned habit of looking narrowly and going down and in.

Looking narrowly and going down and in might be helpful in understanding why your toaster is not toasting. But this approach will never tell you how it made sense for an associate to open the drain valve rather than the feed valve, leading to a batch loss.

Recall the news headline mentioned earlier, the one that stated The Smiler crash was caused by human error. This perspective, where a person is blamed, is called a *first story*, and such a story is created without systems thinking. It expects people to perform flawlessly, which is not realistic. A more helpful story is the *second story*, which is based on systems thinking. In a second story, an error is seen as an output of the system. The error reveals systemic vulnerabilities, and the people part of the story explains how their actions made sense at the time of the incident. The second story describes the impact of complexity in the system.

It's worth noting the difference between a human error and an error. The term human error places blame on an individual or team. It is an unhelpful, generalized label that does not contribute to improvements or change. We must remove the term human error from our vocabulary as much as possible. The term error is less damaging to learning and is defined as the unintentional deviation from an expected outcome. Notice how this definition of error focuses on outcome rather than cause.

To learn the second story, establish a helpful mental model for leaders and investigators. The Sharp-End / Blunt-End Model of Performance, for example, will help people break out of linear Newtonian thinking:

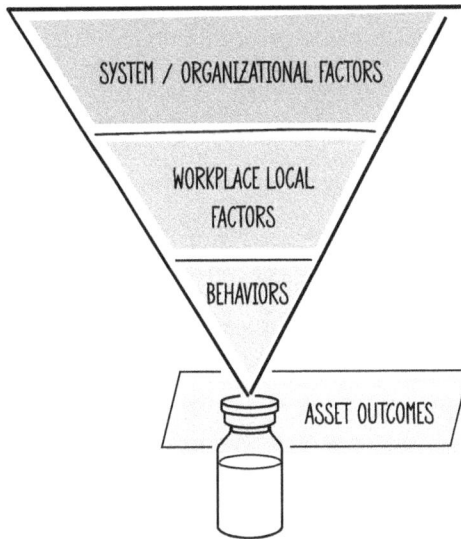

Illustration of Sharp-End / Blunt-End Model of Performance
adapted from Figure 6.1 in *Risk-Based Thinking* by Tony Muschara,
published by Routledge, 2018.

The *asset* the organization is interested in protecting is at the bottom of the model. Above the asset are the *behaviors*, the assessments and actions of the people directly involved with the sequence of events that lead to an outcome. This is essentially a timeline comprised of sequential actions, assessments, and events.

Above behaviors are the *workplace local factors*, which are the conditions present in the workplace at the time work was performed. Workplace local factors influence behavior. Workplace local factors help explain the local rationality[44] of people during the incident. In retrospect, what might seem like irrational or careless actions and assessments are actually reasonable when

---

44   The local rationality principle is that people will do things that they believe are reasonable given their goals, knowledge, understanding of the situation and focus of attention at a particular moment. This is consistent with American economist and political scientist Herbert Simon's principle of bounded rationality, where good enough decisions are made through satisficing as the natural result of lack of omniscience.

the knowledge, mindset, work environment, and multiple interacting goals that guided the behavior are considered.

Above the workplace local factors are the *system / organizational factors*, which include management decisions and business processes that influence workplace local factors. Think of system / organizational factors as being created by people in a different place and time than those doing the work.

At the sharp end of the system are the people close to the asset, conducting Work As Done, adapting to cope with complexity—the blue line. At the blunt end are the managers, regulators, and designers who have more power to dictate how Work Is Imagined—the black line. The decisions made by the people at the blunt end appear as outputs that influence workplace local factors.

When considering The Smiler accident, think of the behaviors that resulted from all four engineers believing the track was clear. The workplace local factors that may have influenced their assessment might have included the informal practice of tracking in-service trains, the CCTV line of sight, the stalled train being indistinct or partially obscured, and the engineers feeling pressure to return the ride to service quickly. The system / organization factors could have included management's ride downtime targets, monetary bonuses linked to achieving acceptable low levels of ride downtime, the use of shadowing rather than formal training for critical safety tasks, and the design of the PLC. Most of these relied on human infallibility as a control—a person pressing the EVAC mode button based on the visual assurance the track was free of trains.

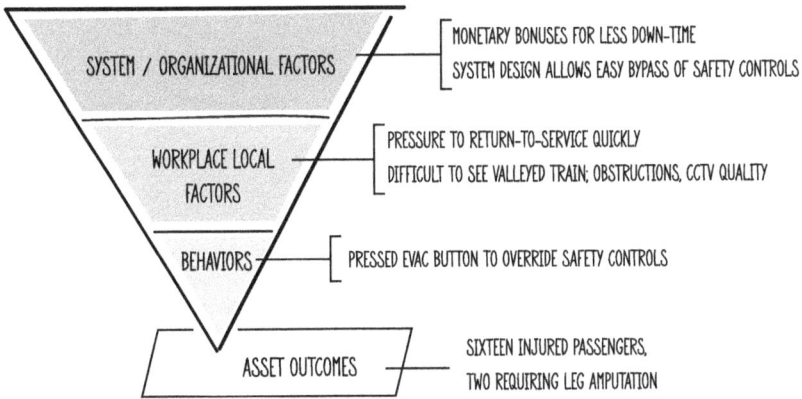

```
SYSTEM / ORGANIZATIONAL FACTORS    ┌ MONETARY BONUSES FOR LESS DOWN-TIME
                                   └ SYSTEM DESIGN ALLOWS EASY BYPASS OF SAFETY CONTROLS

WORKPLACE LOCAL                    ┌ PRESSURE TO RETURN-TO-SERVICE QUICKLY
FACTORS                            └ DIFFICULT TO SEE VALLEYED TRAIN; OBSTRUCTIONS, CCTV QUALITY

BEHAVIORS                          ┤ PRESSED EVAC BUTTON TO OVERRIDE SAFETY CONTROLS

ASSET OUTCOMES                       SIXTEEN INJURED PASSENGERS,
                                     TWO REQUIRING LEG AMPUTATION
```

Illustration of Sharp-End / Blunt-End Model of Performance applied to The Smiler incident, subset of relevant factors and conditions.

Systems thinking also better equips people to apply resilience engineering principles to understand and improve complex systems. According to David Woods, Erik Hollnagel, and Nancy Leveson, authors of *Resilience Engineering: Concepts and Precepts*, resilience engineering is a safety management paradigm that helps people cope with complexity under pressure to achieve success. Resilience is generally defined by Hollnagel and others as the ability of a system to adjust its functioning prior to, during, or following changes and disturbances so that it can sustain required operations, even after a major mishap or in the presence of continuous stress.

For a system to have the necessary resilience, the following resilience potentials must be optimized: *anticipating, monitoring, responding,* and *learning.* While a few paragraphs on resilience engineering are inadequate to develop enough knowledge to aid practitioners in understanding and improving systems, points made in regard to The Smiler are perhaps a way to create interest in further study.

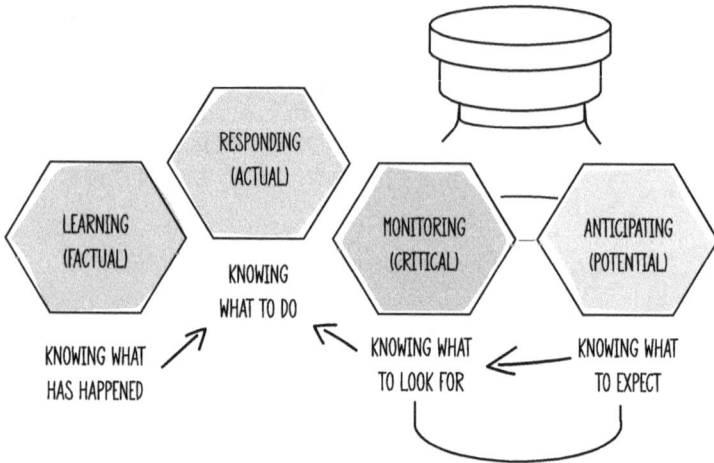

Illustration of the four resilience potentials, the cornerstones of resilience
engineering, adapted from The Scope of Resilience Engineering
in *Resilience Engineering in Practice: A Guidebook*
by Erik Hollnagel et al, published by Ashgate 2011

The resilience potential to *learn* can be described as an active process in
which organizations modify or acquire new knowledge to enhance the potential
to *anticipate, monitor, respond,* and *learn*. For example, the day of the rollercoaster crash was not the first time an empty train on The Smiler had stalled
in the Cobra Loop. This had happened at least once before. Unfortunately,
that information had not been disseminated to all of The Smiler staff and
management so new ways of anticipating, monitoring, and responding could
be designed into the system to enhance resilience. The previous near miss did
not become part of The Smiler operations knowledge, so future performance
could not be changed.

The resilience potential of *monitoring* can be described as focused attention on what is happening within operations and the organization to know
when a threshold has been reached. Technology can be used to monitor, as
was the purpose of the twenty-five CCTV cameras for The Smiler. However,

in this case, the CCTV cameras were not enough. Instead of adding more CCTV cameras, which was one of the corrective actions taken by the ride owner, maybe reframing[45] the problem associated with monitoring would have yielded different solutions. For example, using technology with time-out and alert functions when a train fails to return to the station after a set time. Making complexity more visible improves monitoring and tames complexity.

The resilience potential of monitoring can be applied to more than just machines. Your biopharmaceutical site has a safety reporting system where people can report injuries, near misses, and hazards. There may even be positive reports where controls are noted when in place and effective. Essentially, your safety reporting system is part of how your complex system is monitored by people. Information is reported, shared, and decisions are made to take action by focusing resources on parts of the system that need attention and improvement.

Unfortunately, it is very likely your site does not have a similar monitoring system for quality. Most biopharmaceutical sites have a deviation management system that is only used to report deviations from quality. Near misses, hazards, and risks below the threshold of a deviation are seldom effectively reported and acted upon in a systematic manner. Commercial nuclear power plants have open reporting systems where undesirable outcomes, near misses, and hazards are reported. The U.S. commercial aviation industry uses an Aviation Safety Reporting System (ASRS)—a confidential, voluntary, and nonpunitive process—to report hazards, close calls, and safety-related incidents. The current paradigm for limiting reporting to only deviations in biopharmaceutical manufacturing restrains learning.

---

45 As described by Thomas Wedell-Wedellsborg in his book What's Your Problem?, reframing helps to ensure that you are solving the right problem by exploring different ways to see the problem. Wedell-Wedellsborg suggests a five-step process of: Look outside the frame, Rethink the goal, Examine bright spots, Look in the mirror, and Take their perspective.

Chapter Summary

The risk of a stalled empty train on the Cobra Loop existed well before the accident on June 2, 2015.

The factors that live at the blunt end of a system are latent in nature, and there is no Newtonian causal chain that instantly alerts an organization to the risks created at the sharp end.

Complex systems are deceptive. An organization can be lulled into a sense of process mastery from a long run of performance success—only to be tragically surprised by the system they mistakenly and wishfully believed was perfect.

The Sharp-End / Blunt-End Model of Performance helps in telling the second story of a failure, as well as telling stories about how success occurs every day in biopharmaceutical manufacturing despite our imperfect systems. Moving to the second story is a recognition of the complexity in our biopharmaceutical systems. The integration of human and organizational performance principles and practices into biopharma operations and methods to institutionalize the Sharp-End / Blunt-End Model when troubleshooting and investigating will help organizations see conditions and interconnections between system elements that would be missed in a linear-thinking approach.

Maturity Assessment

Consider using the following statements to assess the maturity of your organization on the subject of complex systems. Each statement has three possible choices. A higher total score indicates a higher maturity.

1. Human error is never an acceptable explanation for how failures occur.
   Agree 20, Sometimes 10, Disagree 0

2. Context drives behaviors. Systems drive outcomes.
   Agree 20, Sometimes 10, Disagree 0

3. The socio-technical system interactions that produce success and failure within the workplace are not a linear cause-and-effect chain.
   Agree 20, Sometimes 10, Disagree 0

4. There is no such thing as one, true root cause when it comes to complex systems.
   Agree 20, Sometimes 10, Disagree 0

CHAPTER SIX

Real Accountability

The downstream manufacturing head had assembled the manufacturing supervisor, the manufacturing lead, and two manufacturing associates in the conference room to discuss the recent batch loss. Also in the room was the newly hired head of human and organizational performance. The head of human and organizational performance had two goals for the meeting. The first was to watch and learn about the effectiveness of this type of meeting. The second was to help the organization learn from the recent batch loss.

The batch loss occurred during the pooling storage stage, between purification steps. One of the manufacturing associates used the automation HMI to initiate the cooling of product contained in a tote. All the indications at the time seemed to confirm that cooling had been started. The HMI had responded the same way it always had, and the temperature began to lower, just as the associates expected.

The crew left to perform work elsewhere. They finished their shift thinking the work they had performed was successful. When they returned to work on their next scheduled day, they were told the cooling had not started, and the batch was lost. It didn't make sense. Everything had gone right that day.

The downstream manufacturing head kicked off the meeting by underscoring the significance of the failure. He explained that the chromatography elution pool could be held at room temperature for forty-five minutes or less, after which it must be maintained at a temperature between two and eight degrees Celsius. The actual hold temperature had been eighteen degrees Celsius for over twelve hours when the problem was discovered. The downstream manufacturing head asked the manufacturing team members to explain why they had failed to start the cooling.

Initially, nobody spoke. Eyes were downcast, and based on the team's facial expressions, everyone felt dejected. Sadly, this scenario is not unusual for members of a biopharma manufacturing organization. When things go wrong, multimillion-dollar losses occur, which potentially impact supply to patients.

The manufacturing associate who operated the HMI spoke first. "I was complacent and should have been paying better attention," he said. "I was sure the temperature was going down. But clearly, I was wrong."

The manufacturing associate who witnessed the procedure added, "I should have done a better job as a witness. I should have made certain the cooling was working before leaving."

The downstream manufacturing head nodded in approval. He was pleased to hear the crew accepting blame for the failure. "I am proud of you," he said, "for being accountable for this failure. I have some ideas that will strengthen performer and witness execution, and we can also add an end-of-shift checklist as part of our standard work to catch future mistakes like this."

The conversation could have ended there with zero learning. As usual, the deviation investigator would have been told to write the investigation report and CAPAs to match what was agreed to in that room. However, this day was different. The head of human and organizational performance said, "Wait, we don't know how this happened. We are talking about what we think the team did or did not do, but we do not understand how the failure occurred." Using the whiteboard in the room and drawing the Sharp-End / Blunt-End Model of Performance, he reframed their thinking.

This mental model and the concept of systems thinking were entirely new to the team. As part of the discussion, the human and organizational performance principle of *blame fixes nothing* was introduced. They discussed real accountability, not blindly assigning and accepting blame, and how the organization could learn to think differently to learn. This reframing helped the team start over and make a better attempt at learning how this event happened.

Following the meeting, an effective investigation was performed that involved the manufacturing team as partners in learning, and the workplace was visited so unit operations could be observed. The people who designed the automated cooling system were also engaged so they could learn and share their knowledge with the manufacturing team. That led to the following essential learnings:

The Purification Suite 1 control system HMI associated with this event was recently upgraded with software from another vendor and designed to look like the previous HMI. The steps used in the previous HMI would not initiate cooling in the new HMI. The upgrade to the control system focused on mirroring the past user's visual experience while altering the interaction experience, setting users up for errors. This might be considered an error trap[46].

The Purification Suite 1 control module associated with this event differed from the Purification Suite 2 control module. The Purification Suite 2

---

46   An error trap is an unfavorable condition in the workplace that increases the likelihood for people to make a mistake that may trigger an undesired outcome. Performance shaping factors is another term that is sometimes used instead of error trap, though performance shaping factors also includes favorable conditions that increase the likelihood of successful performance.

automation was designed within the upgraded system utilizing the improved functionality and constraining the variability that led to the undesired outcome.

The procedure change was not walked through with users before implementing the HMI change, and training for the upgrade was assigned as read and understand (RAU) with no on-the-job component.

The manufacturing associates relied on experience to set up the temperature control module (TCM) as done in the past successfully through a faceplate that was still available but not used by the new HMI as the start sequence.

After setting up the TCM, the control system response indicated the manufacturing associates were successful. "Green text, followed by grey text, and system temperature began to lower as expected," they said. The temperature change was likely due to a slug of glycol moving in the system as a result of repositioned valves. While the cooling automation had not started, there were no alarms to alert the manufacturing associates to the unusual temperature conditions since the recipe had not been loaded.

The batch record referred to the new control system procedure to set up the TCM. However, the procedure guidance for the TCM was underspecified and did not include detailed step guidance. There were no clear instructions on how to set the TCM. In addition, the Work As Done did not include using a procedure for the very simple and frequently performed activity of setting up the TCM. The automation engineering crew had limited engagement with end users, and timeline pressures influenced the design and testing.

A similar near miss previously occurred with a different crew. The crew detected the failure and had the automation engineering staff establish cooling in time to avoid a batch loss. Yet, the near miss was not shared with other manufacturing crews or the automation engineering department. Had the near miss been reported and the organization acted upon the operational learning, this batch loss might not have occurred.

The Ritual of Faux Accountability

Sadly, manufacturing associates accepting the blame for system failures is common in the biopharmaceutical industry. Organizations have made it clear over many years that employees at the sharp end must play their part in the symbolic ritual of *faux accountability*. Sometimes faux accountability is only a verbal agreement on who is at fault. Other times it includes sanctions and disciplinary measures, depending on the outcome severity[47].

Workers who resist playing their part in the ritual are treated as insubordinate. Some are eventually excommunicated or fired. While the people conducting the Work As Done carry a great burden, the organization as a whole loses also. This symbolic ritual of faux accountability ends the learning before it begins. It jumps directly to a correction without knowing what needs to be fixed, addressing the wrong problem. It focuses on quick, inexpensive, yet ineffective fixes. The jump insulates management from the embarrassment of learning the truth about their role in the problem, anchoring the organization in outcome-focused individual blame rather than system accountability. In this scenario, everyone in the company loses. And so do the people who depend on the products the company produces.

Following the examples provided by Jocko Willink and Leif Babin in their book *Extreme Ownership*, which is based on leadership lessons learned from their experiences as U.S. Navy Seals, a leader is always responsible for owning the failures or problems experienced by the team. A leader should never blame the team or individual members for a mistake. Despite Willink and Babin's emphatic and extensive use of the word *blame* as a synonym for

---

47 Sometimes people incorrectly judge behaviors as more blameworthy and requiring harsher punishment when the behaviors lead to significant undesirable outcomes. Those same behaviors might be deemed acceptable when there were no undesirable outcomes. This is a form of outcome bias, where the outcome influences the attribution of blame.

leader accountability, this high degree of system accountability on the part of the leader sets a positive example. Leaders should acknowledge their mistakes while pushing the organization to dig into the details of system ownership and design within the control of management.

Accountability requires sharing in the ownership of a team's problems and also the inherent risk, according to Max DePree in the book *Leadership Is an Art*. Everyone's contributions are measured according to previously understood and accepted performance standards. That includes leaders, who possess the most power over system design. And most importantly, in the words of DePree, "Leaders don't inflict pain; they bear pain."

Marilyn Paul, an independent organizational consultant, suggests that a helpful way to assess whether your organization is confusing accountability with blame is to look at the attributes that are present when it occurs. The attributes of accountability are respect, trust, inquiry, curiosity, and mutualness. When blame occurs, the attributes present are judgment, anger, fear, retribution, and self-righteousness.

To test how accountability is understood and applied in your organization, reflect on the last significant operational failure where people at the sharp end were sanctioned or disciplined—blamed. Did the sanction extend to the supervisor, manager, and director? How did the manufacturing head and site head take ownership of the failure? Did management's response promote learning? How was the system fixed?

Regrettably, in organizations across all industries, the word *accountability* is synonymous with discipline. Sometimes teams who work at the sharp end will even agree to take turns accepting blame for system failures, ensuring the pain is spread evenly over the years. When told, "There needs to be accountability for this event," leaders really mean the event's outcome is so significant the workers involved must be punished to send a message to others. But workers don't learn what management thinks they learn. This kind of faux accountability only sends a message to workers to be afraid and hide the details of failures that could be used to implicate them or their workplace friends.

There are some organizations where blame is even documented as a business process. At these biopharmaceutical organizations, business processes exist where punitive action is prescribed based on the number of deviations attributed to a worker over a year. These measures are cumulative over the time span in the role. Records are maintained showing how many so-called *preventable deviations* a worker has been involved with. These numbers are used during annual performance reviews, merit increases, bonuses, and future promotions. Organizations with such processes learn little to nothing valuable from undesirable outcomes while eroding their workers' trust and loyalty.

James Reason's Culpability Tree, found in the book *Managing the Risk of Organizational Accidents,* is often used to provide the appearance of objectivity and exactness to the business process of blaming. The Culpability Tree was a sketch intended to help readers recognize situational factors, and not as flowchart on how much to blame. Sadly, the importance of the *substitution test* in Reason's Culpability Tree is missed or ignored by many.

Here is an excerpt from James Reason's book, *Managing the Risk of Organizational Accidents* that describes the substitution test:

"When faced with an accident or serious incident in which the unsafe acts of a particular person were implicated, we should perform the following mental test. Substitute the individual concerned with someone else coming from the same domain of activity and possessing comparable qualifications and experience. Then ask the following question: 'In light of how events unfolded and were perceived by those involved in real time, is it likely that this new individual would have behaved any differently?' If the answer is 'probably not' then... apportioning blame has no material role to play, other than to obscure systematic deficiencies and to blame one of the victims."

The original intent of Reason's Culpability Tree was to promote justice for people at the sharp end. Yet some in the biopharmaceutical industry use it to justify placing blame on workers. Perhaps organizations should hide or lock up this dangerous culpability tool as we do household poisons and sharp knives in homes with children. Maybe affixing a warning label to the culpability tool would help.

Warning: Blame may feel good initially, but it will destroy psychological safety, stunt operational learning, and lead to event recurrence.

Acknowledging a mistake—a zig versus a zag—is a doorway to learning. Failure is a feature of learning for individuals, teams, and organizations. When people acknowledge mistakes, everyone can begin looking for how the system influenced performance and the outcome. But to recognize a mistake, we must first understand the step or combination of actions and assessments that played a part in the activity going sideways. This is quite different from an outcome-based attribution of general negligence. For example, the manufacturing associates noted in the case study opening this chapter did not acknowledge a mistake. They acknowledged being involved in a failure. They admitted the obvious, but did not feel obligated, encouraged, and safe to share their candid account of the work or explore alternative explanations. They confessed without even knowing how the failure happened.

If an organization wants workers to participate in reaching positive outcomes, leaders must treat mistakes as an opportunity to learn—and stop chastising or placing blame to explain the cause of a failure.

A Better Way to Learn

There is a more helpful manner in which the downstream manufacturing head could have kicked off that meeting with the team involved with the pooling batch loss. By helpful, we mean encouraging people to be candid about their work. First, he could have acknowledged the difference between learning and fixing—and assured the team the meeting was about learning. As Todd Conklin states, "The problem comes when the pressure to fix outweighs the pressure to learn." Combining learning and fixing into the same conversation almost always ends with little to no learning and not fixing what really needs to be fixed. Second, the downstream manufacturing head could have set the stage for maximum learning by acknowledging the past management missteps during failures associated with blaming while reminding the team about the challenges they collectively face working within a complex system.

Next time you find yourself in a meeting like this, demonstrate empathy for people in attendance who may be embarrassed or blaming themselves. Share an example of when you were involved with a significant failure in the workplace. Remind the group of the human and organizational performance principles: *error is normal* and *blame fixes nothing*. Set the stage for psychological safety by noting how complex work environments include resource constraints, goal conflicts, trade-offs, and interdependencies within the system. Explain that your goal, and the goal of the organization, is to learn so negative outcomes can be prevented, teammates are supported, and the company can produce quality products for patients.

It is critical for the leader of a post-event meeting to set a positive tone. Emotional reactions to failure are never productive. They come from a place of hindsight and judgment that fails to consider the situational context. To maximize learning, people must feel safe. They must be given voice to effectively share their valuable perspectives as the experts closest to the work.

Leaders in biopharmaceutical manufacturing may refer to the necessity of frontline workers to tell management about problems as *Speak Up Culture*.

Speak Up Culture

Unfortunately, a primary emphasis on Speak Up Culture in biopharmaceutical organizations is often the expectation for workers to report their colleagues for violations rather than a mindset of candid sharing to support operational learning that helps the organization to improve. Assuming your organization wants more than an increase in informants, let's consider what it takes to create a culture where workers feel safe to share information.

You will fail if you try to change culture by tackling culture directly. Attempts to act on culture directly often include posters and other reminders to speak up—as if the responsibility falls on the workers. Instead, think like Edgar Schein, who stated, "Given that culture is the past, present, and future of the whole system, what specifically needs changing: what, if anything, is wrong where; what is upsetting or disconfirming; what would you like to see different tomorrow in this fluid, dynamic system?" Define what it is about the culture that is bothersome—the pinpoint behavior, including the time and place of occurrence or nonoccurrence. Then ask questions. You want to know which business processes must be adjusted to better impact culture so a specific performance change can happen. Posters on walls and chiding workers to speak up will not improve openness and trust within an organization.

Psychological Safety

Biopharmaceutical organizations should revise the description of speak up culture to include *psychological safety*. Amy Edmondson, a scholar of leadership, teaming, and organizational learning, defines psychological safety as a belief that one will not be punished or humiliated for speaking up with ideas, questions, concerns, or mistakes. Essentially, psychological safety is a shared sense of candor. Without psychological safety, people will rightfully withhold the details of how their work is done and avoid asking related questions to protect themselves from embarrassment, sanction, or reprimand.

How do you know if your workplace is weak in psychological safety? Consider looking for some of these warning flags:

- Workers are blamed for mistakes.
- Employees hold back from voicing concerns.
- People voice their opinion only moments before the problem is revealed.
- People provide vague explanations rather than detailed, candid explanations.
- Issues linger due to conflict avoidance.
- Open conversations about concerns or problems are shut down by management.

Psychological safety makes post-event learning more effective, and shared trust and openness makes it possible for productive disagreement and the free exchange of ideas. Organizations with psychologically safe work environments enjoy improved talent retention and higher revenue per employee. The positive emotions associated with psychological safety, like trust and confidence, help employees improve their inner drive, situational flexibility, open-mindedness, and creativity while problem-solving. These are all strong reasons to invest in building psychological safety.

Diversity, Equity, and Inclusion

In 2022, when writing this book, your organization was likely beginning or possibly already on a diversity, equity, and inclusion (DEI) journey. Your leadership was providing resources for DEI, and the human resources department was developing and executing plans to improve DEI. There likely was an employee council and employee resource group working at the grassroots. They no doubt were working to enhance psychological safety since it is a contributing factor to improved diversity, equity, and inclusion.

Psychological safety sets the stage for better DEI learning. People are less likely to self-censor when offering contributions that challenge the status quo. And remember, innovation and improvements only happen when everyone looks past old habits and conventions. You may already have allies (in your organization) working on improving psychological safety for DEI, so find them, help them, and let them help you in your human and organizational performance integration.

Amy Edmondson suggests the following guidance for leaders on how to achieve psychological safety in the workplace:

- Create shared expectations and meaning regarding failure, uncertainty, and interdependence to clarify the need for voice and by emphasizing purpose.
- Invite participation by acknowledging gaps, asking good questions, modeling intense listening, and creating forums for input.
- Respond productively by expressing appreciation, destigmatizing failure, and maintaining an orientation toward continuous learning.

Respond Versus React

How leaders respond to significant undesired outcomes tells the organization what to expect next. The response is so consequential that it is captured as one of the five human and organizational performance principles: *how you respond to failure matters*. It's normal for emotions to be a bit high following a batch loss or major failure, so it makes sense to have a predetermined response in the form of a set of questions to ensure that leaders get it right.

Below are three questions to get you started. You will notice these questions are open-ended. That is intentional, to give people a voice and encourage free dialogue.

1. **How are the people and the facility?**

   This must always be the first question, even if you think you already know the answer. Show you care about your people. This question applies not only to an industrial safety event but also to quality events. Following a batch loss or significant event, some will feel embarrassed and ashamed, which can impact their mental well-being and future performance. People should always be a priority. Asking about the facility ensures that any immediate action to control hazards, such as spills and equipment damage, are addressed.

2. **How can I help support activities for return to operations?**

   Offer to provide help and support. If a worker or team's needs are unclear, seek to understand what support is needed. Sometimes people will reject help to avoid the appearance of weakness. Provide reassurance and encouragement. You may need to ask follow-up questions to explore the challenges they face and how you can make their job easier.

3. **How can I help ensure we learn what we need to learn?**

   Set the tone for effective post-event learning. Whether the failure led to an investigation or an after-action review, let the workers involved know you have their back. Give them time, space, and resources to learn from the event. Accept responsibility as a leader, and share in discovering better ways to learn.

Humble Inquiry

Edgar Schein, author of the book *Humble Inquiry*, defines humble inquiry as "The fine art of drawing someone out, asking questions to which the answers are unknown, building a relationship based on curiosity and genuine interest in the other person and their work." The use of humble inquiry is a very effective way to improve psychological safety in an organization, as well as achieve maximum learning with workers. Humble inquiry can be used by a leader at gemba[48], a colleague leading an investigation, or in any conversation where somebody else has knowledge that can be shared.

Humble inquiry embraces the perspective that the modern workplace has become complex, and leaders depend on workers' knowledge and experience. By asking open-ended questions that are not judgmental, leaders can engage with workers to learn about what goes right and how it goes right. Leaders can elicit ideas and concerns, and share in problem-solving and ownership. This, in turn, helps to foster an environment that promotes psychological safety.

The use of humble inquiry acknowledges local rationality and the power of learning another person's perspective about the context of their workplace. To understand a person's rationality, one must know about their mindset, motivations, knowledge, demands, goals, and work context. Humble inquiry creates the possibility to listen to people's stories and appreciate their perspective of their work.

At its core, humble inquiry involves less telling and more listening. When you ask questions, sincerely listen to the answers, and reiterate what you've learned. This style of questioning uses open-ended questions while showing curiosity, caring, and a commitment to helping the other person. While

---

48 Being humble is an enabling attitude that precedes learning and improvement at gemba. It is characterized by an ability to accurately acknowledge one's limitations and abilities, and an interpersonal stance that is other-oriented rather than self-focused.

discussing work situations, you must make it clear the worker is the expert and you are there to learn from them. In fact, just saying those words and staying true to those words will open doors to learning that you did not know existed.

In his book *Humble Inquiry*, Edgar Schein provides examples of questions or statements that encourage people to engage in a shared conversation. Here are a few to get you started:

- "What do you think?"
- "So . . ." (with an expectant look)
- "What's happening?"
- "What's going on?"
- "What brings you here?"
- "Go on..."

Here are examples from Bob Edwards' book, *Bob's Guide to Operational Learning*:
- "Tell me about..."
- "Describe what it is like when..."
- "Teach me how..."
- "Tell me more..."

The following are our examples of questions that have worked well for us:

1. "How do you think that activity went?"

2. "What conditions make the activity harder than it has to be?"

3. "When this activity goes well, what conditions help create that success?"

4. "At which points of the work have you been surprised that risk, response, or controls were not what you expected?"

Avoid starting questions with the word *why*. Why is often interpreted as a question of judgment and often leads to an answer that is thin on context and thick with excuses. Use words like *how* or *what* to get answers that are richer in context.

Appendix A provides an activity that can help improve your understanding and use of humble inquiry in your organization.

Deviation Cause Codes

A commonly sanctioned destroyer of psychological safety and learning is the misuse of deviation cause codes. The set of cause codes available in most deviation management systems includes an unhelpful subset poorly designed for when people make mistakes during work. By people, we mean the colleagues who work on manufacturing floors, labs, or warehouses—the people at the sharp end who tend to be those who touch things last. As if these are the only people who make mistakes in an organization. These cause codes include unhelpful terms like human error, violation, and sabotage.

Some cause code lists may borrow from the Generic Error Modeling System (GEMS), which is intended to model the *black box* that is the human brain. GEMS categorizes cognitive factors believed to occur during work performance—instead of the observable environment or work context factors that shape performance. If your cause codes contain the terms skill-based, rule-based, or knowledge-based, it is borrowing from GEMS, and it is likely doing more harm than good.

While James Reason may be best known for GEMS, the basis of GEMS originated in 1979 by Jens Rasmussen as the Skill-Rule-Knowledge (SRK) model, which explained categories of human performance processes—how nuclear plant operators transitioned between modes of control while executing work. Rasmussen explained the SRK model as "The degree of conscious control exercised by the individual over his or her activities, depending on the degree of familiarity with the task and the environment." Skill-based was associated with highly practiced tasks with little to no conscious monitoring. Rule-based was associated with mindful attention to familiar tasks. And knowledge-based was related to unfamiliar situations where no known solutions were available.

While this model might have been helpful to the cognitive engineering community following the Three Mile Island accident, in the early days of exploring human error and when practical frameworks did not exist, the SRK model or GEMS is not well suited for biopharma manufacturing deviation investigations. First, these labels unintentionally support the blaming of workers. Secondly, what is the organization really going to do with the information where a person was in knowledge-based performance and in hindsight we wished the person would have stopped work? If this information drives the organization to change the design of work, that is super. However, that is not often the case when programmatically assigning synonyms to error. Third, trying to gain insight from skill-based, rule-based, and knowledge-based error frequencies is misleading—confusing classification with analysis and understanding. Such a classification scheme will only confirm that most performance is skill-based and the least common is knowledge-based—despite the error rates.

In the end, using GEMS as a basis for deviation cause codes does little more than describe an error with another name while failing to explain how it happened. What is needed is a rich description of the work context and the local rationality of the people involved.

A more helpful design for cause codes would be based on environmental and work context factors. This information would encourage actionable learning so the organization could make choices and invest in improvements that shape future performance. Also, assigning causes to workplace performance shaping factors avoids organizationally sanctioned blaming that damages employees' psychological safety and short-circuits learning.

A good starting point can be found in Erik Hollnagel's Cognitive Reliability and Error Analysis Method (CREAM). The CREAM classification scheme is intended to be used by an analyst to predict and describe how errors could potentially occur. Although the method was developed for the nuclear power industry, Hollnagel claims that it is a generic technique that can be applied in a number of domains involving the operation of complex dynamic systems.

The part of the model that would lend itself best to deviation cause codes is the *common performance conditions*. Of course, in the majority of instances, more than one common performance condition might apply to an undesired outcome where a person made a mistake. Some of the potentially more useful common performance conditions are: adequacy of organization, working conditions, adequacy of 'Man Machine Interface' and operational support, availability of procedure/plans, number of simultaneous goals, time of day (circadian rhythm), and adequacy of training and experience. In addition to these, consideration should be given to adding cause codes that characterize the presence and function of controls in a system that prevents significant adverse outcomes when people fail—because people *will* fail.

Fundamentally, cause codes should be used as trending attributes and should not dictate a limited set of conclusions, prescribe preset possibilities for learning outcomes, or be stated verbatim as *the cause* in investigation reports. Simply put, cause codes are not causes. Recognize that some people will use cause codes incorrectly—as an endpoint for an investigation or as a quick pick that short-circuits learning.

As you determine appropriate cause codes for your organization, consider how they might be used—as intended, for trending and pattern identification—and as not intended, to fully describe analysis outcomes.

Playing Cops and Robbers

Another organizationally sanctioned destroyer of psychological safety in the biopharmaceutical industry is the Cressey Fraud Model, used as part of the industry's focus on data integrity. Data integrity is the maintenance and assurance of data accuracy and consistency over its lifecycle. It is certainly necessary that complete, consistent, and accurate data be attributable, legible, recorded in original/true copy, and accurate—especially when it comes to making medicines for patients. Biopharmaceutical organizations rightfully must commit attention and resources to that end. However, when describing reasons for people not following data integrity principles, using a model based on bank fraud created in the 1950s by a criminologist is both misguided and destructive. What internet word search did somebody do to find this inappropriate model? It's akin to suggesting that casting chicken bones or pulling tarot cards are predictive of the future.

The Cressey Fraud Model suggests the industry looks at workers at the sharp end as potential wrongdoers. Using this model compares valuable employees to people who may commit bank fraud when pressure, opportunity, and rationalization are present.

A complete explanation of the Cressey Fraud Model's three factors is a non-shareable financial problem, the opportunity to commit a trust violation, and rationalization by the trust violator. Clearly the biopharmaceutical industry has leveraged an incorrect and simplistic interpretation of an inapplicable behavioral model to try to solve an important problem. On a positive note, the instinct of organizations that focus on improving systems through the use of controls to improve data integrity is sound.

A model that is helpful and supportive to openness and trust is Jens Rasmussen's model of the natural migration of activities toward the boundary of acceptable performance. Rasmussen's model can be used to explain data integrity challenges and most other operational challenges where an asset must be protected. Normal changes in local work conditions lead to frequent strategy and work adaptation modifications. Workers and leaders may naturally choose the least effort gradient during that adaptive search, and organizations tend to take the least cost gradient. The result is a systematic migration of the system operating state toward the boundary of acceptable performance where if crossing the boundary is irreversible and catastrophic a significant undesired outcome will occur. In the case of data integrity, counter gradients would be organizational investments in design and controls based on the risks.

The model provided here is a simpler version of Jens Rasmussen's original model. We've named this simplified version of the model the Cost-Effort-Controls System Model:

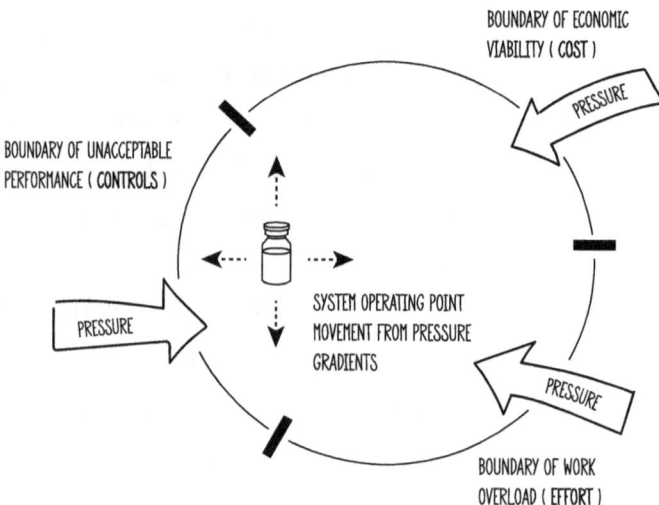

Illustration of the Cost-Effort-Controls System Model adapted from Figure 3 in
Risk Management in a Dynamic Society: A Modelling Problem
by J. Rasmussen and published by Pergamon: Safety Science in 1997.

Accountability In Practice

Some readers may still not be entirely convinced of this different approach to accountability. In most situations, if people are honest and explain what they did and how it made sense at the time, and there was no malicious intent, then there should be acceptance and goodwill on the part of the organization. The organization makes the wise decision to learn instead of blame, and the learning opportunity leads to operational improvement. That win-win on the part of the people and organization will create momentum for future win-wins.

When the situation demands a more nuanced approach, there are options covered in chapter thirteen.

We recognize that results count, which applies to the business and every person in the organization. Psychological safety does not replace performance management[49], which ideally must take place in association with desirable and undesirable work performance. If the totality of a worker's performance does not measure up to standards met by coworkers—be it observed behaviors or repeated mistakes—then perhaps the person is in the wrong job. If occurring over an extended period, it also may indicate a failure in leadership, coaching, or performance management.

Dishonesty and malicious intent are always grounds for discipline. Both should be extremely rare—or the organization has a different and much bigger problem to solve than human and organizational performance integration. In addition, when dishonesty or malicious intent is revealed, hiring and leadership practices should be assessed.

---

49 Effective and timely feedback is a critical component of successful performance management. Feedback includes appreciation, evaluation, and coaching.

Chapter Summary

Psychological safety in your organization will be supported by how leaders respond to failures, how questions are posed as part of your investigation process and work observations, how your investigation documentation system is structured, and what models are used to describe how failures occur. Pay attention to what your organization means when the word accountability is used. Is it faux or is it real?

Maturity Assessment

Consider using the following statements to assess the maturity of your organization regarding psychological safety. Each statement has three possible choices. A higher total score indicates a higher maturity.

1. Accountability is forward-looking and not synonymous with blame.
   Agree 20, Sometimes 10, Disagree 0

2. Cause codes in a deviation management system are understood to not be synonymous with cause statements that are rich in context.
   Agree 20, Sometimes 10, Disagree 0

3. Coaching, counseling, and awareness discussions are never acceptable corrective actions for a deviation.
   Agree 20, Sometimes 10, Disagree 0

4. Workers are treated like partners in learning, and are never considered wrongdoers during an investigation.
   Agree 20, Sometimes 10, Disagree 0

5. Our organization does not have an institutionalized process or culture where workers are systematically disciplined for mistakes to improve operational performance.

    Agree 20, Sometimes 10, Disagree 0

CHAPTER SEVEN

A Better Way to Learn About Work

Today at 9:30 a.m., the site head and the head of human and organizational performance are going to gemba[50]. The two-hour meeting on both their calendars is titled *Operational Learning in Purification*. Leaders at the site have found that scheduling time at gemba assures they go to gemba. Otherwise, competing priorities creep in and steal the necessary time away from going to where the work happens for operational learning.

They are going to gemba with human and organizational performance in mind, which means they will focus on managing risk to the product. They are not conducting an inspection readiness walkthrough or a process confirmation. While both of these leaders also go to the gemba for those activities, the purpose and method of operational learning are very different and add unique and essential value to the organization.

Remember, *operational learning* is defined as the capacity of an organization to understand how people and systems perform within the context created

---

50 Gemba is a Japanese word for the actual place. When used as part of Lean the term gemba walk is often used. When performing operational learning, we are not going for a walk of the value stream. We are going to where work takes place and then we will stand there to watch the performance of that work.

by the organization. Operational learning is learning about work from the perspective of the people performing the work. Operational learning at gemba is about leaders going to where the work occurs to learn about the difference between Work As Imagined and Work As Done. Again, *Work As Imagined* refers to the various assumptions that people who do not perform the work have about how the work should be done. *Work As Done* refers to how a task is actually performed by the people who do the work. These two terms describing different work perspectives are often used in contemporary approaches to safety management and were presented in more detail in chapter two.

The site head and head of human and organizational performance will be watching a process performance qualification (PPQ) run on the new purification skid. Yesterday they reached out to the manufacturing manager to let him know they would be visiting that manufacturing space. They asked what work they would see in action. As is typical in manufacturing operations, production schedules shift, and it is helpful to be flexible based on what work is available to watch during a leader's available time. Two hours may seem like a lot of time to spend at gemba. When the people doing the work know and trust their leaders, less time is needed—one hour, for example. In this case, this will be the first time the people involved with the work have encountered the site head on the floor—especially two site leadership team members at once.

It will not be surprising if some people are initially anxious and quiet. Some will first try to perform their work in a manner that is not typical; closer to Work as Imagined. Some will try hard to comply with written procedures just to meet expectations, even when the procedures are not conducive to the work. The first hour of the two-hour block will be spent building relationships and showing the people that the site head and the head of human and organizational performance are interested in learning and helping the team, as opposed to judging them and trying to fix their behaviors.

The site head and head of human and organizational performance enter the suite. All eyes turn their way. While the manufacturing manager notified his workers of the visit, the two leaders are not part of the work team and are hard to recognize wearing the ISO 7 aseptic gowning required for the suite. They scan the area. Two manufacturing associates are standing in front of the HMI for the purification skid gazing at the colored screen and their documentation. There are three validation engineers standing in front of a laptop and a stack of documentation. The manufacturing manager gives a wave and walks over to greet the site head and head of human and organizational performance before they reach the people in the work area.

"Is the work in a good place for introductions?" asks the site head.

"Absolutely," says the manufacturing manager. The introduction is brief and intended for everyone in the work area. He shares everyone's full names and their roles within the company.

"Nice to meet you all," says the head of human and organizational performance. She explains the purpose of the visit is to learn about the work the team performs from the perspective of the experts—the workers. "Where is the best place to stand so we won't interfere with your tasks?" she asks. They are guided to a good spot nearby where they can watch and listen well.

After watching the tasks for a few minutes, the site head asks, "What written guidance are you using and what step are you on? I would like to follow along." He is genuinely curious and wants to learn. His interest also emphasizes the importance of procedure use.

The first hour of watching the work is a combination of learning something personal about the people doing the tasks and seeing the workers' interactions as part of the system. This is a key focus of operational learning at gemba. Initially, it's about building rapport and creating psychological safety. Once mutual respect is established, the focus will shift more to watching the work performed. Seeing workers' interactions as part of the system includes noting what people are looking at and talking about in relation to the work. These two leaders know it's important they understand how workers feel about the work from the words they use, tone of voice, and facial expressions. With this knowledge, they can better assess how processes, procedures, and all the system elements support the people in managing risk and creating success.

The site head and head of human and organizational performance split up to watch from different perspectives. When the work pauses, they take the opportunity to get to know the workers more personally. They also share tidbits about themselves.

"I'm quite new here," says one of the validation engineers.

"Welcome to the team," says the head of human and organizational performance. "Where did you work before here?" They discuss their backgrounds.

"I've been at this site for twelve years," says a manufacturing associate.

"Wonderful," says the site head. "Such loyalty is appreciated. May I ask what you like about working here and why you've stayed for twelve years?"

The head of human and organizational performance sees a manufacturing associate wearing a New England Patriots shirt under his coveralls. She points to the logo that is somewhat distinguishable through the gowning material. "What are the chances of the Pats going to the Super Bowl again this year?"

Before the site head and head of human and organizational performance arrived on the floor, they discussed what they would do and not do as part of this operational learning gemba. They wanted to show engagement and make the visit a positive experience for the people doing the work.

A good list of how leaders should show up at gemba can be found in the *Field Guide to Effective Leadership Engagements* created by the Construction Safety Research Alliance. Key points are:

1. Make it clear that the visit is not an audit.

2. Do not correct or attempt to coach the people doing the work.

3. Learn and use the first names of employees.

4. Learn something personal about each person.

5. Share something personal about yourself.

6. Ask questions to learn what motivates them in their job.

7. Ask questions to better understand tasks.

8. Ask about challenges that make the job more difficult and riskier than necessary.

9. Ask what will make the work better, easier, and reduce risks to the product.

10. Share information that explains how their role supports the company mission.

These key points are necessary to create psychological safety for the people doing the work. Psychological safety is essential as part of an operational learning gemba. For positive results, the people doing the work must choose to teach leaders—the ones present to learn. As soon as workers feel safe, candid sharing will begin. Workers recognize when leaders are there to help them. For that help to happen, they must disclose work knowledge the leader does not possess. Sometimes this will happen quickly, sometimes near the end of the operational learning gemba, and sometimes it may need more time. If there is a lack of psychological safety, the damage might take time to repair. Sometimes entire teams have been disrespected and diminished by other leaders who visited their workplace, setting negative precedence.

The Wrong Approach

Many leaders arrive at gemba with the wrong attitude. They consider themselves *the fixer of bad behaviors* and *the smartest person in the room*. They come looking for evidence of wrongdoing and incompetence. A leader like this undermines learning on a grand scale.

If you are a leader unsure if these labels apply to you, consider collecting data to support or refute your belief before totally rejecting the possibility. Asking manufacturing associates how they feel about you may not yield reliable data. They may have had bad experiences in the past when providing candid feedback to management, or perhaps they lack the skill or experience to safely manage the *ugly baby* conversation. Instead, pay attention to how manufacturing associates react when you arrive at their workplace. Notice if the work slows, concerned eyes dart between the team, and workers avoid eye contact with you. Watch to see if communication with you is strained and meager. You might notice answers to questions are short and vague, and the team looks relieved when you say goodbye. This data indicates you may have some self-improvement work to do.

During good times and challenging times, many leaders' instinct is to engage in a direct manner through questioning that feels like an oral examination. Some managers use corrective feedback that asserts their expectations based on ill-conceived beliefs about what workers should be doing. This approach is contrary to what Lean Six Sigma practitioners cite as desired behaviors, such as those in the Shingo Model described by the Jon M. Huntsman School of Business at Utah State University. The cultural enablers of *respect every individual* and *lead with humility* are absent when leaders show up at gemba with an authoritative command-and-control mindset.

When workers are not respected and leaders are not humble, very little operational learning can occur. The amygdala hijack[51] shuts down productive conversations and further damages relationships. While a *fight reaction* may be rare on the part of manufacturing associates, they will withdraw, reluctantly, and do whatever they can to ensure the speedy departure of management from their workplace.

There certainly is a time and a place when behaviors must be addressed. Like when there is an immediate risk of harm to employees or the product. To test if such a time is happening when you are at gemba, apply *the pointy stick-in the-eye rule*. Figuratively speaking, if somebody is about to poke themselves in the eye with a sharp stick, you should stop them and provide an explanation of the risk. State your good intent and try to understand how it made sense to align the stick so close to their eye. But choose wisely. Choosing not to intercede during an operational learning gemba may lead to you learning how it makes sense to the people doing the work. That learning is invaluable.

While at gemba, work hard to resist the instinct to correct behaviors and give advice. Instead, be curious about what is shaping the behaviors. This is not easy to do. It will take self-control and practice. You will also

---

51 An amygdala hijack is an emotional response that is immediate, overwhelming, and out of measure with the actual stimulus because it has triggered a much more significant emotional threat. Human ancestors developed this response to deal with threats and dangerous situations, to release stress hormones that prepare the body to either face the threat or flee from it.

need to gauge whether or not the behaviors you are seeing has any impact or risk to product, because it may not in many cases. If you find it impossible to remain in a learning mindset and repeatedly correct workers at gemba, consider applying Hackworth's Two Rule Plan. Choose two simple rules you previously communicated as necessary and where you explained the why. Then give feedback on only those two rules. Even someone as hardcore as Colonel David Hackworth[52], often thought of as a transformational leader, did not correct his soldiers every time a rule was broken or when performance slightly missed the standard. Hackworth recognized that people needed space to fail and learn from their errors. He also recognized that taking care of your people is foundational, seeing things through the eyes of your team is paramount, and the chain of command is not always right. So, being thoughtful and deliberately infrequent in correcting behaviors you deem undesirable is essential if your goal is to learn about Work as Done.

If you resist correcting behaviors, you have the opportunity to learn what factors are shaping behaviors, which will put you in an ideal position to adjust systems. In his book *Out Of The Crisis*, W. Edwards Deming stated, "The supposition is prevalent throughout the world that there would be no problems in production or service if only our production workers would do their jobs in the way that we taught. The workers are handicapped by the system, and the system belongs to management." If we take the advice of Deming, systems would be optimized for successful outcomes. Worker behaviors would change because behaviors are a byproduct of the system.

The idea that the environment influences behavior is not new. Yet, sometimes leaders forget or choose to take the quicker and less expensive

---

52 David Hackworth was a U.S. Colonel and writer known for his service in Vietnam, which included the transformation of the 4th Battalion's 39th Infantry. Hackworth may be most well-known for later opposing America's military involvement in Vietnam.

path—despite not getting the desired sustained results. For a situation where a leader is troubled by an observed behavior, a good first step is to think of Kurt Lewin's equation to describe what determines behavior, where $B = f(P, E)$. To change a *behavior* (B), one must either change the *person* (P) or the *environment* (E) or both. It is far easier to change the environment. We all know how hard it is to change people, including ourselves. As stated by James Reason, "We cannot change the human condition, but we can change the conditions under which humans work." And, of course, since Lewin's model is an open system, changing the environment may influence the person or people by creating new attitudes and motivations.

Also consider the Blumberg and Pringle model of performance: Performance $= f$(Willingness X Capacity X Opportunity). The term *performance* in the Blumberg and Pringle model is interchangeable with behavior. *Opportunity* is about changing the work environment to better influence the desired behavior. *Capacity* includes factors such as competence, and *willingness* includes factors related to well-being and motivation. The bottom line is that leaders cannot change behavior by force. Leaders must learn what factors drive or shape behavior and then adjust those factors.

A good way to begin is to remind yourself of the quote by Wayne Dyer[53]. "If you change the way you look at things, the things you look at change." Changing the way you look at things is similar to a concept in Zen Buddhism known as *shoshin*, or a *beginner's mind*. A beginner's mind refers to a paradox where the more you know about something, the higher the likelihood you may miss something new due to your mind being closed.

In the words of Zen monk Shunryu Suzuki, "In the beginner's mind there are many possibilities, but in the expert's there are few." What Zen monks

---

53 Wayne Dyer was a professor, therapist, and author whose early work focused on psychological themes that included motivation, self-actualization, and assertiveness.

recognized hundreds of years ago is now known as the Earned Dogmatism Effect. A study in 2015 found that giving people the impression that they were experts on various subjects led them to dismiss other viewpoints. At gemba, leaders desire what is known as *open-minded cognition*. This involves directionally unbiased information processing and the tendency to select, interpret, retrieve, weigh, and elaborate upon information in a manner that is not biased by the individual's prior opinion or expectation. So, when going to gemba, remind yourself that it's hard to learn if you already know.

Another way to change how you look at things is to literally change how you look at things by changing your observational methods. Changing your observational method is helpful as a check against your biases[54]. To get a more complete and accurate understanding of what you are looking at, aggregate the information from multiple perspectives. In basic terms, look at things twice. First without any external influence and then consulting preexisting information and opinions when looking again for the second time. To apply this concept to operational learning at gemba, try to watch work with an unbiased and unjudging mind. Look at everything in the area without forming a judgment of the people, process, and technology. Look for details such as where people are standing in relation to each other and the equipment, the ergonomic posture of the people, the items held in the hands, the units on a gauge face, and the details of documentation in use. Pause to consider the context of the workplace and the interconnectedness of all the parts of the system. Then look again. This time, tell a story that contains both the details and how the people are experiencing the work

---

54 Bias is a disproportionate weight in favor of or against an idea or thing. Another term for bias is cognitive biases, which are systematic patterns of deviation from norm and/or rationality in judgment. Examples of cognitive biases studied by Amos Tversky and Daniel Kahneman included anchoring, the availability heuristic, representative heuristic, regression to the mean, and hindsight bias.

as part of the system. This second look will form your assessment of risk management.

Generally, the first half of your time at gemba should be dedicated to the first look. The remainder of your time is used for the second look. However, you may also find yourself bouncing back and forth between details and the story context multiple times as the work progresses and the situation changes.

Another way to change how you look at things while at gemba is by applying a Safety-II mindset. According to Hollnagel, "Safety-II assumes that everyday performance variability provides the adaptations that are needed to respond to varying conditions, and hence is the reason why things go right." A Safety-I perspective assumes that things go wrong because of identifiable failures or malfunctions and does not consider why human performance practically always goes right. A Safety-II perspective seeks to understand work adaptations to learn how performance usually goes right despite the situations often present during complex work involving uncertainty, ambiguity, and goal conflicts. When watching work from a Safety-II perspective, observe the Work As Done, then consider the Work As Imagined. Now you have a basis for asking better questions about the difference between Work As Imagined and Work As Done relative to risk management and work adaptations necessary to create success.

While extreme failure and extreme success are both the minority of work outcomes and easy to see, everyday work is the majority of outcomes and difficult to see. If we can better understand everyday work, we will create more success.

The Story of Operational Risk

In this chapter's opening example of the site head and the head of human and organization performance going to gemba, the following story details were identified:

1. The compressed HMI scaling made performance changes and trends difficult for the manufacturing associates to see. They seemed to tolerate the issue until the head of human and organizational performance asked what they were monitoring on the screen.

2. A validation engineer overheard the conversation and explained that the HMI software was updated and the installation used factory defaults. The preferred settings used by the manufacturing associates had been lost, and they were unsure how to modify the scaling while the PPQ run was in progress. The validation engineer provided assistance through a brief tutorial and improved the displayed scaling.

3. At one point in the operation, the manufacturing associates and the validation engineer began questioning who was logged into the HMI. They were worried about data integrity. Since the head of human and organizational performance was familiar with the issue due to previous concerns at a different factory and an unhelpful meeting with the vendor who refused to improve the design, she shared where (on the screen) information could be found to identify who was logged in to the system.

4. The team was attentive and monitored the process by standing close to the HMI to watch and discuss the trend. The column was taking an unusually long time to reach equilibrium compared to the previous skid and column.

5. At one point in the process, a manufacturing associate had to walk to the back of the skid to operate a valve as another manufacturing associate called out total volume values as the process approached the target.

6. The local pressure gauge range was zero to eighty pounds, while the process pressure barely displayed on the gauge at 0.5 psi.

7. The manufacturing associates struggled to monitor the flow through the opaque tubing. They needed to hold the tubing up to the light close to their eyes to see the liquid as it flowed into the tubing.

8. The manufacturing associates verbalized the name of the device they were operating and the status to which the device was being changed as valves were repositioned.

9. One of the manufacturing associates was on overtime from a previous shift to cover for a colleague who was out sick.

10. The batch record had five performer steps that took an hour to execute. Data was recorded for three of the steps, and there was only one witness signature for the entire series.

11. There was only a single floor scale in the suite, and it was out of service. The manufacturing associates could either wheel totes to an adjacent suite or move an operational scale into the area, requiring calibration with 750 kg weights. A replacement control board was on order for the out of service scale.

The story the site head and the head of human and organizational performance could tell, based on their learning in gemba, was a *story of operational risk.*

What is *risk?* For human and organizational performance, we define risk as the static and dynamic conditions that impact the exposure of assets to hazards[55].

Getting good at spotting risk requires what is known as *chronic unease.* Chronic unease is thinking about awful stuff, the worst things that can happen with an unusual or unexpected condition or behavior discovered during an operational learning gemba. Chronic unease is a preoccupation with failure, even when operational performance is going well. A preoccupation with failure includes looking for *weak signals.* The term weak signals originated in 1975 by H. Igor Ansoff. As Ansoff defined it, "Weak signals are the first symptoms of strategic discontinuities; they are symptoms of possible change in the future." Ansoff's use of the term primarily applied to strategic business planning, concepts of a turbulent environment, strategic discontinuity, and strategic surprise. Weick and Sutcliffe later adopted weak signals in 2001 as part of their High Reliability Organization (HRO) Theory[56]. The theory suggested a necessary element of anticipation was a preoccupation with failure. A preoccupation with failure is when you look for and are sensitive to early signs of failure.

Strong signals are what people know they must pay attention to and are, therefore, what they mostly notice. The out-of-service floor scale stood out as a strong signal in our example.

---

55 Assets are anything of value to the organization. Hazards are anything that can cause harm to an asset.

56 A high reliability organization is an organization that has succeeded in avoiding catastrophic failures where normal accidents can be expected due to risk and complexity. According to Weick and Sutcliffe in their book Managing the Unexpected, high reliability organizations share five characteristics: preoccupation with failure, reluctance to simplify interpretations, sensitivity to operations, commitment to resilience, and deference to expertise. Examples of high reliability organizations include nuclear aircraft carriers, air traffic control systems, and nuclear-powered electric generating stations.

Weak signals in contrast include information that people are not prepared for, or that they do not expect, or that they otherwise might fail to notice. The futurist Elina Hiltunen suggests a subjective test can be used to assess if something might qualify as a weak signal. She thinks if the information causes a reaction among experts, it may be a weak signal, and a reaction may include any of the following:

- Does the information make your colleagues laugh?
- Do your colleagues insist this will never happen?
- Does the information make people think?
- Has anyone heard of this before?
- Do people remain quiet because it is taboo?

Erik Hollnagel describes weak signals as performance patterns over time, using an analogy of time-lapse photography where the strong signal is the last photograph in the series. Weak signals are usually ambiguous, and the first reaction may be to assume normalcy and move on. In our example, the leaders observed a process that uses an 80 psi gauge to monitor a 0.5 psi process. This could be considered a weak signal because the gauge still functions to enable people to do their job, though the range is not ideal for the application. The leaders would need to determine how impactful or widespread the situation could be.

Another weak signal from the leaders' observations was the designed location for a valve that needed to be operated at an exact moment based on information displayed on the HMI screen that was located on the opposite side of the skid. Upon discovering a weak signal, a degree of research and interpretation is necessary before dismissing the information as nonactionable or a sign of potential failure.

Since the site head and the head of human and organization performance were at gemba to learn about operational risk, they could practice humble inquiry. They asked the following questions:

1. What workplace factors create a risk of failure for the task?

2. What is the worst possible thing that will happen if a failure occurs?

3. How are the steps that must go right performed?

4. How is the process monitored to ensure success?

5. Where in the task have manufacturing associates experienced past surprises or unexpected results?

6. Where in the task are workers having to make do, improvise, or adapt to create success?

7. Where else have they experienced or heard of a similar situation?

When the site head and the head of human and organizational performance completed their operational learning at gemba, they thanked the team for their experienced perspectives. While no actions were intentionally assigned to the team, the site head and the head of human and organizational performance documented and shared their learnings with others who could improve the situation associated with the strong signals or connect some dots in order to refute or validate the weak signals.

Chapter Summary

When you go to gemba in your organization, if you don't watch the work performed, and your relationship with the people doing the work is based on organizational hierarchy and obedience, it is unlikely you'll learn from your gemba experience. How would people in your organization describe the purpose of going to gemba and how best to learn from work? While there is a need for management to check in on issues related to inspection readiness, workplace safety conditions, and efficiency, if you are only going to gemba for these reasons, you are missing valuable opportunities to learn about your site's state of risk and controls. Continuing this way will lead to ongoing failure.

Try a different approach. Go to gemba with open eyes, curiosity, and the willingness to learn from your frontline workers. A leader who understands how the system operates will catch possible problems before they occur. A leader who acknowledges, involves, and appreciates workers at the sharp end will see the challenges they face and contribute to solutions. The result will be a robust and resilient system with minimal operational risks.

Maturity Assessment

Consider using the following statements to assess the maturity of your organization regarding operational learning at gemba. Each statement has three possible choices. A higher total score indicates a higher maturity.

1. We understand it is impossible to learn about operational risk while at gemba if workers are constantly corrected.
   Agree 20, Sometimes 10, Disagree 0

2. Psychological safety is essential if we are to maximize learning at gemba.

    Agree 20, Sometimes 10, Disagree 0

3. We often go to gemba to watch work activities.

    Agree 20, Sometimes 10, Disagree 0

4. To assess risk, we must check the factors that shape performance.

    Agree 20, Sometimes 10, Disagree 0

5. We get to know our manufacturing associates and share information about ourselves at gemba.

    Agree 20, Sometimes 10, Disagree 0

Human-Focused Written Guidance

Beth is an experienced manufacturing associate. Her crew regards her as a subject matter expert on ultrafiltration (UF) skid operations. Juan is less experienced and not yet qualified to operate the UF skid. Today, Beth and Juan are assigned to the UF work activity. This morning is their crew's first day back after being off for three days, and the next shift can't support bottling operations due to several staff members taking vacations simultaneously. Beth and the supervisor agree to perform the UF skid operation quickly so the team can also complete the bottling operations.

Beth and Juan place the batch record paperwork and the electronic tablet used to view the procedure on a podium next to the UF skid. Juan is the performer, and Beth is the witness. Juan is also the trainee, and Beth is the qualified trainer. Beth is reading and directing while Juan executes the steps required by the written guidance.

The UF human-machine interface (HMI) prompt reads, "Ready to begin transfer out." Since the next three steps (numbered 9.9, 9.10, and 9.11) start with, "When the prompt reads 'Ready to begin transfer out,'" Beth and Juan work ahead in the batch record. It is accepted practice to complete the tare weight of the product collection vessel according to step 9.10 before taking the bioburden and endotoxin sample from the product tank at step 9.9. The written guidance steps for taking the endotoxin sample and performing the tare weight must be performed before starting product collection at step 9.11. Many manufacturing associates prefer performing the tare weight at step 9.10, prior to the sampling step of 9.9. From the workers' perspective, the work flows better by performing the tare before the sample and product collection, and crews have been doing the work this way for years. The detailed sub-steps and data recording fields for step 9.9 (sample) are on a separate page, while the sub-steps and data recording fields for steps 9.10 (tare) and 9.11 (transfer out) are on the next page of the batch record. The written guidance describes Work As Imagined, and how the manufacturing associates perform the activity is Work As Done.

While Juan is working, Beth notices two issues that require resolution—slowing progress and shifting the focus of the two-person team. The first is a broken NovaSeptum sample bag on the product tank. As part of the tank assembly performed by the previous shift, three NovaSeptum bags were installed onto the product tank—two for planned samples and one as a backup. Beth steps out of her witness role to crimp off and discard the damaged bag. At the same time, she deals with the second issue by installing the product collection filter onto the product addition valve on the collection vessel. The product addition valve installed on the vessel did not have the 1.5-inch sanitary connection required to install the filter. Beth notified the supervisor, and a clean 0.5-inch to 1.5-inch reducer was installed onto the product addition valve to facilitate the installation of the product addition filter.

Once the product collection vessel tare weight is performed, Beth follows the automation prompt to transfer out—an irreversible step that transfers product from the product tank to the product collection vessel. Juan notes the sample step in the batch record has not been performed and asks Beth about the missing step.

Realizing the problem, Beth attempts to take a sample from the product tank using an installed NovaSeptum bag, but she can't get a sample because the tank contents have already transferred out. The required sample for bioburden and endotoxin was missed. The batch is now at risk and may need to be discarded.

Here is a visual to better understand the ultrafiltration system Beth and Juan are working with:

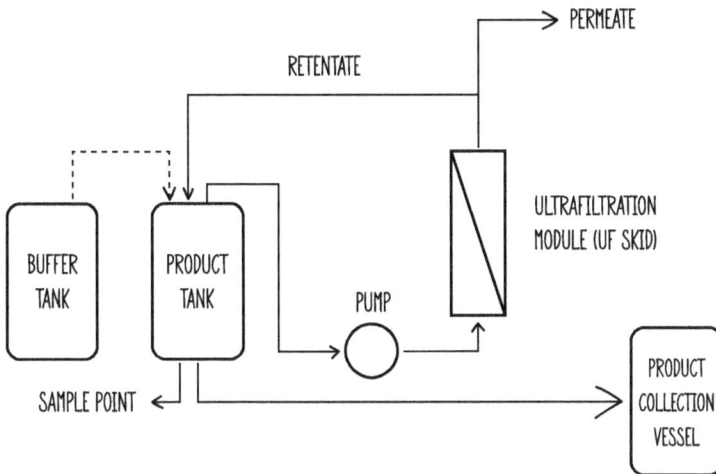

Simplified diagram of an ultrafiltration system.

This story example contains multiple factors that influence system performance:

1. Poorly organized employee days off created a staffing issue.

2. Three workers reduces the risk when training a new employee. One qualified person teaches the employee who is the performer while the other is a witness.

3. The unplanned role swap between the performer and the witness increased the complexity of the task.

4. The lack of an automated Manufacturing Execution System (MES) that would force the sample to be taken before the prompt that allows the transfer out to begin.

Written Documentation

Many organizations have not yet made the jump to appropriate integration of automation to check the performance of humans and reassign tasks better suited to machines. Until a manufacturing facility can take this step, paper documentation must be optimized to create success. Small or start-up bio-pharmaceutical manufacturers may be locked into working with paper for many years before they can progress to elaborate automated solutions. In these situations, optimizing paper procedures, instructions, and batch records to better match the capabilities and limitations of workers is essential.

It is typical in situations like the one with Beth and Juan for management to assume they were not following procedures and should be disciplined by applying faux accountability. Yet, if management and workplace designers did not know manufacturing associates performed the work differently than the clumsily prescribed batch record, they did not have an accurate understanding of the Work As Done. All biopharmaceutical manufacturing organizations have written expectations that procedures are followed, yet many also have tacit agreements that allow procedure steps or sections to be performed in parallel or out of sequence in order to keep operations moving smoothly without interruption.

Biopharma manufacturing operations—whether upstream, downstream, or fill-finish—are not like an automobile assembly line where workers tend to perform assigned repetitive tasks during their shift. The work performed in biopharma manufacturing often includes segments where batch record pages or sections for a unit operation can be split out and performed in parallel by different people or teams when necessary or preferred. This creates little risk depending on design of the batch record. This ability to vary the sequence of activities within a unit operation enhances operational resilience by allowing people to respond to surprises and abnormal situations so production can proceed in a complex system. The ability to perform activities in parallel also affords efficiency benefits. A negative, of course, is that the variability in work sequencing may increase the risks associated with irreversible actions leading to deviations and lost batches.

Commercial nuclear power plants provide *Level of Use* guidance for all procedures in order to institutionalize minimum requirements for how specific procedures should be used based on risk. As part of that guidance, procedures are designed to make users aware the sequence of steps must be followed in order unless otherwise specified. One method for informing workers a procedure segment does not require the sequential performance of steps is using bullets rather than numbers.

For example, Pacific Gas & Electric, the company that owns and operates the Diablo Canyon Nuclear Power Plant, uses the following *Level of Use* guidance:

- Continuous Use (In Hand) - Read each step prior to performing that step.
- Periodic Use - Use the procedure either before, while, or after performing each procedure segment to ensure all steps are performed in accordance with the procedure.

- Reference Use - Perform activities from memory and in accordance with procedures.
- Multiple Levels of Use - May incorporate more than one level of use, as described above. An example would be *continuous use* for the removal of equipment from service. Once the equipment is removed from service, *periodic use* may be allowed. Restoring the equipment may require continuous use of the procedure.

Within the commercial nuclear power industry, procedures that immediately impact the integrity of the reactor core, especially its cooling, are designated for *continuous use*. If a procedure has no immediate impact on the state of the reactor core and is within the skills and knowledge of the workers to be performed by memory, it is designated as *reference use*. If the procedure does not meet the criteria for continuous use or reference use, and the task can be broken into smaller segments easily memorized, it can be designated as *periodic use*.

Such concepts would benefit biopharmaceutical manufacturing as a way for leaders to provide better clarity on using written guidance. Such a design is clearly risk-based and reflects the real world—how people interact with written documentation. The change is necessary since the prevailing guideline in the biopharmaceutical industry is simply to *follow procedures*.

Involve End Users

The design and format of written guidance is a major factor in how helpful it is to end users. Always involve the end user in creating or revising written guidance. This includes procedures, batch records, and automation prompts. End-user input should be solicited for the sequence of the written guidance to best match Work As Done. The words used to describe the work are important; they ensure the process intent and requirements are met. Also, when multiple written guidance sources are used to perform an activity, it must be clear which source is used at which point. The written documentation must allow the user to smoothly transition from the batch record to procedures and back again.

When it comes to formatting procedures and batch records, documentation writers often lean towards a format that is easier for them to create and maintain. These choices may counter what makes the documentation helpful to end users. While end users sometimes resist a new design or format standard for their procedures and batch records, the change is usually beneficial to improve work performance. Experienced end users may initially dislike a new design and format because they will need to relearn where specific information is located. Less experienced end users will have an immediate appreciation for the changes and provide that feedback.

The bottom line: Clear written guidance makes everyone's job easier and increases the likelihood of successful performance.

Look to Ikea for inspiration. Ikea was one of the first companies to pair written guidance with helpful images, eliminating language barriers. Also look at passenger safety cards on your next flight. Airlines use thoughtfully designed graphics that require little or no text to convey lifesaving instructions. However you structure your written documentation, let your users try the new design and listen to their feedback.

Procedure Formatting

While procedure formatting sounds simple enough, there are tips for making documents easy to read and follow. Here are several great tips:

1. Use ample white space in margins, between sections, and around headings and other items on the page.

2. Place helpful and often-referenced information in the front of the document. The least helpful and least referenced information should be at the back. For example, the glossary, reference list, and history of changes are best at the back of the document.

3. An Arial, Calibri, or Times New Roman font is easily read in most biopharmaceutical environments. At least twelve-point fonts should be used, in black only.

4. Use simple yet informative titles, headings, and subheadings to divide content.

5. Consider breaking a unit operation into chunks, where each chunk contains the applicable steps.

6. Consider using color to make sections and chunking more obvious to the user. Put section and chunking titles on light blue or darker background, while written steps are on a lighter gray background.

7. Use short, simple sentences that don't trip the reader.

8. Write using an active, positive voice.

9. Avoid weak words like maybe, possibly, could, and might. Weak words can be easily misinterpreted.

10. Avoid filler words such as the, that, more, some, and most. Get right to the point.

11. Begin steps with an action verb like close, open, press, lower, or raise.

12. There should only be one action per step, and the instructions must be clearly written.

13. Be consistent with conditional steps, and use uppercase for logic words like IF, THEN, and ELSE.

14. Use tables to group similar steps performed together as part of a chunked section of a unit operation.

15. Use simple images as attention activators to indicate steps with higher risk, for example irreversible steps with immediate and intolerable product harm.

Here is an example of a procedure with steps, levels, activity chunking, an attention activator to indicate risk, and shading:

1. PROCEDURE SECTION NAME	
Chunked Activity Brief Description	1.1. Step Level 2 • Step Level 2 bullet 1.2. Step Level 2
⚠	Risk Critical Step
Chunked Activity Brief Description	1.3. Step Level 2 • Step Level 2 bullet 1.4. Step Level 2 　1.4.1. Step Level 3 – use sparingly. Stay at 2 levels when possible. 　• Step Level 3 bullet – use sparingly

Illustration of procedural documentation where risk is identified.

Notes, precautions, and warnings are not steps, and written guidance should be designed for successful completion even if the user skips over them. Notes, precautions, and warnings should precede the applicable step—written in a positive, passive voice. A note provides supplemental information helpful to less experienced users, such as the location of a valve. Precautions or cautions describe hazards to equipment or the process. Warnings explain dangers to people.

Here is an example of a procedural document showing notes and cautions:

2. PROCEDURE SECTION NAME	
→ NOTE: Use this note placement if note, warning, caution applies to entire section below	
Chunked Activity Brief Description	21. Step Level 2 • Step Level 2 bullet • Step Level 2 bullet 22. Step Level 2
Chunked Activity Brief Description	CAUTION: Use this placement if note, warning, or caution applies only to steps below ←
	23. Step Level 2 24. Step Level 2

Illustration of procedural documentation with a note and caution.

Images are useful in clarifying steps with multiple objects or multiple locations on an object. Images used in procedural documents must be easily understood and visible. Locate images immediately after the applicable step. Consider using photo editing software to include labels, arrows, or text on images. Use callouts to draw attention and shapes to communicate movement, actions, or locations.

When providing directions on the use of software or a human-machine interface (HMI), use bold text to represent menu items selected, typed, or clicked by the user. Consider also using single quotes around menu items if that helps to clarify the step.

Batch Record Formatting

Batch records in biopharmaceutical manufacturing are essentially forms to record critical information with some performance direction. How you design a batch record matters. Think about internet forms you have encountered in your personal life. Think about paper forms used by the state and federal government, such as your tax return form. How are shading and color used in relation to white space? How does the design help you complete the form correctly and completely? Consider a badly designed form you have used in your personal life, and what attributes made it difficult to complete correctly?

Here is an example of a U.S. income tax return form. Notice the use of shading and white space to indicate where data is required to be recorded. Notice the left to right and downward flow of the form that your eye and action will follow.

Image of U.S. Internal Revenue Service (IRS) Form 1040,
https://www.irs.gov/pub/irs-pdf/f1040.pdf.

Batch records would be easier to use and more robust if they were designed with a similar format. See additional guidance below.

1. Use multiple tables shaped and sized to fit the specific chunked steps where data or actions are recorded and signed for.

2. Put written guidance on a light gray background, and data fields on a white background.

3. When the batch record needs to point to a procedure section, make the section title match the landing procedure section title.

4. Make the size of fields for data and signatures large enough to allow for documenting required information legibly.

5. Where a section requires a witness, use an attention activator image near the top of the table to alert the performer, so they know to obtain a second worker before proceeding with the steps.

6. Locate the signature field for performer and witness at the end and to the right of the table that contains the recorded work performed.

7. For data that requires rounding, use a field to record the instrument value or calculated value before rounding and then an additional field for the rounded results.

8. High and low parameter ranges should appear beneath the field where the data is recorded for quick and easy comparison.

9. Where data is recorded in a field containing a long string of characters, such as a number, consider using a string of boxes or comb-style lines so that it is clear how many characters are to be recorded.

10. Chunk long character strings into groups of three or four using delimiters, such as the account number on a credit card. This design feature reduces both recording errors and reviewing errors.

Avoid batch record designs where multiple performer steps span an extended period of time and data recorded or steps performed only have one witness signature for the entirety. This design sets up manufacturing associates for poor performer and witness execution. Consider the possibility of making some of those steps reviewed or checked rather than witnessed. While reviewing a group of data fields recorded over an extended duration is reasonable, attempting the same with a single witness signature is not. If a witness signature is required as part of a performer step, each performer step should have its own signature, as well as a corresponding witness signature.

Here is an example of a batch record with attention activators, shading, and helpfully designed data fields:

SOP - 17893		📑	MEDIA SAMPLE

6.4 ALIQUOT Media sample into 50ml conical tube.

	Sample Time	

6.5 MEASURE media pH.

	pH Meter ID#	

	Measured Media pH		.		
			7.0 – 7.4 Range		

6.6 IF pH is out of range THEN:
- Notify Supervisor
- Do Not Proceed

Performed By/Date		Witnessed By/Date	

Illustration of a batch record.

A mistake often found in batch record design is using under-sized fields to reduce the number of batch record pages. The page length of a batch record is of little significance, while the usability of a batch record for the end user is of primary significance. If batch record length becomes an issue, then consider breaking batch records into multiple records based on logical breaks between unit operations.

Critical Steps

Though all steps may be created equal from a compliance perspective, from a risk or operational outcome perspective, they are not. Building off the idea of a warning as part of written guidance for issues related to worker safety, consider a similar concept for when a step may trigger harm to the product if performed improperly.

Going back to the UF skid example presented at the start of this chapter, the transfer out step required human action that triggered immediate, irreversible, and intolerable harm to the product when performed improperly. According to Tony Muschara, a human performance consultant and author, this is known as a *critical step*. The word critical is used within the biopharmaceutical industry for multiple purposes, so it is important to recognize the distinctions of its use. We recommend adding the word risk to the critical step, setting it apart from other terms where the word critical is used. Thus, *risk critical step* is a better option. A risk critical step is not the same as a *critical quality attribute*, defined as a physical, chemical, biological, or microbiological property or characteristic that should be within an appropriate limit, range, or distribution to ensure the desired product quality. Also, a risk critical step is not a *critical process parameter*, which is defined as a process variable that impact a critical quality attribute. However, a risk critical step may impact a critical quality attribute, such as a step that loads product onto a column or washes buffer across a loaded column.

The origin of risk critical steps can be found in the commercial nuclear power industry in the concept known as *critical steps*. The basis of the idea was borrowed from the pages of James Reason's *Managing the Risks of Organizational Accidents*, where actions that were hands on and posed higher criticality to system safety would theoretically be more likely to generate human performance problems.

Commercial nuclear power's critical steps were steps that solely relied on individual worker performance, and the outcome of a mistake being intolerable for personnel safety or the plant. The identification of critical steps at nuclear power plants is used as a heuristic by workers to have richer risk-based conversations before a work activity begins. The aim is to improve the anticipation of error-likely situations[57] with high-severity consequences.

Tony Muschara later developed the idea of critical steps further by adding the criteria of certain unavoidable harm triggered by human action, which is also immediate, irreversible, and intolerable. Another important aspect of this new definition is recognizing the action as a trigger to cause harm if a preceding action is performed improperly. These preceding steps are often referred to as risk important steps. Biopharmaceutical examples of risk important steps include the wrong buffer connected during column operations or the flow path intended to load the column going to drain. In these examples, there would be critical quality attribute implications once the risk critical step is performed.

The following are examples of biopharmaceutical risk critical steps and related risk important steps:

1. Unit Operation: Inoculation into a bottle or flask.

   Risk Critical Step: Pour / pipette inoculum.

   Risk Important Steps: Pre-transfer sample complete, calculation for medium working volume, medium is warmed and not expired, and medium dispensed into bottle or flask.

2. Unit Operation: Bioreactor transfer.

   Risk Critical Step: Acknowledge the prompt on the receiving bioreactor.

---

57 The U.S. commercial nuclear industry defines an error-likely situation as a work situation in which there is a greater opportunity for error when performing a specific action or task due to error traps or error precursors. An error-likely situation typically exists when task-related factors exceed the capability of the individual (mismatch) at the point of "touching" the physical plant.

Risk Important Steps: Sterilization of transfer line, pre-transfer sample complete, transfer volume calculation, target addition volume entered into digital automation system, flow path established, transfer line cool to touch, acknowledge to start transfer from sending bioreactor.

3. Unit Operation: Column elution.
   Risk Critical Step: Acknowledge prompt to begin elution.
   Risk Important Steps: UV operating correctly, collection vessel connected to outlet, elution hose free of kinks, flow path established by positioning valves and pinch clamps, and correct buffer connected.

When the risk critical steps for a unit operation are identified, the written guidance must be modified to include that information for the end user, similar to a caution or warning preceding a step or section. Well-designed written guidance uses symbols as attention activators instead of solely relying on words. Studies have shown that warnings with symbols are more noticeable than a warning without symbols.

According to the *Handbook of Warnings*, edited by Michael S. Wogalter, images and symbols convey a great deal of information using less space and require less cognitive processing by the user. The brain processes mental representations of images faster than text. Symbols are more salient than text because of visual variations of shape, size, and color. For example, some biopharmaceutical companies use the image of an alarm beacon to identify risk critical steps. The effectiveness of a symbol depends on the utility of the represented context and the end user's knowledge.

Consider the following four factors when choosing symbols for written guidance:

- Does it call attention to itself?
- Is it elegant yet simple in design?
- Is it legible?
- Is it understandable and intuitive?

Risk critical steps are most often verified or witnessed steps in a batch record, requiring a real-time witness as the step is executed. Risk important steps are often a checked or reviewed step, where real-time witnessing is not required because correct performance of the step can be confirmed later in time. From a risk-based perspective, performing the check of completed risk important steps immediately before the performance of the risk critical step adds a measure of control when procedures or batch records are performed out of sequence. Where the risk critical step is the response to an automation prompt, consider placing the completion check of the risk important steps as a prompt before the risk critical step prompt.

Witness Steps

While we are on the topic of real time witness steps in documentation, there is little else in the biopharmaceutical industry so well intended yet often destructive in its application to a smooth and even workflow that supports reliable performance as the real time witness step. The runner-up is data integrity forced workarounds. In both instances, the workers' focus shifts from the performance of high-risk work to documentation compliance. This change in focus creates opportunities for errors, impacts product safety, and adds to staffing challenges by forcing a second worker to become available at an exact moment to watch work in real time. Considering that this need for a second worker often occurs dozens of times over a shift, interrupting their smooth workflow, the resulting problems are obvious.

Work design that requires repeated stops and starts to record data influences error. This is a strong driver for moving from paper batch records to an automated Manufacturing Execution System (MES) and obtaining instrumentation designed to create the necessary data trail that ensures data integrity. It should also be a strong driver to design the risk out of work, like alternatives to real time witness verifications. Considering the importance of successful execution and complete documentation, the work must be designed to achieve both with minimal risk.

Witness verification, when implemented effectively, can support reliability. Before adding witness steps in response to a deviation associated with a procedure or batch record step, consider the following questions:

1. What work task was the assigned worker doing before the witness step was introduced?

2. How will the new witness step change the work? Will workers need to pause, restart, come and go, or change roles?

3. What risks are created?

4. Is this new witness step a means of compensating for a work design problem?

Witness steps are not always a good idea for two reasons. One, as Sidney Dekker explains in *Patient Safety: A Human Factors Approach*, unlike a second engine on an aircraft or a backup diesel generator at a nuclear power plant, adding more people to a work process does not always add the safety margin hoped. This is known as the fallacy of social redundancy. When checks by a second person are performed, errors can still go undetected, especially in settings where experienced personnel perform repetitive routine actions. Since in such cases those checking or witnessing know that the work has almost always been done correctly, they will tend to see what they expect. This is true even when the witness is confirming that information matches between two sources, and no interpretation is required. People's expectancy can nullify human redundancy.

The fallacy of social redundancy contributed to the friendly fire[58] event that shot down a U.S. Black Hawk helicopter in 1994 as described in the book, *Friendly Fire,* written by Scott Snook. This is likely also a contributor to mishaps in biopharma, and chiding workers to focus harder when checking or witnessing will not fix that. Such checking by a second person is least effective when conducted routinely for a process with a low error rate. This is the characteristic of most unit operations in biopharmaceutical manufacturing. Vigilance is difficult during processes or tasks that go right most of the time. Also, the ability of the less experienced worker to identify problems or intervene as a real time witness during a task performed by a more experienced worker may lead to less effective checking. In situations with a significant experience gradient between workers, the more senior worker should be the real time witness for the less experienced worker.

The second reason witness steps are not always an effective way to support reliable performance is due to work design. There are multiple situations that require a team of two workers to temporarily split up to support work in different locations in the suite. In those cases the witness step will not be performed as intended or the interruption of work required for the two people to come together creates a different problem.

---

58 Friendly fire is military terminology that refers to a military unit attacking friendly troops while attempting to attack enemy or hostile targets.

Chapter Summary

Biopharmaceutical manufacturing documentation serves multiple purposes. It guides work, documents processes and practices, allows inspection and review, and demonstrates compliance with regulatory expectations. Regulation and compliance often overshadow documentation design, pushing useability to the back burner. Depending on the current state of documentation at your site, it may take several months or years to improve written guidance.

The amount of time and resources required to apply human-focused design to your site's procedures and batch records can feel daunting. An appropriate way to begin is to focus your efforts on the unit operation that has the most documentation-related deviations. Use that unit operation to establish your new standards and templates. Engage the end users in resequencing written guidance to match Work As Done while meeting the process intent and remove the clutter of unnecessary witness steps and notes that have been added over the years as band-aids for deviations. Look holistically at how documentation such as procedures, batch records, and automation combine to match the workflow. Finally, perform a workplace walkthrough with the end users to ensure the final product flows with how work is performed. Then move to the next unit operation or factory and continue to apply the guidance provided in this chapter.

Maturity Assessment

Consider using the following statements to assess the maturity of your organization regarding human-focused written guidance. Each statement has three possible choices. A higher total score indicates a higher maturity.

1. Written guidance identifies specific steps that must go right to protect the product from harm.
   Agree 20, Sometimes 10, Disagree 0

2. End users are involved in creating, revising, and field-testing written guidance.
   Agree 20, Sometimes 10, Disagree 0

3. End users speak positively regarding written guidance.
   Agree 20, Sometimes 10, Disagree 0

4. Improvements and corrections to written guidance documentation are made promptly.
   Agree 20, Sometimes 10, Disagree 0

5. There is a standard used by documentation writers that provides human factors practices that make written guidance more helpful to end-users.
   Agree 20, Sometimes 10, Disagree 0

6. There is clear guidance on how to use procedures and batch records, including which steps can be performed out of sequence and which require continuous use.
   Agree 20, Sometimes 10, Disagree 0

CHAPTER NINE

Better Investigations

Two manufacturing associates, two manufacturing leads, and a supervisor were gathered in a small suite for downstream unit operation. The vessel containing product was positioned against the far wall. Tubing ran from the vessel and through a peristaltic pump to the container of polysorbate solution on a scale. The pump and scale were on the floor where the colleagues would need to squat or kneel to interact with either device. This was an unusually large team for what might be considered the fairly straightforward and quick operation of pumping thirty-one grams of polysorbate solution into the vessel containing the product. The team was very focused on getting this step right. Less than six months ago, an over-addition resulted in a batch loss.

The previous batch loss investigation found that a math error had led to adding more polysorbate solution than allowed. Following the investigation, the batch record was revised to make calculations and field-to-field manual data duplications[59] less prone to error. A supervisor was now also required to check the calculated result.

---

59 Batch records sometimes require copying data recorded on earlier pages to later pages to perform calculations that determine volume, weight, time, or other information to perform a step as part of a unit operation.

As the supervisor and the manufacturing leads peered over the shoulder of the manufacturing associates, the newly revised batch record was used to perform the calculation. One manufacturing associate was the performer, and the other was the witness checking the math. The supervisor rechecked the calculation as prescribed by the batch record. Now all the team had to do was execute the polysorbate solution addition. The manufacturing associate acting as the performer switched on the pump and began to monitor the scale display in preparation for stopping the pump as soon as the scale displayed the target weight. The pump had been operating for less than 30 seconds, when the displayed weight bounced up and down, and the witness noted the displayed weight seemed to be going up rather than down.

The performer stopped the pump so the team could troubleshoot. One of the lead manufacturing associates discovered the tubing retainer clip was attached to the outlet side of the pump head rather than the inlet side. The tubing had been pulled into the pump head when the pump was switched on, causing the weight to increase as the tubing slid through the pump head and pulled the ten-liter bottle containing the seven liters of polysorbate solution downward. The manufacturing associate readjusted the tubing, the tubing clip was attached on the inlet side of the pump, and the new initial scale weight and target weight was recorded in the batch record.

Back on track, the team added the polysorbate solution and ended their shift. They were pleased the unit operation was successful and they'd avoided another batch loss.

Two weeks later, a product sample analysis indicated an abnormal result. A manufacturing investigation was initiated after confirmation the analysis result was valid. An investigator talked with the team involved. They realized that any polysorbate solution added to the product during the initial attempted addition, before the process was stopped to fix the tubing, hadn't been subtracted from the weight target. The thirty-one grams were added on top of the unknown quantity.

Now, some might think this was the root cause. But there was much more to this story.

This story did not begin and end on this one day. In fact, the story started many years before. The first incident of an incorrect addition for this process step occurred twelve years earlier. An investigation determined it was due to a calculation error. The corrective action included an *Awareness CAPA*. That's when managers tell workers to be more careful and try harder next time, yet nothing changes within the system.

Two years after that incident, there were another two over-additions. The causes were deemed operator errors. A revision was made to the batch record—a note reminding people to be more careful—and workers were again reminded by management not to make the same mistake.

There were three more over-additions across the next five years. The first and second were deemed operator errors, while another change was made to the batch record after the third incident, lowering the speed of the manual pump.

One would think by this point, lessons were learned. Yet, the same over-addition error occurred three more times over the next four years, leading to two more batch record wording changes and a replaced pump head. In case you weren't doing the math, there were ten batch losses due to over-additions across twelve years—all at the same process step.

How could this happen, you might ask? Easily.

Cause and Root Cause

Cause is codified in FDA regulations like Title 21 of the Code of Federal Regulations governing food and drugs within the United States. Part 820 states, "Investigating the cause of nonconformities relating to product, processes, and the quality system." The International Council for Harmonization of Technical Requirements for Pharmaceuticals for Human Use (ICH) says, "A structured approach to the investigation process should be used with the objective of determining the root cause."

As Dekker and Conklin say in *Do Safety Differently*, "Sadly, there is never one root cause that must be removed or fixed." The belief that a single root cause exists gets in the way of learning. In most cases, many factors within the complex system combine to lead to the undesired outcome.

A great deal of caution is necessary when using the word cause in relation to operational failures in complex systems. The word cause is associated with Newtonian cause and effect assumptions, which are deterministic. Given this association, when used to describe a failure, cause may indicate the organization did not consider emergent properties of complex systems.

Other problems with the word cause include its use in the news for phenomena we have little to no control over, such as weather. The air of finality it creates may discourage further learning and reinforce blame. There is a high level of abstraction associated with cause, like the causes chosen from lists of investigation database cause codes and the taxonomies of causes prescribed within some well-known root cause analysis methods.

Rather than suggesting an alternative for the word cause, be mindful of the need for details and situational context that must always accompany cause statements.

Let's return to the case study presented at the beginning of this chapter. The biopharmaceutical manufacturing facility lost ten batches over twelve years, all at the same process step. They failed to learn from failure. Like many in the biopharmaceutical industry, they looked at complex systems using an inappropriate and simplistic linear-thinking mental model rather than a systems perspective.

Here is an example of an inappropriate and simplistic linear-thinking mental model:

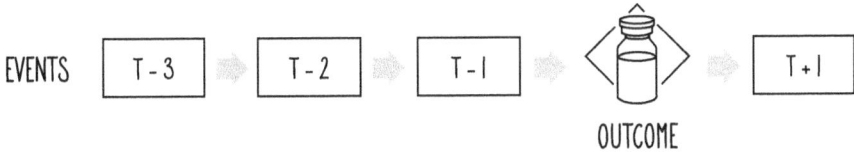

EVENTS | T - 3 | ⇒ | T - 2 | ⇒ | T - I | ⇒ | ◁▯▷ | ⇒ | T + I |

OUTCOME

Management often expects investigators to use a reductionist[60] component level analysis, which often ends with identifying a single so-called root cause. A reductionist approach looks for the faulty component rather than considering interactions between components. This approach also ignores that complex systems will likely have *multiple contributors, each necessary but only jointly sufficient.*

The Methodology

Using a complex system mental model is essential when learning about how systems function and how systems create both good and undesired outcomes. Complex system learning is about going up and out, not down and in, and not strictly looking backwards at the fanciful so-called causal chain. Dekker, Cilliers, and Hofmeyr explain that the difference in thinking is, "We mean by linear thinking a process that follows a chain of causal reasoning from a premise to a single outcome. In contrast, systems thinking regards an outcome as emerging from a complex network of causal interactions, and therefore, not the result of a single factor."

Here is an example of a complex system mental model:

---

60 Reductionism holds that systems can always be understood by breaking them down into simpler or more fundamental components.

SYSTEM ELEMENTS AND RELATIONSHIPS

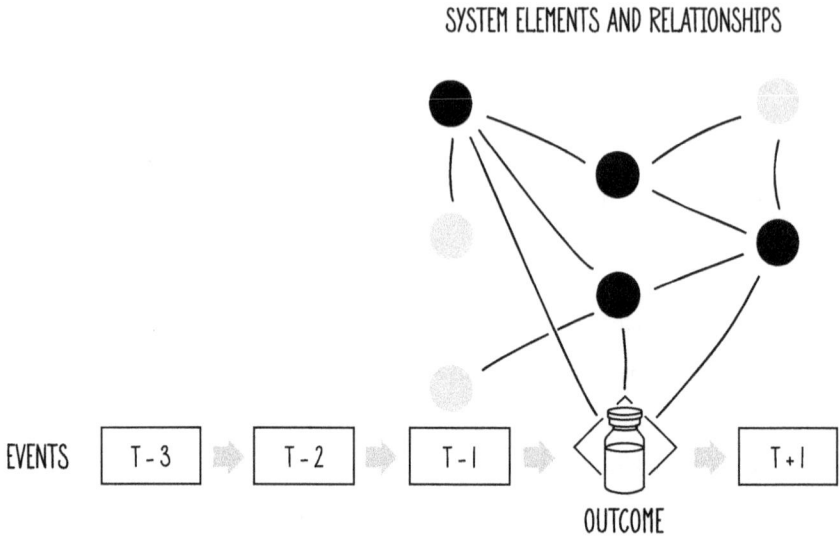

EVENTS | T-3 | ➡ | T-2 | ➡ | T-1 | ➡ | ◇ | ➡ | T+1 |

OUTCOME

A failure to learn in biopharmaceutical manufacturing can also derive from the over-reliance on methods typically a part of Lean Six Sigma to solve all problems. This marriage of convenience between ideas originating from the Toyota Production System to eliminate waste and Motorola's binning of methods, techniques and tools for improvement in variation has proven successful for industries dealing with problems of variation, waste issues, and process flows. Success in improving efficiencies and variation issues using Lean Six Sigma has led to a belief that the methodology can be applied to all problems with equal success. This belief is wrong. As noted in *Four Types of Problems* by Art Smalley, though there are similarities in how to approach different problems, including a need to observe and go through cycles to learn and progress, specific methodologies and approaches are better suited for different types of problems.

Chapter five explained how the 5 Whys problem-solving method widely used in Lean Six Sigma efforts might work well in cases with simple machines but is not very helpful when used to learn about complex systems. The 5

Whys method was used for the analysis in the previous nine investigations of the polysorbate solution over-additions in the case study that opened this chapter. All nine of those investigations resulted in single so-called root causes, and many of those investigations identified human error as the single failed component in the system.

Even when an investigator using the 5 Whys method multiple times comes up with more than one so-called root cause for component-level failure, another Lean Six Sigma tool may further limit improving the system. Often a PICK Matrix[61] will be used to identify a single corrective action while ruling out all other potential corrective actions. A corrective action considered easy to do will be implemented if the payoff is categorized as either high or low. In contrast, a corrective action considered hard to do will be challenged or killed if the payoff is categorized as low, as well as high if another corrective action considered easy to implement is believed to exist. Difficult corrective actions involve engineering work, validation work, or even regulatory filing changes. Easy actions involve the addition of notes or witness steps within written guidance or telling workers to be more careful next time. Use of a PICK Matrix may be appropriate as part of weeding through a long list of brainstormed ideas associated with improving efficiency, but its use can be highly destructive for situations involving catastrophic failures where the workplace, processes, and systems must be redesigned.

Another well-known Lean Six Sigma method used in those nine investigations was an Ishikawa 6M Fishbone diagram, sometimes called a 6M Fishbone diagram. The 6M Fishbone diagram is a visual way to organize and

---

61 PICK stands for Possible, Implement, Challenge, Kill. These are labels for four quadrants of a matrix where the x-axis is Payoff and y-axis is Difficulty. The PICK matrix is a Lean Six Sigma tool that is intended to help categorize the feasibility of possible improvement ideas.

record brainstorming ideas. When the direct[62] cause of an undesired outcome is not known, there may be some benefit to using the 6M Fishbone diagram or the rational and efficient Kepner-Tregoe Problem Analysis method. The centrifuge was working last week, and now it is not. Microbial bioburden samples of the product in the bioreactor were within limits three days ago, but now microbial bioburden is too numerous to count. These are examples of the direct cause not being known and are potential candidates for the use of the Ishikawa 6M Fishbone diagram or the Kepner-Tregoe Problem Analysis.

If what occurred to trigger the undesired outcome is known, brainstorming can be skipped. Move right to trying to understand how actions made sense to the people involved—especially the activities that had a direct impact on occurrence, detection, or severity. Examples may include the selection of an automation recipe, the opening of a valve, or the mix-up of components that resulted in a failure. To learn about this, we must observe the work as it is performed and engage in dialogue with the people who do the work.

Many biopharmaceutical manufacturing organizations mandate that DMAIC is used for quality investigations. The DMAIC acronym stands for Define, Measure, Analyze, Improve, and Control. DMAIC, reportedly created by W. Edwards Deming in the 1950s, is a data-driven improvement cycle process used for improving, optimizing, and stabilizing business processes. Some say Walter Shewhart's Plan-Do-Study-Act (PDSA) cycle, developed in the 1930s, was the basis of DMAIC. Regardless, DMAIC and PDSA are both intended for use with improvement processes that are data-driven. For problems where the direct cause is not known, DMAIC may indeed be a good place to begin. However, shoehorning DMAIC into investigations

---

62 A direct cause is also known as a proximal cause, occurring immediately before the undesirable outcome. Causes that are upstream from the undesired outcome are sometimes referred to as distal causes.

where the direct cause is known is not appropriate and will likely lead to inadequate operational learning.

A Better Framework

For investigations where the direct cause is known, there are useful frameworks that can be used to ensure the organization learns what it needs to. These frameworks also work well for investigations where the direct cause is unknown. The typical stages of an investigation are:

1. Develop problem statement

2. Create plan

3. Collect information

4. Organize & analyze information

5. Create recommendations,

6. Write report, and

7. Select recommendations

A primary source of information must be watching work and engaging with colleagues to leverage their work insights. When the direct cause is known, the information collected for investigations should include observations, conversations, interviews, reviews of documents, and reviews of any other applicable artifacts.

The analysis will be influenced or biased based on the accident model or mental model used. Thus, the need to think about your thinking is vital. One must recognize the system is a complex adaptive system[63]. The Sharp-End / Blunt-End Model of Performance described in chapter five is a helpful model to apply during investigation analysis.

Event & Causal Factor (E&CF) Charting has been used as a method for investigation analysis for decades. An E&CF Chart is not a process map or an Ishikawa-esque cause-and-effect diagram—although some may wrongly insist it is. E&CF Charting should not be confused with cause mapping, which is basically the diagramming of multiple 5 Whys chains without using a useful mental model or creating an understanding of context. E&CF Charting should also not be confused with Management Oversight and Risk Tree (MORT) or TapRoot, which rely on cause taxonomies with an engineering Fault Tree look and feel, leading to findings selected from a list with high levels of abstraction.

One of the first known mentions of E&CF Charting was in 1978 by the U.S. Department of Energy, where J.R. Buys and J.L. Clark, doing work for Edgerton, Germeshausen, and Grier (EG&G), describe the method in a technical document. Buys and Clark cite the work of Ludwig Benner and his colleagues at the National Transportation Safety Board (NTSB) as the originators of E&CF Charting. Page fifty-nine of the NTSB Report, HAR-71-06, documents the investigation of a liquified oxygen tank truck explosion that killed two people in Brooklyn in May of 1970. Figure N in this document, titled *Relationship of Event and Causal Factors,* is a good example of the early use of E&CF Charting. Later interpretations of E&CF Charting can be found in Ammerman's *The Root Cause Analysis Handbook*

---

63 It is important to realize that a complex system always adapts to a changing environment. Thus the description, complex adaptive system.

and *Guidelines for Investigating Chemical Process Incidents* by the Center for Chemical Process Safety.

There are common features shared between the NTSB Report HAR-71-06, the EG&G technical documents, and the two books mentioned where E&CF Charting is described. One common feature is the use of a timeline that details the sequence of events pertaining to the mishap. Another common feature is the diagramming and coding that lists conditions and factors that influenced specific events on that timeline. Benner's original idea was that the timeline would be comprised of events that describe the *what*, and the conditions listed adjacent to an event would describe the *how*. Buys and Clark added more distinctions to Benner's concept by suggesting that the events on the timeline were direct factors, conditions closer in proximity to events on the chart were contributing factors, and conditions further in proximity to events on the chart were systemic factors. The concept of a condition's proximity from the event it influenced allows the investigator to use coding similar to the Sharp-End / Blunt-End Model of Performance described in chapter five. Workplace local factors would be closer to the timeline, and system and organizational factors would be farther away from the timeline.

Buys and Clark also provided guidance on what shapes to use on the chart to better distinguish conditions (ovals) from events (rectangles). These shapes help investigators and stakeholders understand the coding and relationships in an E&CF Chart, which sometimes resembles a spaghetti-like drawing of rectangles and connecting lines with conditions both above and below the timeline.

In an effort to make the E&CF Chart even more user-friendly and better understood, the guidance provided in this book recommends that: 1) conditions are only placed above the timeline to mirror the schema of the Sharp-End / Blunt-End Model, and 2) lines are not used to connect the events and ovals, rather the horizontal proximity between objects on the timeline and the vertical proximity of conditions above an event are sufficient to suggest relationships in the visual representation. Additional context concerning the relationship between events and conditions can be described in the written narrative of the report.

The steps that follow provide a useful process for how to conduct operational learning using E&CF Charting:

Step One: *Define The Problem Statement*
Similar to other methods, a problem statement is critical to aligning participants. Be mindful that the deviation statement (statement of what happened) is not a problem statement. The problem statement should clearly and concisely identify the object, defect, and consequence. Where the consequence was not severe, consider stating the potential consequence instead. For example, *the product in the bioreactor exceeded allowed pH which potentially placed the batch at risk.*

The problem statement is critical because it shapes the focus of an investigation. It is not uncommon for a given deviation to present multiple problem statements, such as when a new undesired outcome suggests that prior corrective actions were ineffective. It's good to note the actual problem, what occurred, as well as the problem introduced by CAPA—especially when a recurrence was not prevented. Those might be two different yet related problem statements.

Step Two: *Watch Everyday Work*
A major step forward in learning about events can be made by simply talking to the workers involved in an event. Do not call workers to your office or conference room, and stop sending meeting invitations with the word *interview* in the subject line. Instead, go to gemba and watch the work. There are several problems with interviews conducted in an office or conference room—especially those that take place days or weeks after an event. Memories are prone to decay.

162

Stressed workers herded from their work area to a conference room become overly agreeable and unintentionally fall prey to leading questions.

Work is the subject of an investigation, so watch the work to learn about it. If the investigation is about a bioreactor transfer, go watch a bioreactor transfer. If the investigation concerns a component mix-up during media preparation, watch media preparation. Keep in mind, the investigation is not about learning what people did wrong. It's about learning how people create success despite imperfect, complex systems. Again, this is an important distinction, and you will likely need to think differently about the word cause. When you watch everyday work, you'll notice where performance might be challenged, where existing controls are insufficient to manage risk, and where there is the possibility for failure.

The following image depicts various areas of focus for operational learning when you watch everyday work:

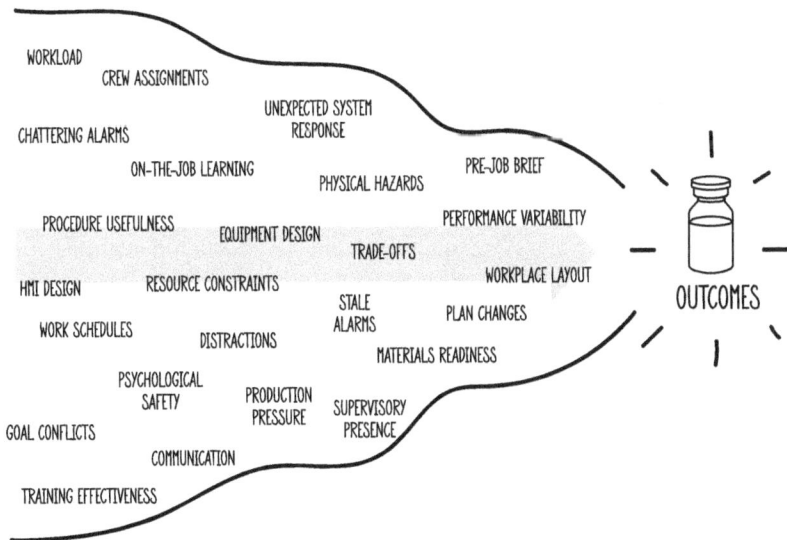

Illustration of operational learning areas of focus, adapted from Chart 4.4 in *Bob's Guide to Operational Learning* by B. Edwards and A. Baker, published by Pre-Accident Investigation Media in 2020.

As stated earlier, one could think of these as causes, but this approach is different than the typical ingrained notions of finding causes. Use failure to improve the relevant work, recognizing that multiple conditions likely contributed to the specific failure.

Step Three: *Create a Sequence of Events Timeline*
Gather the experts of the work, the people who perform the procedures and processes every day. Together, build a timeline showing the sequence of events of Work As Done. Build from left to right, including actions and assessments that led up to the undesired outcome, as well as what happened afterwards in response.

For some, it may seem strange to build the investigation timeline from left to right, in the direction of time, but this is how people tell stories. Building a timeline in reverse order, from right to left, may be a warning flag that you're backsliding to the 5 Whys and causal chains, which will negate the effective use of E&CF Charting. Post-It Notes work well for building timelines. So does visual collaboration software like Miro. Let everyone create and place events on the timeline, rearranging the timeline as necessary. Check your timeline for sufficiency by asking questions like, "What happens immediately before that?" and "What happens after that?"

Step Four: *List the Conditions That Influenced Specific Events*
Working with the experts of the work, list conditions that may influence specific events in the timeline. If using Post-It Notes, consider using different colors to identify the conditions above the particular events they influenced. While events were placed in sequential order, conditions are not necessarily time-based. Many vulnerabilities were present long before the incident occurred and are often referred to as latent.

To tease out conditions, draw the team's attention to specific events and ask questions that seek descriptions versus explanations. Here are several questions to get you started:

1. What makes that part of the operation more challenging sometimes?

2. What system response is expected at this point?

3. How can you tell when something is not going as expected?

4. How does that action typically occur when fully staffed compared to when not fully staffed?

5. Where is the team's focus just prior to that?

6. How does the team realize whether the situation is different compared to previous times it was performed?

In general, you want to ask questions[64] that reveal work context and the local rationality of the people. The *Etsy Debriefing Facilitation Guide* suggests the following as examples of information valuable to learning:

- The status of necessary materials, equipment, and resources.
- Situations in the workplace that make work execution difficult.
- Context for assessments or judgments.

---

64 How these questions are asked is critically important to the level of openness and candidness you will get in response. Refer back to Chapter 6 and 7 for more information about ensuring psychological safety in how this is done.

- Rationale for choices or decisions.

- People's states of mind at the time.

- Factors that lead to specific actions.

- Signals that bring people to ask for help.

- Aspects of work and work design that create a need for adaptation.

Step Five: *Organize the Conditions*

Draw a horizontal line above the timeline, through the middle of the collection of conditions. Now begin organizing your conditions. Move the conditions that are *system / organizational factors* above the line. Leave the conditions that are *workplace local factors* below the line. This should resemble the schema of the Sharp-End / Blunt-End Model. A system / organizational factor is a management decision and process that influences workplace local factors. Examples of system / organizational factors may include issues related to staffing, process development, and system design. A workplace local factor is a condition present in the workplace at the time work was performed that influenced behavior. Examples of workplace local factors include the work environment, time of shift, mental states, competence, and the availability and usability of items necessary to work performance.

The addition of the horizontal line to create two separate areas for mapping causal factors above the timeline is similar to how an AcciMap[65] is drawn. An AcciMap is a systems-based technique for accident analysis, specifically for analyzing the causes of accidents that occur in complex sociotechnical

---

65   The AcciMap method is frequently used by the Chemical Safety Board (CSB). An example of a recent CSB investigation that uses AcciMap is the Husky Energy Superior Refinery Explosion and Fire final accident report (https://www.csb.gov/husky-energy-superior-re-finery-explosion-and-fire/). More information on the AcciMap method can be found on the Loughborough Design Systems Thinking Design website at https://systemsthinkinglab. wordpress.com/accimap/

systems. The AcciMap concept was developed by Jens Rasmussen. The flexible approach inherent in the AcciMap method to graphically represent the interrelationships of conditions across multiple system levels is beneficial to E&CF Charting, adding additional power to an already effective analysis method.

At this point in the development of the E&CF Chart, there may be many more workplace local factors than system / organizational factors. Review the workplace local factors and explore what system / organizational factors enabled them to exist. Place additional system / organizational factors above the workplace local factors they influenced.

Here is an illustration of a general format for E&CF Charting:

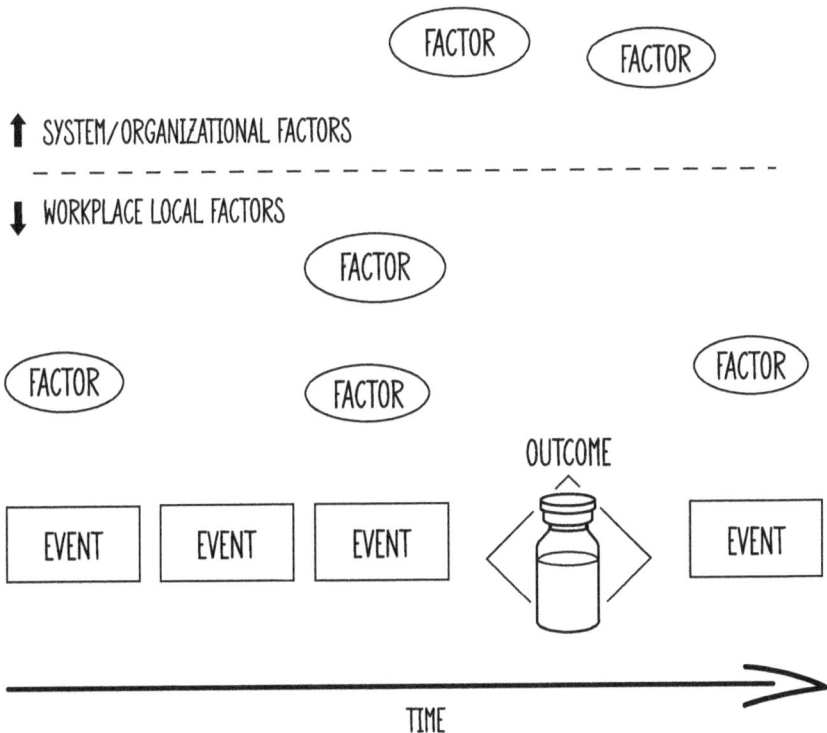

Step Six: *Check Your E&CF Chart for Sufficiency*

Ask the following questions to assess if more workplace local factors or system / organizational factors are necessary to tell the story but are missing. Then add additional factors as necessary:

1. What elements or components did we decide were part of this complex system?

2. What did we choose not to include as part of this complex system and why?

3. Where in the story were there failures to control a product hazard, and did we explain how they happened?

4. How does the organization enable sufficient anticipation of risk, monitoring what is important to success, and guided response for abnormal situations?

5. Have similar incidents occurred before, and how did the organization learn from them?

Step Seven: *Identify Root Causes and Contributing Causes*

Review all the system / organizational factors and workplace local factors to identify *root causes* and *contributing causes*. At the start of this chapter, we discussed the challenges in using the terms cause and root cause. In relation to E&CF Charting, the definition of *root cause* is a fundamental, underlying, system-related issue that, if eliminated or modified, will prevent the recurrence of a similar event. Based on this definition your root causes are more likely to be system / organizational factors. We define a *contributing cause* as an issue that shaped the outcome of the incident, making it more severe, making it more widespread, or masking detection.

It cannot be stated enough—human error is never a cause, root or contributing. The actions and assessments of people are recorded in the E&CF Chart timeline. Not as factors that might be causal.

Step Eight: *Create Recommendations*

The recommendations stage is where the investigation can get tricky and possibly go off the rails. Recommendations may be influenced by political and economic considerations, local traditions, expediency, and the regulatory environment. For this reason, it is helpful to document all recommendations and then identify which recommendations are accepted by stakeholders with decision-making authority. Including all recommendations provides a mechanism to record differing professional opinions and creates a helpful history of business decisions made if the organization needs to revisit the learnings and choices in the future.

Step Nine: *Investigation Documentation*

If possible, include your E&CF Chart as an attachment to your investigation. If built with Post-It Notes, take photos of the final chart. If built in Miro, save your work as a PDF file. If you really want to impress future readers of your report, consider converting your learnings into a Visio file format. The benefit of adding your completed E&CF Chart to your investigation report is that you show the readers the accident model you used, the analysis outcomes, and visual artifacts supplementing the report's written narrative.

Step Ten: *Tell the story*

Avoid providing a collection of disconnected data that lacks context. Reports written in this manner often lead to confusion and nonconfidence in the investigation. Just as a book or movie is more than a list of characters, an inciting event, and a conclusion, an investigation report must contain context, surprises, and zigs and zags leading to the outcome.

When writing an investigation report, you write a story about an undesired outcome. Tell that story in enough detail and context so your reader can appreciate the situation experienced by the people involved. Give the system a starring role as both the protagonist and the antagonist.

Case Study Learnings

Returning to the over-addition case study from the beginning of this chapter, let's look at the workplace local factors:

- Written guidance lacked visual aids to provide guidance on how to set up the pump head.
- Written guidance lacked visual aids to show how to configure the equipment from the polysorbate solution bottle to the product vessel.
- There was no prescribed pump setup check before starting of the operation.
- The large range of the scale display relative to the small amount of polysorbate solution being added made it difficult to monitor for the target weight.
- Ventilation in the room was directed at the scale, causing the scale display to fluctuate.
- The lack of a suitable working surface like a table made monitoring the operation physically difficult for the team.

- The pump was manually operated to start and stop the process, making over-additions a possible outcome.

From a system / organization factor aspect, some of the conditions revealed included:

- The system design lacked the necessary controls to prevent the potential for over-additions due to the manual nature of the process. An example of better control would be the use of a metered pump that could be programmed to transfer specific low volumes of liquid.
- The room layout prohibited the use of a table that would improve the ergonomics of the task and conduct the work in a location less impacted by ventilation supply.
- The organization preferred causes that were simple and quick to implement, avoiding system redesigns that would require validation work.

While the actual investigation E&CF Chart had a longer and more granular timeline with workplace local factors and system / organizational factors, here is a simplified version of an E&CF Chart for the event:

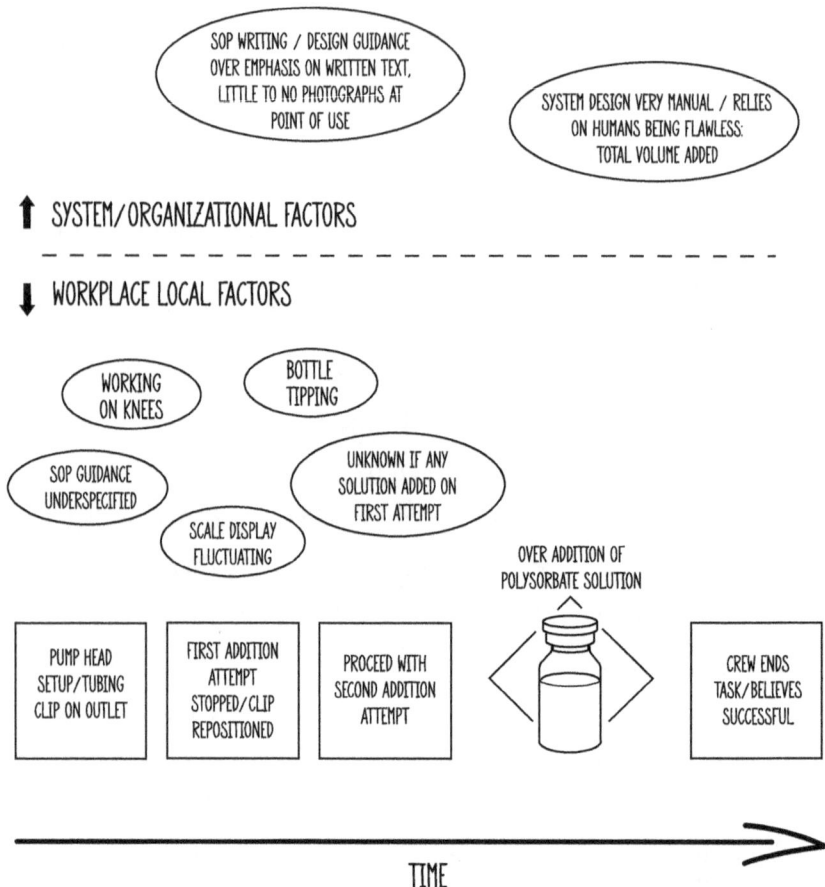

Illustration of an Event & Causal Factor Charting diagram
for the polysorbate over-addition event.

Consider when reviewing your completed E&CF Chart and the subsequent written report the following traps as described by Sidney Dekker:

1. "Explaining what people could have done to avoid the incident." Counterfactuals that describe what people could have done to prevent a particular outcome do not explain why they did what they did. Describing what was not done as the cause of an event explains nothing about what actually happened or how. When an investigator uses

counterfactuals, it is like discussing an incident that never happened. Clues that counterfactuals have been used include terms such as *did not* or *would have* when describing people's actions. An example of a counterfactual might be the statement, "If the associate had read the procedure more closely, they would have recognized that the displayed value was out of range."

2. "Judging people for what they did not do based on what others believe they should have done"

    Making normative judgments about a person's behavior during an incident does not explain why they did what they did. Inserting one's values into the analysis of another's performance does nothing to explain how the incident happened. For example, stating that a person was complacent while monitoring a unit operation does nothing to explain why the person did what they did given their surrounding circumstances. Besides, is it even possible to determine if a person is complacent—smug or exhibiting uncritical satisfaction with oneself or one's achievements? And how could you correct that in every person if you somehow were able to detect complacency?

3. "Assessing the system using mechanistic reasoning."

    Mechanistic reasoning is based on the belief that the incident was the result of a malfunctioning component in a well-designed system. If all the components are in place and working as intended, the system is safe and reliable, so one of the components must not have been working to have a failure. Mechanistic reasoning ignores the relationships and interdependencies between the elements in the system. A cue that mechanistic reasoning has been used is when an investigation report lists all the components that were checked and determined to be working properly. This type of reasoning is often the report output found when an Ishikawa 6M Fishbone model was relied upon for analysis, and often will end with human error as the cause in the Manpower bone segment.

Chapter Summary

The method we have described above for E&CF Charting differs from traditional root cause analysis. The method proposed leverages what is known as learning team[66] practices, such as learning from those closest to the work and focusing on the conditions necessary for things to go right. Include designers when building the timeline and teasing out influencing conditions. These practices move investigations away from person-focused improvements toward system-focus improvement actions. A 2021 study found that for traditional root cause analysis investigations, system focused actions were identified 30 percent of the time, versus 57 percent when learning team approaches were applied. So, there is value in using learning team practices.

The conditions and complexity that create the context of work experienced in both success and failures cannot be ignored or simplified through analysis methodologies if we want to learn the right lessons to improve systems. Event and Causal Factor Charting is a straightforward, standard approach that effectively reveals factors at both local and organizational / system levels when applied to problems where the immediate trigger might be easily identified as a behavior, but how it made sense at the time is not clear.

It takes teamwork to create success and failure. Serious events are

---

66 A learning team is a facilitated conversation between those who do the work and those who design the work, to share operational intelligence between the two groups and improve system design.

organizational failures—the severity of events driven by the absence, weaknesses, or circumvention of controls, not specific individual action. Engaging those who do the work and watching Work As Done increases the likelihood that your analysis will uncover what needs to be addressed to prevent a recurrence.

Telling that story in a relatable way will help those with decision-making authority to provide the resources necessary to take action, making a difference.

Maturity Assessment

Consider using the following statements to assess the maturity of your organization regarding investigations of complex systems events. Each statement has three possible choices. A higher total score indicates a higher maturity.

1. Complex systems require a mental model that accounts for complexity.
   Agree 20, Sometimes 10, Disagree 0

2. DMAIC is for continuous improvement, not for investigations of complex systems where the direct cause is known.
   Agree 20, Sometimes 10, Disagree 0

3. Investigations use appropriate models that guide our analysis.
   Agree 20, Sometimes 10, Disagree 0

4. We do not use mechanistic reasoning to assess complex system failures.
   Agree 20, Sometimes 10, Disagree 0

5. We watch everyday work as part of the investigation process.
   Agree 20, Sometimes 10, Disagree 0

Creating Systems That Work Better With People

The chromatography column packing activity progressed after the unantici-pated challenges experienced earlier in the shift—not to mention the failed packing attempt from seven days earlier. The in-service column was experi-encing unexpected performance issues, so today's attempt to pack this column with resin had to go well if the production schedule was to be maintained. This particular chromatography column was very much like the others used in the factory; its major components consisted of a cylinder of borosilicate glass, a stainless steel bottom plate, a manually adjusted head plate, and ports for connections that allowed for flow through the column.

When setting up for the activity earlier in the day, the two manufac-turing associates were unable to remove the column head plate from the thirty-centimeter column when the O-ring did not release from the column wall. The two manufacturing associates recognized that the O-ring did not perform as expected by its visual appearance. They expected that once tension was removed from the O-ring, it would be short and thin; it was actually still tall and wide. The two manufacturing associates retightened the head plate and tried again to release the O-ring by backing out on the head plate adjuster knob. They were successful on the second attempt and removed the head plate.

Next, the two manufacturing associates filled the column with buffer and then slurried the resin into the column. The head plate and O-ring were reinstalled, and the manual adjuster was manipulated to secure the head plate in position. The column packing activity was now humming along smoothly. The column upflow was performed, and then the downflow was performed. A manufacturing associate monitored the skid and column pressure with the local pressure gauge and noted the readings were in the normal range. Everything seemed to be going as expected.

After completing the column pack, the manufacturing associates observed that one side of the resin bed was three centimeters higher than the other. They discussed the situation and agreed that the column would not pass qualification. They agreed to correct the issue by initiating a repack of the column. The team of two again removed the head plate from the column to re-slurry the resin. After slurrying the resin, the team replaced the head plate on the column without sealing the O-ring because they would need to add buffer, requiring air to be displaced while filling the column.

As the two manufacturing associates were adding buffer using the pump on the newly commissioned chromatography skid, they closely monitored the addition so that as soon as the buffer level passed the frit, they would seal the O-ring and head plate. Dividing their attention between the rising buffer level in the column and the local pressure gauge, everything appeared normal.

Minutes into the buffer addition, the chromatography column suddenly burst, sending shards of glass, buffer, and resin flying across the room. A shard of flying glass lacerated the head of one of the manufacturing associates, and he began to bleed heavily. The work ceased, first aid was provided to the injured person, a supervisor was notified, and medical assistance was called. The laceration required sutures, and the injured worker would return to work after a few days away.

Nobody at the site had ever experienced or heard of a chromatography column bursting from overpressure. The event challenged the production schedule and added cost through rework and resin loss. And most importantly an employee was injured. The site had recently commissioned two new chromatography skids, and this was the first use of one of the new skids for a commercial unit operation. Or rather, the setup for a unit operation, as no product was being run through the column. The two new skids had recently completed their validation, and the engineering staff was very proud of the new design and its capabilities. The engineering staff had also recently performed preventive maintenance on the column that shattered and the head plate that was in use at the time. The local pressure gauge had recently been calibrated.

Designer Perspective

Two engineers went to the scene of the incident the next morning to have a look at the setup. The four-way valve at the bottom of the column was not in the position they expected, so the immediate conclusion was that the manufacturing associates had deadheaded the process during the downflow. Their finding was shared with the head of engineering and the site leadership team (SLT) was informed. Although the findings were nothing more than hearsay, the story began to be accepted as fact.

The engineers didn't investigate further. An unusual event occurred, they found the first thing that did not appear as expected, from their perspective, and they stopped there. In this case, the atypical finding was an apparent mistake by a person performing the work—human error. The anomalous condition or behavior was discovered by narrowing in on a very small segment of the system while blithely ignoring all other parts of the system.

This is a common challenge in many workplaces. People, including designers of systems, need help understanding the importance of what elements they believe are part of the system. This includes humans.

Did the chromatography system designers at this plant believe the new chromatography skid was an element of the system? Or did they think it was the entire system? What about the chromatography column and associated valves, gauges, and tubing? What about the human operators? Did they understand the workers were part of the system they'd designed and that human involvement was vital to system function and outcome? When people forget that humans are part of the system, they say things that sound like the character Finnegan from Kurt Vonnegut's novel *Player Piano*[67]. "If it weren't for the people, the goddamn people always getting tangled up in the machinery. If it weren't for them, the world would be an engineer's paradise."

The story the engineers believed and spread was only their perspective. To them, the workers were not part of the system—they were hazards to their well-designed machinery. Their confirmation bias ended further inquiry or learning. The workers did wrong, and that was it.

Safeguards

As described in chapter nine, when an unexpected or undesired outcome happens, there is a lot to uncover and learn with respect to conditions, like workplace local factors and system / organizational factors that create the necessary and jointly sufficient conditions for the event and its outcome to occur as it did. From a system design perspective, safeguards should always be a key element. When the column burst, the most important question

---

67 The reference to Player Piano related to human factors and system safety was originally made by Steven Shorrock in a blog post from 2014. http://radar.oreilly.com/2014/11/if-it-werent-for-the-people.html

that needed to be asked about the event was, "Did the safeguard function?"[68] The presence of safeguards—often referred to as controls, barriers, or defenses—prevents or mitigates high-consequence outcomes. In the case of the chromatography column burst event, the safeguard could have been a rupture disc or pressure relief valve, but neither was a design feature on this column or any other column in this factory. After all, nobody had ever heard of a chromatography column bursting from overpressure before. Yet, one of these would have protected the borosilicate glass column from overpressure.

This is a classic case where the concepts of *asset*, *hazard*, and *risk* can be applied. While these are safety domain concepts, they can be applied to significant quality failures (and proactively through design) in biopharmaceutical manufacturing. Hazards in biopharmaceutical manufacturing include biological, chemical, temperature, pressure and other hazards. In the column burst case study, the assets were the worker and the column. The risk is the static and dynamic conditions that impact the exposure of assets to hazards. In the column burst case study, the organization believed the risk of overpressure did not exist, and in reality the safety margin was driven to zero.

Controls, often referred to as barriers, are a means that guide, separate, coordinate, defend, or safeguard in order to increase the likelihood of protecting an asset from harm and accomplishing work successfully. The term *safety barrier*—a barrier providing protection from energy—originated in 1973. In William Haddon's now classic paper on injury control, he suggested the sixth of ten countermeasure strategies used to reduce human and economic losses from energy damage was using a material barrier to provide separation between energy and susceptible bodies or structures. The theory

---

68 This safeguard functionality question is attributed to Todd Conklin who mentioned its use during an episode of his Pre-Accident Investigations Podcast.

and application of the barriers concept have evolved since 1973 to include physical and nonphysical barriers. However, no single agreed-upon source currently provides clarity on the definitions.

Snorre Sklet provided a suitable definition for our use. He wrote, "Safety barriers are physical and nonphysical means planned to prevent, control, or mitigate undesired events or accidents."

A helpful distinction between different barriers is based on their functions. James Reason uses the term *defense* rather than barrier, and he specifies six different functions that a defense may serve: protect, detect, warn, recover, contain, and escape. Let's look at these in more detail:

Protection: To provide a barrier between the hazards and the potential victims under normal operating conditions.

Detection: To detect and identify the occurrence of an abnormal condition, an unsafe act, or the presence of hazardous substances.

Warning: To signal the presence and the nature of the hazard to all those likely to be exposed to its dangers.

Recovery: To restore the system to a safe state as quickly as possible.

Containment: To restrict the spread of the hazard in the event of a failure in any or all of the prior defensive functions.

Escape: To ensure the safe evacuation of all potential victims after an accident.

In the case study a missing feature of the system was a rupture disc or pressure relief valve to protect the borosilicate glass column from overpressure. Using Reason's taxonomy of defense functions, either device would be categorized as recovery.

Mistake Proofing

A common statement heard following a failure in biopharmaceutical manufacturing is, "We need to poka-yoke that!" Sometimes that statement is appropriate, and other times it is not. Taiichi Ohno[69] explains poka-yoke, or *baka-yoke*,[70] as he calls it, in his book *Toyota Production System*. He suggests it's a means to mistake-proof work processes by installing devices on tools and equipment to prevent defects. In all the examples provided by Ohno in his book, a mistake has already occurred, resulting in a defect, and the poka-yoke device stops the work to contain the problem.

In its purest form, and how many in the biopharmaceutical industry understand it today, poka-yoke can be a simple mechanical device that prevents incorrect part placement during an assembly activity—a guide pin on a filter housing, for example.

Shigeo Shingo provides more detail on poka-yoke in his book, *A Study of the Toyota Production System*, where he states that 100 percent inspection can be achieved through mechanical or physical control. The poka-yoke can detect defects in multiple ways—including how a machine will respond when a defect is detected. In Shingo's 1989 book, he suggests machines should monitor humans. Fitts and Chapanis[71] proposed the same in 1951 within the aviation industry.

---

69 Taiichi Ohno is considered to be the father of the Toyota Production System, which inspired Lean Manufacturing in the United States.

70 Poka-yoke or poka-yoka has replaced the term baka-yoke in the Western usage of the term. Changing baka to poka was likely driven by political correctness and Western interpretation. Baka is a word for chump, idiot, or fool. While yokeru is a word that means to avoid bad situations or to move out of the way to avoid being in danger. Baka-yoka literally means fool-proofing. Poka-yoka means mistake-proofing.

71 Paul Fitts and Alphonse Chapanis are recognized as two of the founding fathers of human factors. Much of their work was in the area of aviation safety during World War II and in the decades that followed.

In our experience, it is common in biopharmaceutical manufacturing to conflate poka-yoke with human factors engineering or system safety via engineering process controls. The distinctions are important to understand; otherwise, application and effectiveness will suffer. Human factors engineering is a discipline that considers the cognitive, physical, and organizational influences on human behavior to improve human interaction with products and processes. Designing the mental aspects of perceptual, attentional, and decision-making workplace requirements is not poka-yoke.

Engineering process controls are also quite different than poka-yoke. Again, this distinction is important. In the context of health and safety, process engineering control is a physical modification to a process or process equipment to prevent the release of energy or harmful materials into the workplace. The Center for Chemical Process Safety describes the levels of inherent safety measures from most effective to least effective for process controls as follows:

First Order Inherent Safety Measures: Avoid Hazards Through Elimination

Second Order Inherent Safety Measures: Reduce Severity; Reduce Likelihood

Layers of Protection: Apply Passive Safeguards; Apply Active (Engineered) Safeguards; Apply Procedural Safeguards

The process safety concept of process controls that protect people can also apply to product safety in biopharmaceutical manufacturing. For example, the process controls associated with pH monitoring, temperature control and monitoring, and bioburden control and monitoring, are all forms of process controls.

As for poka-yoke, it is desirable to design work so mistakes don't happen. But other human considerations will be missed if human factors engineering is not utilized in system design. And safeguards must be present for when those mistakes occur—because they *will* occur.

Designing for Humans

Designing for humans means more than mistake-proofing. When designing systems where humans are an element of the system, one must design with an understanding of the capabilities and limitations of humans. People make between one to fifteen mistakes per hour while ensuring safety and productivity when working in imperfectly designed systems. Humans have a 2 in 10,000 chance of misreading an alphanumeric, a 1 in 1,000 chance of reading a checklist incorrectly, a 1 in 100 chance of recording information improperly, and a 1 in 4 chance of making a mistake performing a task under high stress.

As Agent Smith says in the movie, *The Matrix*, "Never send a human to do a machine's job." There is some truth to that line. However, there is equal truth to the statement, *never assign a machine to a job better suited for a human.* There are indeed some tasks that humans are better suited for than machines. Paul Fitts, Alphonse Chapanis and the other coauthors of *Human Engineering for an Effective Air-Navigation and Traffic-Control System* explained this well in 1951. Humans can improvise and use flexible procedures. They can recall relevant facts at the appropriate time, reason inductively, and exercise judgment. Machines can respond quickly to control signals and apply great forces smoothly and precisely. Machines can also perform repetitive, routine tasks. Machines store information briefly and then erase it completely. Machines can reason deductively and have superior computational abilities. They are expert multitaskers.

When deciding which tasks are assigned to a human or a machine, first consider the significance of the consequences if the task is performed incorrectly. If the task requires flawless execution or alertness, it may not be suited for a human. Tasks for humans should provide activity and should be intrinsically interesting. If the task is not active or interesting, expect humans to make mistakes.

Remember the fallibility of humans. Fitts believed that, as a general rule, machines should monitor humans instead of humans monitoring machines. He claimed machines, including automated equipment, were better teammates for humans when their strengths and weaknesses were thoughtfully leveraged.

In our column burst case study, an important factor discovered after the initial investigation was that the new chromatography skid had an alarm and protective trip feature set at ten bar by the manufacturer. The previous chromatography skid had an alarm and protective trip feature set at three bar. The chromatography column glass was rated at four bar. A review of yearly historical chromatography skid system data showed that the process alarms *had never* been set for any past column packing activity. Yet the written guidance for the column packing had a section where process alarms were set manually at two-and-a-half bar. This procedure section was located near the end of the document and was not branched to or referenced as part of the section steps for packing the column.

The system design required humans to follow the poorly designed written procedure and manually set the process alarms. Because human involvement in the application of the safeguard created risk, a system design that had preset process alarms based on the recipe selection would have been a better teammate for the humans.

Creating Systems That Work Better With People

Designer Bias

When designing any workplace system, especially systems associated with high hazards and unacceptable risks, human factors engineering must be applied so technology works well with people. The first goal is safety, where risk is managed to protect an asset from harm. The asset might be people, products, or both. The second goal is performance, where productivity and efficiency are enhanced. The third goal is end user satisfaction, where increasing acceptance, comfort, and well-being is achieved. The design must ensure people can do their jobs in a manner that delivers a quality product. And design features should protect the asset from harm when the human fails. Because, after all, failure is normal.

According to David Meister, a distinguished ergonomist, "Design is at bottom a highly judgmental process in which all the engineers' biases and predilections have the opportunity to influence the final configuration." However, the designers of your workplace are everywhere, and their work is not exclusive to engineering. Designers include management, Lean Six Sigma practitioners, scientists, engineers, and others who attempt to impose order in systems. The book *Human Factors in Engineering and Design*, written by Ernest J. McCormick and Mark S. Sanders, explains that when designs miss the mark it is often due to one or more of the following factors:

1. Designers are experience oriented and tend to repeat design approaches previously thought to be effective.

2. Designers are often intuitive in their thinking and don't apply multiple criteria or involve end users enough.

3. Designers get down to the nitty gritty aspects of hardware and software design as quickly as possible, neglecting prototyping and human factors testing.

4. Designers often do not know where to find behavioral information related to human factors or choose not to seek out that information.

To assess the current state of your systems and how they work with people, take a walk to the manufacturing floor and assess multiple human-machine interface (HMI) workstations. If computer screens are overloaded with shapes and colors that resemble the dazzle camouflage[72] used on ships during World War II, there's a problem. There shouldn't be multiple stale alarms[73] displayed, and the layout between screens should be standardized. Audible alarms should not be muted or low, and visual alarm notifications should be visible from anywhere within the work area. The workstation should be logically placed near the equipment under its control. Displays should inform the user of the current operating mode and indicate the name of the user currently logged in. All of these examples describe weaknesses of systems design. Where do you see room for improved design in your systems?

The Big Picture

The chromatography skid was not the entire system for the shattered column event. As noted, the workers required to set up and operate the column and

---

72 Unlike other forms of camouflage, the intention of dazzle is not to conceal, but to make it difficult to estimate a target's range, speed, and heading.

73 A stale alarm is an alarm that remains annunciated for an extended period of time. A common contributor to stale alarms are routine transitions between process states where the alarm system is not designed to adapt and therefore provides false indications of an abnormal condition.

everything attached to it were part of the system. The procedures and automation that supported the unit operation were also part of the system. So, what do we see when we evaluate a system? In this case study, a cross-functional team was given the time and space to learn more about the incident. They visited the manufacturing area to watch column packing work activity using the same skid, same head plate, and a new column. They used Event & Causal Factor (E&CF) Charting to learn about all the factors present during system successes and failures. And they used the Kepner-Tregoe Situation Appraisal and Problem Analysis to identify probable causes.

Here is what the team learned:

1. The most probable direct cause was that the head plate became stuck.

2. It was difficult to see a stuck head plate before adding the buffer to the column.

3. The four-way valve at the bottom of the column was determined to be in the appropriate position for filling the column with buffer, nullifying the earlier information reported by the engineers.

4. The local pressure gauge was damaged, and since the gauge lacked a bottom stop pin, the actual pressure was higher than displayed.

5. The system lacked a protection feature like a rupture disc or relief valve.

6. The manufacturing associates had no idea the new chromatography skid had an alarm and protective trip feature set at ten bar by the manufacturer versus the usual three bar.

7. The chromatography column glass was rated to four bar—much lower than the chromatography skid manufacturer's preset rating of ten bar.

8. The written guidance had a section where process alarms were set manually at two-and-a-half bar. However, these instructions were located near the end of the procedure and were not branched to or referenced as part of the section steps for packing the column.

9. A review of chromatography skid system data for this column packing activity and another packing activity seven days earlier with the new skid revealed that the process alarms had not been set.

10. The column packing activity seven days earlier had spurred multiple high-pressure alarms and pump trips. The alarm occurrences were reported to the manufacturing supervisor but were not relayed to engineers or management.

11. A review of the years of historical chromatography skid system data for the old skid found that process alarms had never been set for any column packing activity.

So, *did the safeguard function?* You might be saying, "Obviously, no." But what, exactly, was not present or did not function, and to what consequence?

Evaluating Safeguards

One method to evaluate and explain the functioning of safeguards is Hazard Barrier Target (HBT) Analysis, or what some refer to as Defense Analysis. HBT Analysis is not particularly effective as an investigation technique for complex systems, but it is helpful in communicating safeguard information to stakeholders after the investigation is complete. The hazard is the property in a process that can harm the target. The target is the asset the organization is trying to protect, such as people, the product, or the environment. The hazard must get past all the barriers to cause harm to the target.

A HBT Analysis for the chromatography column packing case study is provided in the table that follows below:

HAZARD	BARRIER	ASSESSMENT	TARGET
Pressure	Rupture Disc / Relief Valve	Not Provided	Column / People
	Skid Pressure Trip	Not Effective	
	Process Alarms	Not Used	
	Local Pressure Gage	Failed	

As in most undesired outcomes and accidents, failure is a loss of control of a hazard during a work activity executed by people. The story of how the barriers failed to control the hazard is a more complex story than the words in the table provides the reader. The story begins with the system design and the testing of that design. When the two new chromatography skids were designed, the skid components and pumps were upgraded and the skid pressure protection alarms and high-pressure pump trips were raised from three bar to ten bar based on the increased robustness of the new design. The chromatography skid was considered to be the sole element of the system, and the risk of column damage from pressure was not effectively considered.

The chromatography skid system design included a Failure Modes and Effects Analysis (FMEA), which did not consider the chromatography column as part of the system, and also did not consider the human operator as part of the system. While FMEA is effective in analyzing the potential reliability of a machine, it is not appropriate for analyzing operational risk where humans are part of the system. A more appropriate analysis to assess risk would be either a Hazard and Operability Study (HAZOP) or a Failure Modes and Effects Criticality Analysis (FMECA), where guide words (e.g., no, more, less, early, late, etc.) are used to systematically determine possible failures that could result from the operation of the equipment outside of design conditions. Also, the analysis must consider all modes of operation, including the setup of the system, as was missed in the case study where only column operations were assessed, while column packing was not assessed. When using a HAZOP or FMECA, avoid recommendations that are intended to reduce risks dependent upon flawless human behavior rather than engineering process controls and hardware or software design features.

Remember, a failed column packing attempt occurred seven days earlier when multiple high-pressure alarms were received, and the pump tripped. It is likely this previous performance damaged the local pressure gauge and weakened the column to a point where a lower pressure beneath the alarm and pump trip setpoint led to the column bursting. The problems experienced during that earlier column packing attempt were reported to a manufacturing supervisor, but the escalation stopped there. Others were not informed of the event. How was it that engineering and manufacturing management were not made aware of the problems?

Reporting processes, expectations, and behaviors are, of course, a part of a broader operating system. Though rarely addressed in specific system design or during investigation processes (though we think it should be), one can see how improved information sharing and learning may have created different conditions than those present the day this column burst. How might one learn about conditions that drive a specific behavior? In chapter four, we described two different frameworks to drive change in behavior: Schein's cultural embedding mechanisms and Gilbert's Behavior Engineering Model. Here, we introduce another: Force Field Analysis[74]. Force Field Analysis can be used in conjunction with Gilbert's Behavior Engineering Model. An example template of how these can be used together can be found in Appendix E.

To perform a Force Field Analysis, first, write a specific behavior at the top of a piece of paper. For example, "Notify manufacturing management and engineering of process alarms that occurred during the work shift." Then, draw a dashed line from just below the written specific behavior to the bottom of the page, dividing the page into two halves. Now, begin brainstorming about the *driving forces* that would enable the behavior and the *resisting forces* that would inhibit the behavior. Record the driving forces on the left side of the page where the description of the force will be written above an arrow drawn horizontally left to right with the arrowhead touching the vertically drawn dashed line. Record the resisting forces on the right side of the page, where the description of the force will be written above an arrow drawn horizontally from right to left with the arrowhead touching the vertically drawn dashed line. The thickness and length of the arrows can be adjusted to depict stronger and weaker forces, or you could assign numbers to the arrows to depict relative strength. The analysis will help in the understanding of what must be adjusted through either strengthening driving forces or weakening resisting forces to shift the equilibrium of the desired behavior. Weakening or removing resisting forces is often the best way to shift performance.

---

74   Kurt Lewin was a social psychologist who created the Force Field Theory in 1951. Lewin used Force Field Theory to define the causes of human and group behaviors in group conflict, learning, hatred, and morale. The concept of Force Field Theory was later adopted by practitioners of corporate change management.

Here is a diagram showing a Force Field Analysis:

MANUFACTURING STAFF REPORT PROCESS ALARMS TO MANAGERS AND SUPPORT FUNCTIONS.

FORCES DRIVING CHANGE	FORCES RESISTING CHANGE
WE HAVE SYSTEMS THAT MAKE REPORTING EASY	WEEKEND / HOLIDAY — PEOPLE ARE OUT OF OFFICE
WE ASK PEOPLE TO SUBMIT THESE ISSUES	WORK SLOWS DOWN WHILE I MAKE CALLS
WE REWARD / RECOGNIZE PEOPLE	LACK OF SYSTEM UNDERSTANDING OF IMPLICATIONS
	QUESTIONS ABOUT MY COMPETENCE
	THERE ARE MANY ALARMS HAPPENING OFTEN
	VAGUE EXPECTATIONS ON REPORTING

In regards to the forces within the case study, here are a few to consider:

- The first packing attempt occurred on Christmas Eve, and the second packing attempt occurred on New Year's Eve. Very few people beyond essential staff were onsite.
- Workers feel a sense of pride and competence when solving a problem without engaging others or management for help.
- There was no formal process for escalating the notification of alarms.
- Alarm reports were reviewed as part of the process for batch release. These alarm reports were sometimes hundreds of pages in length, containing thousands of instances of alarms.

- Many nuisance alarms[75] occur during manufacturing operations. Most require no response or escalation due to the alarm management design.

Insisting that all manufacturing associates and manufacturing supervisors report alarms experienced during their shifts will have little to no long-term impact on performance. The organization designed the system that led to the current level of reporting or non-reporting, and behavior changes require adjustments to the system. Multiple conditions or factors associated with the chromatography column over-pressurization will need adjusting, including the addition of controls to protect the equipment and employees from high-pressure accidents.

If you hear someone say, "We're going to poka-yoke that column," they may need help shifting their thinking.

Reframing

The way a problem is stated often frames the problem-solving and solutions explored. For example, an engineering design course professor noted a problem with wrinkled bed sheets. The issue was initially framed for students as irons not effectively or efficiently getting wrinkles out of bed sheets. This led to brainstorming focused on improving the iron. A breakthrough came, however, when the problem was framed differently—why were bed sheets wrinkled at all? What was the solution to that problem? Permanent press fabric.

There are times the problems people ask designers to solve are not the ideal problems. An example is the slow elevator problem in the book, *What's Your*

---

75 A nuisance alarm is an alarm that does not meet the definition or purpose of an alarm according to the ISA-18.2 / IEC 62682 alarm management standards. Defined as alarms that annunciate excessively, unnecessarily, or do not return to normal after the correct response is taken.

Problem? Rather than focus on the elevator being slow, which would likely yield costly solutions to make the elevator faster, the problem was reframed. Was the problem the elevator? No, it worked fine. The problem was how the wait time made people feel. They were bored and impatient. This reframing led to solutions that made the wait feel shorter, like installing mirrors, playing music, and hanging art near the elevator.

Reframing tackles a conventional organization syndrome described by Kees Dorst in *Frame Innovation: Create New Thinking by Design*—the syndrome of the *self-made box*. We are sometimes trapped by how we approach problems with habits. We don't always think past the ways that worked in the past. It is helpful to remind yourself that problems are often different from problems experienced in the past. It may also be the case that past problems were not addressed as well as we like to imagine. Like people, organizations get stuck in this self-made box. But rather than expecting people to perform an intended behavior flawlessly, innovation involves creating new approaches that could lead to people performing new actions. Innovation will achieve the desired outcome with a more robust design. As Dorst explains, innovation is found through *design abduction,* where the how (pattern of relationships) and the what (elements of the system) are treated as unknowns to achieve an outcome. The outcome may need to be abstract to allow for a reframing of the problem by removing details that constrain the possible solutions. Then, beginning with the known desired outcome, the designer works backwards by first solving *the how* and then solving *the what.*

Take a look at this concept as a formula, and remember to work right to left:

What? + How? = Abstract Outcome

A biopharmaceutical manufacturing example of an opportunity to reframe is the self-made box of thinking they must prevent error by driving compliant performance. Rather, what if the work design was changed such that the risk was removed and the verbatim compliance to manage the risk was no longer necessary?

Consider the task of swapping media totes that feed an in-service bioreactor located behind a wall in a different room. The work design requires a manufacturing associate to identify the tubing of the empty media tote and sever it using scissors so that the tote can be rolled out of the room. The disconnected empty media tote tubing is located next to the tubing of the in-service media tote connected to the bioreactor. This work design led to multiple batch losses when the tubing of the in-service media tote was mistakenly cut instead of the empty media tote's tubing. This was despite awareness communications, retraining, and a procedure change to add a second worker. What ultimately changed performance and completely stopped batch losses at this step was a reframing of the problem that led to a work design change. Rather than cutting the tubing, the work was changed to coil the tubing and pass it though the bottom of the empty tote, allowing the tote to be rolled out of the room without cutting the tubing. This eliminated the risk entirely.

Chapter Summary

Your organization likely has some work to do to improve systems so that they are more helpful to people. In order to do that well, designers need to stay humble and guard against pride. Understand the right problem to be solved and always have an open mind to new possibilities. Identify where people can go wrong and safeguards are necessary. Listen to and focus on the needs of the end-user, remembering that the system is often larger than we initially think.

Maturity Assessment

Consider using the following statements to assess the maturity of your organization regarding user-friendly systems. Each statement has three possible choices. A higher total score indicates a higher maturity.

1. Our organization includes at least one person with training and experience in human factors engineering.
   Agree 20, Sometimes 10, Disagree 0

2. Our organization believes people are part of the system.
   Agree 20, Sometimes 10, Disagree 0

3. Necessary safeguards and controls are in place, verifiable, and working effectively before work begins.
   Agree 20, Sometimes 10, Disagree 0

4. We design our systems to ensure humans perform what they are better at, and machines perform what they are better at.
   Agree 20, Sometimes 10, Disagree 0

5. Our design process ensures end users are involved from the beginning.
   Agree 20, Sometimes 10, Disagree 0

CHAPTER ELEVEN

Risk-Based Response Triggers

It was a near miss that turned into a catastrophic failure. The crew from the previous shift had set up the viral filter in preparation for the next downstream unit operation. The workers now performing the unit operation primed the filter as directed in the procedure. While priming the filter, a manufacturing associate noticed an unusual delay between the opening of the bleed valve and the flow of liquid from the valve. Another manufacturing associate closed the valve upstream of the filter to segregate the viral filter and then depressurized the system. The manufacturing associate then traced the flow path looking for anything unusual. The filter housing base was installed in an incorrect orientation. The filter's inlet was attached to the outlet piping, and the outlet was connected to the inlet piping.

The manufacturing associate discussed the situation with the manufacturing supervisor who joined the team in the suite. The manufacturing supervisor then called the downstream manufacturing manager to notify them of the situation and discuss how best to proceed. The manufacturing supervisor and the downstream manufacturing manager agreed to remove the filter housing and reinstall it in the correct orientation. The downstream manufacturing manager called a member of the manufacturing sciences team and a member of the quality department, so everyone was abreast of the situation and next steps. All agreed with the fix. It was also decided that later in the shift a deviation would be originated in the deviation management system by the manufacturing supervisor in accordance with quality systems procedural guidance.

The filter housing was gravity drained and reoriented per the agreed-upon plan. Viral filtration unit operations recommenced.

The next day, the downstream manufacturing head learned about the viral filter situation and the actions taken. He and the downstream manufacturing manager discussed how the incorrect filter housing orientation placed pre-viral material in contact with the post-viral side during the pre-use filter bleed. The manufacturing process did not have additional downstream controls or sampling for viral contamination. While the downstream manufacturing head knew this, the downstream manufacturing manager did not. As a result, the batch was discarded, and an investigation began to learn more about the failure.

It is common for investigators and management to fixate on the action that usually goes right but this time went wrong. In this case the viral filter housing being installed backwards. Leadership teams judge work processes as well designed when there are no known instances where things don't go as planned. They haven't watched the work performed or asked workers about risks and previous near misses. Their assumption the system is well designed means the worker who did the wrong thing (this time) is to blame. He or she should have done the right thing like everyone else before. Speculation begins circulating. The worker is considered incompetent or complacent. "The worker didn't follow the written guidance accurately," they say. "That person should have known."

In this case, workplace conditions told a different and more complete story. The etched flow direction arrow on the filter housing was faded as a result of frequent cleaning. Investigators noted the lack of helpful written guidance for the filter housing orientation. Also there was no photo of the correct orientation at point of use in the procedure. There was a piping and instrumentation diagram (P&ID) located near the back of the procedure, but it wasn't easy to find or understand. These conditions could be easily improved through corrective actions. In addition, in this case, since leadership chose to listen to workers' ideas, location pins were affixed onto the filter housing that only allowed the inlet and outlet valves to be installed to the correct corresponding connections. Yes, poka-yoke.

But there was more to learn. Investigators wanted to understand how it made sense to two manufacturing leaders, a scientist, and a quality professional, to flip the viral filter housing and proceed with the unit operation—ultimately ending in the batch loss. After all, the manufacturing associates caught the incorrect installation of the filter housing, and the work was stopped. If that is where the story ended, the situation would have been classified as a near miss, though the happy ending would have relied on luck rather than effective controls.

The decision to flip the filter and proceed, agreed to by four competent people from three different functions, perplexed many of the more experienced site leaders. The four people involved had dozens of combined years of industry experience, had come from multiple companies, and represented different specialties (e.g., Quality Control, Process Engineering, Manufacturing, etc.). Most had been in their current role for less than two years, which is not unusual in the biopharmaceutical industry. Voluntary turnover can be 15 percent or higher. At the time of writing this book, it was not uncommon to see voluntary turnover rates between 20 and 30 percent at some sites, with the most impacted departments between 40 and 50 percent.

Staff turnover is a significant factor that challenges workforce competence. The turnover is largely due to a very competitive talent market, expanding companies, and new startups offering compensation packages and position opportunities[76]. While job-jumping can be a financial boon for workers, it creates a challenge to operational performance at manufacturing sites. Turnover depletes the institutional memory that is so important when faced with the unanticipated and unknown associated with an operational mishap. The mental models and cause maps acquired through informal learning leave the organization when an employee leaves the company or the team. The new employee, hired as a backfill or internally promoted to fill the role of a more experienced departed leader, may have fewer and less appropriate mental models and cause maps, leading to limited and inaccurate perceptions during abnormal situations.

According to a paper by Julian Decius, an organizational psychologist, some studies have found that 70 to 90 percent of learning in the modern workplace occurs informally. As Weick explains, this informal learning includes work experiences that create rich memories of categories and assumptions stored as mental models and heuristics[77] that can be retrieved to address problems quickly and correctly.

The small team of professionals involved with the decision-making to correct the misoriented viral filter housing all recognized they were outside of existing procedures. They may not have realized they were all relying on intuition to create a path forward. According to Daniel Kahneman, psychologist and author renowned for his work in judgement and decision-making,

---

76 There is some truth to people leaving companies because of bad managers. Skilled leaders do make a difference in retention. However, people also leave because of compensation and development opportunities, with development opportunities being the biggest driver. A 2021 Pew Research Center survey found that workers who quit a job in 2021 say low pay (63%), no opportunities for advancement (63%) and feeling disrespected at work (57%) were reasons why they quit.

77 Heuristics are mental shortcuts that allow people to solve problems more quickly and with minimal mental effort.

"Intuition is thinking you know without knowing why you do." Kahneman suggests intuition is wrong unless three conditions are met:

1. There must be a regularity of experience, so people have an opportunity to learn.

2. Intuition comes with lots of practice by taking advantage of the regularity of experiences.

3. The person needs immediate feedback on whether their decision was right or wrong in order to establish that mental model and cause map.

It appeared the viral filter housing decision-making team did not have the necessary expert intuition for the situation. As Kahneman explains, the danger in such a situation is that "Intuition feels just the same when it's wrong and when it's right. That's the problem."

Other factors contributed to the decision to reorient the viral filter housing and recommence the unit operation. While there was no approaching expiry associated with the drug substance as part of the unit operation, there is always a mindset of *keeping the product moving* in biopharmaceutical manufacturing. This is the pressure from the Economic Viability (Cost) boundary from Rasmussen's model, as described in chapter six. There may be no conversations that reveal the mindset, yet the self-imposed time pressure exists as part of everyone's thinking. And the action driven by that thinking is frequently rewarded by the organization. Workers avoid the risk of creating a bottleneck that would stall other operations that share equipment and staff.

Groupthink

The final factor to mention is the sense of safety that people and organizations believe exists when more than one person is involved in decision-making and checking the work of others. In the case of the viral filter housing decision-making team, there were four people involved. Adding more people to a decision-making group might seem like a potential solution, but as Dekker explains, it ignores that people are not machine components where system reliability can be improved by adding unreliable duplicate components to compensate for existing same-function unreliable components. A social factor in play with teams of people (not present with machines) is groupthink, where there is a psychological drive for team consensus, preventing the necessary conflict for questioning proposals and alternative solutions. Rather than adding more people, the interrelationships between the people and how they function as a team is a leverage point to change future system performance.

A method to ensure group discussions lead to better solutions is to provide a framework for the conversation. Consider the following list of questions used to guide teams when determining a path forward when they recognize they are outside existing written guidance:

1. What is the purpose of the process step?

2. Does the situation involve a control associated with product quality? (e.g., filter, column, sample, alarm, etc.)

3. Have I ever experienced this exact process step situation previously?

4. Considering what I think I know about the situation and possible paths forward, what else might be true? What am I missing here?

5. If we take this action is it a "point of no return"—not reversible?

Questions one and two help the group align on the situation and the problem to be solved. Without a common understanding of the situation, the group is at risk of making an inappropriate decision. Question three helps the group members be deliberate about the mental models and cause maps created from past experiences. It is important to recognize whether anyone in the group has encountered the exact situation. Question four is designed to nudge the group's discussions toward systems thinking. The situation may include multiple contributors, each necessary but only partially sufficient. Question five is essential to building a complete picture of the decision risk. If the proposed action cannot be undone, failure could harm the product, and the answer to question three indicates no previous experience, this is the cue to engage more experienced colleagues in the decision. Engaging diverse expertise aligns with the high reliability organizing (HRO) principle, Deference to Expertise[78].

Risk-Based Criteria

Provide teams with operational decision-making escalation criteria to engage risk-based expertise. Most biopharmaceutical manufacturing organizations already have outcome-based escalation criteria. Such outcome-based standards are necessary and include outcomes like manufacturing associates notifying manufacturing supervisors of any deviation before proceeding, manufacturing supervisors notifying manufacturing managers before implementing any

---

78 High Reliability Organizing (HRO) as described in Managing the Unexpected recognizes expertise as an HRO principle. "HROs cultivate diversity, not just because it helps them notice more in complex environments, but also because it helps them adapt to the complexities they do spot."

decision that may be outside of approved procedures or batch records, and manufacturing managers notifying area manufacturing heads of product loss.

Escalation is required before implementing decisions outside an approved procedure or batch record, and when the following are true:

1. The exact process step situation has not been previously experienced.

2. The situation involves a control associated with product quality.

3. The action is a "point of no return."

Chapter Summary

While the biopharmaceutical industry has plenty of written guidance for everyday work, there is limited guidance for unexpected and rare occurrences. In contrast, commercial nuclear operating plants have procedures for normal operations in addition to abnormal and emergency operations. The commercial aviation industry has in-flight emergency checklists. Just as a biopharmaceutical site might have procedures for response to contamination or anomalous results, a case can be made for similar procedures to respond to off-normal operational events.

Establishing risk-based triggers to engage expertise enhances the operational resilience of an organization. The right team will respond well to unanticipated conditions. The potential to respond well, according to Erik Hollnagel in *Safety-II in Practice: Developing the Resilience Potentials*, requires a list of regularly maintained unexpected threats, guidance on how teams work together and communicate these threats, and escalation bridges connecting local groups to additional resources in the organization. These should be in place *before* problems happen.

Maturity Assessment

Consider using the following statements to assess the maturity of your organization regarding risk-based triggers. Each statement has three possible choices. A higher total score indicates a higher maturity.

1. The organization has formal guidance for how to identify and manage off-normal conditions.
    Agree 20, Sometimes 10, Disagree 0

2. Our escalation criteria includes risk and is not solely outcome based.
    Agree 20, Sometimes 10, Disagree 0

3. Our organization considers expertise when adding more people to a group to improve decision-making.
    Agree 20, Sometimes 10, Disagree 0

4. We consider institutional memory important to operational decision-making when making staffing changes.
    Agree 20, Sometimes 10, Disagree 0

Non-Technical Risk
Management Practices

Emily and Chris had just installed their tags and locks on the empty ten-thou-sand-liter tank. They verified zero energy from the top of the tank where the tags and locks had been placed nearby. Now that the lockout/tagout (LOTO) was complete, the next step was to descend two flights of stairs in the gray space area to the bottom of the tank, where they would replace the NovaSep-tum sampling system. Emily informed Chris that before proceeding to the next part of the task, she needed to meet a quality analyst to provide a batch record that required review as part of an investigation. Chris replied that he would meet Emily at the bottom of the tank and set up the work area for the NovaSeptum changeout while he waited for her arrival.

Chris was a former member of the U.S. Army, and this was his first job since leaving military service. He had been working in biopharmaceutical manufacturing for almost three years and was known as a get-it-done type. Chris didn't have much use for human and organizational performance stuff. He believed that people needed to pay close attention to their work, and those who made mistakes had only themselves to blame.

When Chris arrived at the bottom floor of the gray space area, he turned right, toward the bottoms of six towering stainless steel tanks. He stopped at the first tank to set up for the NovaSeptum changeout. He checked an identification tag hanging from a valve attached to the bottom of the tank. The tag displayed a ten-character string of numbers and letters—from an engineering database when the plant was originally built. The tag did not include a noun name of the tank. There were no local pressure, temperature, or weight gauges for any of the tanks at this plant level, and there was no HMI control system station in the area.

It did not take long to complete the setup for the job. Chris had the paperwork, the new NovaSeptum sampling system, the wrench, and a rolling worktable for his tools and documents. Chris checked his smartphone for the time—he had been waiting for what seemed like a long time. He decided to begin the work without Emily since it was a simple job that he had performed many times before.

Chris removed three of the four small bolts that connected the old NovaSeptum sampling system to the bottom of the tank. As Chris loosened the last bolt, he suspected he might be at the wrong tank. He paused for a second, then decided he should reinstall the bolts and recheck the tag to be sure he was working on the correct tank. Suddenly, media was spewing out of the tank from where the NovaSeptum was previously fastened securely, hitting Chris in the face and chest. Chris fought to block the media flow with his hands while attempting to reinstall one of the small bolts. People working in an office area adjacent to the gray space heard what they believed was a person wailing, "No, no, no!"

Thankfully, Chris was not injured, aside from his pride. Unfortunately, the media tank was needed for an operating bioreactor, and now, before the tank could be cleaned and new media prepared, the product in the bioreactor would expire. The entire batch was lost.

During the initial investigation meeting, attended by Chris, Emily, and the supervisor, Chris remarked to the investigator and the human and organizational performance lead, "I don't understand how this happened to me."

The human and organizational performance lead replied, "Would you like me to explain how something like this could happen to anyone?"

Chris answered, "Yes."

"Well, you are human, and therefore you are fallible. *People make mistakes.* Those tanks are in close proximity to each other and look very similar. The tag identification system is not easy to follow, and your LOTO, which should be a visual cue, was located two levels up. Also, we don't have sufficient controls established to prevent tank mix-ups. This type of mix-up event happens once a year or so, yet the organization has treated them as one-off events rather than investing in improved controls."

This was a response meant to support positive change.

Human Performance Tools

Non-technical risk management practices are also known as human performance risk management practices or human performance tools. This content is located near the end of this book for a reason. In the past, biopharmaceutical organizations have focused heavily or entirely on asking workers to adopt a new set of human performance tools. Organizations spent little or no effort to improve the management of risk. As a result, performance was mostly unchanged.

Because of this misguided focus, we wanted our readers to learn alternative ways of thinking—ideas presented in previous chapters. That said, there is certainly a place for formal non-technical risk management practices at the sharp end. These practices help workers compensate for the gaps in imperfect systems, adapt to transient changes originating from the dynamic nature of systems, and get work done in the modern workplace.

An accident such as the one described at the beginning of this chapter highlights the need for controls. And improving controls will go a long way to improving performance. However, organizations face the realities of limited resources, the necessity of business efficiencies, and the normal tendency for organizations and humans to follow the path of least effort.

Even in a perfect world, if an organization identified a need for better controls, it would need time to design and execute the solution to put those controls in place. There would be a period of time when the risk is not entirely mitigated.

In addition, it is not always possible to manage every process's risks. It's also impossible to guarantee controls will sustain effectiveness for eternity in a modern workplace where VUCA[79] is present. Recognizing that our systems are always running in a suboptimal manner with surprises being common, aiming for exceptional execution at the sharp end is desirable for positive control, where the only thing that happens is intended to happen, and nothing else happens.

Beware of the trap of thinking that once your system capacity and controls are working pretty well, the job of management is done, and it is now up to the workers to ensure positive control. James Reason states that "Striving for the best attainable level of intrinsic resistance to operational hazards is like fighting a guerrilla war. One can expect no absolute victories. There are no Waterloos in the safety war." He's alluding to entropy in that statement—a probabilistic concept where a system's state of disorder, randomness, or uncertainty increases over time. Just as that bottle of vinaigrette dressing in your refrigerator frequently needs a few shakes to remix the oil-rich layer at

---

79 VUCA is an acronym for Volatile-Uncertain-Complex-Ambiguous. The acronym VUCA was first used in the U.S. Army War College in 1987 as the Cold War was ending to depict a new form of unpredictable military engagement.

the top of the bottle with the vinegar-rich layer at the bottom, systems in an organization require ongoing attention and energy to ensure the necessary capacity and controls to create success are present and effective.

While Reason uses guerilla warfare to make a point, David Hackworth, who wrote the book on counter-insurgency warfare, provides additional insights about managing risk at the sharp end. His ideas translate well to work in the biopharmaceutical industry and other industries where there are high hazards to product. David Hackworth, a much-decorated career Army officer and combat legend in Vietnam, provides the following maxims in the preface of the 2003 edition of *The Vietnam Primer*[80]:

- "Always have a go-to-hell plan."
- "Never assume anything."
- "Always expect the unexpected."
- "Talk to the grunts; they always have the best feel for what's going down."
- "Keep operations sledgehammer simple, and remember, if it can be f***ed[81] up, it will be."
- "Never, never be in a hurry."

These tips and other tactics offered by Hackworth helped win many battles and keep untold American soldiers alive in Vietnam but were not sufficient to overcome the lack of competent strategic leadership by generals

---

80 The Vietnam Primer (1967) is an operational analysis of U.S. Army tactics and command practices in the small combat unit, digested from historical operations from May 1966 to February 1967. The lessons in the Vietnam Primer are the distillate of after action reviews with upward of one hundred rifle companies and many patrols and platoons, led by the authors David Hackworth and Samuel Marshall.

81 Euphemistic spelling of the word used in the original quote.

and government policymakers, as well as the lack of understanding about the motivations and thinking of the adversary engaged in a civil war. The results are similar when a biopharmaceutical organization adopts non-technical risk management practices for workers at the sharp end while neglecting the other topics in the earlier chapters of this book. The organization will swat at the mosquitoes of error versus draining the swamp that hinders capacity and controls, leaving the situation at the sharp end unimproved. Basically, it's a bad strategy.

So, how does an organization select which human performance tools to adopt? Avoid taking the list of human performance tools found in the *Department of Energy Human Performance Handbook* and haphazardly bolting them onto your existing expectations for workers. Depending on how you count, there are twenty or so tools in that handbook used by people and teams, and that is not what Hackworth would call keeping operations simple. Layering these human performance risk management practices onto what your workers already do to manage risk will, in many cases, create confusion and increase complexity. The list generally works well in the nuclear industry because it was created with that specific work in mind. While some nuclear human performance tools can be tailored for the biopharmaceutical industry, practices that consider the context of biopharmaceutical manufacturing are better.

Human performance risk management practices for biopharmaceutical manufacturing can be binned into three general categories associated with how work must be managed to create success:

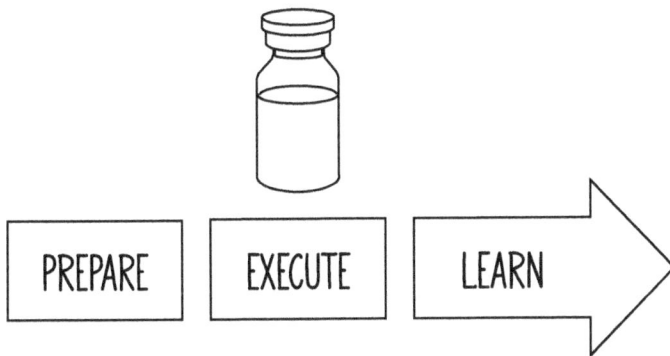

Illustration of the three categories of non-technical
risk management practices.

Human performance tools in the *prepare* category are necessary to anticipate risk. Human performance tools in the *execute* category improve positive
control during the performance of work. Human performance tools in the
learn category are necessary to learn the right lessons from success and failure
in order to improve future work.

PREPARE

Risk-Ready Review

A *risk-ready review* is a simple human performance tool used to anticipate
risk before conducting work with potential risk. A risk-ready review is performed at the location where the work is performed by the people doing the
work. It should be conducted as close as possible to when the work begins.
A risk-ready review consists of four questions asked and answered aloud by
the team. This is a dialogue. A risk-ready review takes between five and ten
minutes to perform.

Here are the risk-ready review questions:

1. What factors create a risk of failure?

2. What is the worst possible failure that can happen?

3. How will steps that must go right be performed and monitored?

4. What is the status of controls that protect the product?

It is common, after explaining the purpose and performance details of a risk-ready review to a manager or a manufacturing associate, they will look at you troubled and state, "We already do that." This is where being sensitive to the words used in conversations and the distinctions around different ideas becomes very important. Unless the organization is already asking and answering the four questions above, they are not doing the same thing. It may be true that a conversation takes place before work begins. However, it is unlikely that factors that create risk are explored, steps that must go right are discussed in detail, and the controls to prevent harm are checked before the work begins.

As Karl Weick said:

If you want to change the way you think, change the words you use.

The practices intended to be human performance tools must have a name and be formally executed. Without a name, people will have different ideas about the practice. Without some formality around the steps to perform the practice, people will have different ideas about what good looks like.

For a risk-ready review to be effective, managers must create time and space for the discussion. Also, as with other human performance tools, managers must abide by the rule, "What's important to my boss is important to me." This means that if a manager never observes risk-ready reviews, infrequently asks about what was discussed when unable to attend a risk-ready review, or does not provide positive reinforcement when a risk-ready review is performed, the practice will not truly exist. Edgar Schein refers to this as "What leaders pay attention to, measure, and control on a regular basis." He listed it as one of the primary embedding mechanisms of organizational culture. Another way of saying this is the well-known maxim attributed to General Bruce C. Clarke,[82] "The organization does well only those things the boss checks."

Finally, don't expect people to memorize the risk-ready review questions. Instead, find ways to make the four questions easy to access where they are intended to be used. One way of doing this is by creating magnets with the four questions. Mark them as non-GMP[83] job aids, and affix them to surfaces in the GMP area.

The Pre-job Brief

If your organization has taken the time to identify risk critical steps and risk important steps, you might consider a more formal discussion to anticipate

---

82 General Bruce C. Clarke served as a combat commander in the 7th and 4th Armored Divisions, 1943 to 1945 (participating in the Battle of the Bulge); commanding general of the 2nd Constabulary Brigade, 1949 to 1951; commanding general of the 1st Armored Division, 1951 to 1953; and was Commander in Chief of the U.S. Army in Europe, 1960 to 1962.

83 GMP refers to the Good Manufacturing Practices regulations of the U.S. Food and Drug Administration (FDA) under the authority of the Federal Food, Drug, and Cosmetic Act. These regulations require manufacturers, processors, and packagers of drugs, medical devices, some food, and blood take proactive steps to ensure that their products are safe, pure, and effective. GMP is also referred to as cGMP. The c stands for current, reminding manufacturers that they must employ technologies and systems that are up-to-date in order to comply with the regulation. Systems and equipment used to prevent contamination, mix-ups, and errors, which may have been first-rate twenty years prior, may be less than adequate by current standards. (Reference https://ispe.org/initiatives/regulatory-resources/gmp/what-is-gmp, accessed on 13Aug22).

the risks for those specific activities. This formal risk discussion would include previously identified risk critical steps and risk important steps in a pre-job brief.

It is helpful to create pre-job brief guidelines for unit operations that list the associated risk critical steps. A pre-job brief guide is typically a two-sided letter-size laminated paper used as a non-GMP job aid and stored in a visible location where work takes place. The guidance on conducting a pre-job brief is on the front side of the job aid, including a list of open-ended questions used to guide the conversation. On the back side are the risk critical steps, risk important steps, and a list of lessons learned.

Here are a few examples of questions:

1. What does success look like for the activity we are about to perform?

2. What are our roles and responsibilities?

3. What workplace local factors and abnormal conditions create a risk of failure?

4. Which steps pose a risk to the product?

5. What is the plan to manage the risks to the product?

6. What is the status of necessary controls to protect the product?

7. What conditions will require us to stop the work?

8. What past experiences and lessons will help us complete the work successfully?

9.   What questions or concerns do you have with our plan?

The information on the back page of the pre-job brief guide is used to help answer the questions on the front page.

Similar to a risk-ready review, a pre-job brief is conducted at the place where the work will occur by the workers doing the work. When using a pre-job brief, there is no reason to perform a risk-ready review—that would be redundant. A pre-job brief is a dialogue best performed when a team member facilitates the discussion by asking open-ended questions from the pre-job brief guide, and the other participants answer the questions and discuss the work to be performed. A pre-job brief will generally take between ten and fifteen minutes to perform.

Be aware of the problems associated with pre-job briefs. Do not use the pre-job brief guide as a checklist or prework requirement that participants must sign. This practice tends to weaponize the pre-job brief process and will detract from creating the necessary helpful dialogue that must take place. Also, discourage workers from reading the pre-job brief guide verbatim. Instead, use the aid to generate an organic conversation about risk and the controls necessary to create success.

EXECUTE

Questioning Attitude

The human performance tool known as *a questioning attitude*[84] is not as easy as it sounds. Even including it in this list may be controversial. The Nuclear Regulatory Commission (NRC) cites a questioning attitude as "A trait

---

84   The basis of a questioning attitude in human and organizational performance is chronic unease. Chronic unease is defined as a preoccupation with failure.

necessary for positive safety culture." The NRC also states that a questioning attitude should be used by both leaders and individual employees, so listing it as a human performance tool to be used at the sharp end may be misleading.

For our purposes in biopharmaceutical manufacturing, we borrow the idea of safety culture and apply it to the main assets we aim to protect—the product and the patient. Think from that perspective in the following paragraphs. Consider it an aspect of quality culture.

While there is no single definition for *safety culture*, the Australian Radiation Protection and Nuclear Safety Agency (ARPANSA) has a pretty good definition. ARPANSA defines safety culture as "The core values, beliefs, and behaviors resulting from a collective commitment by leaders and individuals throughout an organization that appropriately prioritize safety against other organizational goals to allow business objectives to be undertaken without undue risk."

Edgar Schein believes that safety culture is too general, and it is the task and the people doing it that create their own standards, rules, and behavior patterns.

He says, "The risks and dangers that make us want safety do not derive from cultural factors. They derive from the work itself, the actual tasks that have to be performed that bring various kinds of risks and dangers with them. Culture may have influenced the design of those tasks, and cultural factors may influence the kinds and degrees of risk we want to take. But if we want to increase safety itself in a given work situation, it is the designers, operators, and executives aligning their interests and working together to minimize those risks that worry them most that will produce an effective safety program."

Consider replacing safety with quality in Schein's quote and read it again. Imagine the progress that could be made in Quality Culture if we stopped talking so much about culture and instead focused on work risk.

For a questioning attitude to exist in an organization, there must be adequate psychological safety so people feel safe to admit a situation they cannot reconcile with previous experience. The leaders in the organization must have spent the time and resources to communicate expectations, ask questions, model the behavior of asking questions for issues they are not knowledgeable about, and respond positively to questions asked by workers.

Unlike other human performance tools, a questioning attitude is not defined as a series of behaviors executed in a certain sequence. A questioning attitude is more like a set of conditional prompts to execute when the condition arises.

The following is a concise and broadly applicable list of cues for a questioning attitude:

- Challenge unknown and unexpected conditions.
- Challenge assumptions and offer opposing views.
- Stop and escalate when unsure.

When setting the expectation for people to stop and escalate when unsure, remember humans in the workplace—and in life—are seldom faced with a set of two simple and easily defined emotions. There is a wide chasm of feelings between *certain* and *unsure,* including *pretty sure* and *comfortably certain.* With that in mind, for unit operations that include risk critical steps, it is beneficial to establish *start work criteria* and *stop work criteria* specific to the task. Start work criteria is more effective than stop work criteria as a result of certain and unsure not being a simple binary choice for a human in the flow of work within complex systems. A questioning attitude is then left to hopefully catch situations that the organization may not have imagined beforehand.

Performer Eyes on Written Guidance

Throughout the biopharmaceutical manufacturing industry, you will find a practice known as *reader-doer* or *reader-performer*. The practice of reader-doer consists of one worker reading aloud the step to be executed from written guidance and the coworker performing the step. How this practice often looks to an observer is one worker holding the written guidance in their hands and reading aloud, while the second worker executes the steps as they are read aloud. Sometimes the worker performing the steps will verbalize a completed step with a one-word reply that summarizes the action's outcome, like opened, closed, started, or stopped. While reader-doer is helpful when the goal is to perform work quickly, it is also a workplace factor that can detract from positive control, where the only thing that happens is what is intended to happen.

There are multiple problems with reader-doer when the goal is positive control. The wrong step could be read. A step read out loud could be misheard by the person executing the step. Also, when only one person on the team is looking at the written guidance, the opportunity to catch a mistake or question the step's correctness and clarity is lost. The importance of both workers having eyes on the written guidance is amplified when considering how often poorly designed written documentation is present in biopharmaceutical manufacturing.

For steps in unit operations where positive control is essential, having a performer's eyes on written guidance will improve performance. Slight changes to the reader-doer structure are necessary to leverage the second set of eyes on documentation and to largely eliminate the possibility of a communication error. If a single copy of the documentation is used, the reader should hold the documentation so the performer can also see it. The reader may still read the steps aloud as a means of placekeeping[85] and to help focus the performers' attention on the step.

If the performer can hold the documentation while working, this is an opportunity for a set of matching documentation to be used, ensuring the performer reads the steps. For example, if written guidance is provided through electronic tablets, each worker would have their own tablet in hand.

There will be situations where the performer cannot see the written guidance. Maybe they are working in a biological safety cabinet, or the task requires both hands. Perhaps the work environment does not allow the workers to stand close together. In those situations, effective communication between the reader and the performer is essential.

Three-Part Communication

Probably the most misunderstood and difficult to execute human performance tool is *three-part communication*. Often, people think they are involved in three-part communication when they are not. They might even be making the work more complex and adding to risks. Three-part communication has three parts to it, where the sender does parts one and three, and the receiver does part two. For our purposes in biopharmaceutical manufacturing, the reader will be the sender and the performer will be the receiver. The only purpose of three-part communication is to send information to a receiver—the performer, in our case—when the receiver is not able to see the written guidance.

Here is an example of three-part communication:

---

85 Placekeeping is a human performance tool used in the nuclear industry where, as each step is performed as defined by written guidance, the worker uses a pen to mark the step as completed. This practice does not translate well to biopharmaceutical manufacturing due to the industry's interpretation of Good Data and Documentation Practices. Placekeeping can only be used in biopharmaceutical manufacturing if the batch record is designed to include checkboxes corresponding to steps within a section signed by the performer.

Part 1 - Reader (sender) says: "Open the outlet valve located at the bottom of the column."

Part 2 - Performer (receiver) says: "Open the outlet valve located at the bottom of the column."

Part 3 - Reader (sender) says: "Correct."

Notice there are only three parts to the communication example. If the reader did not perform the third part, confirming his or her statement was heard correctly, it's not three-part communication. Skipping the third part is a common problem. Another is when the performer executes the action before the reader confirms or rejects the instructions were heard correctly.

If it feels like using three-part communication slows work, good. Slowing work ensures effective communication takes place for tasks with higher risks. If speed in work execution is necessary, or where an action is low risk, three-part communication may not be the human performance tool to use.

Performer and Witness Stay in Role

Sometimes, during the execution of steps within a unit operation, there is a tendency for the performer and the witness to swap roles without discussion. For example, when a witness is standing closer to the valve or device to be operated so he or she takes action instead of the performer. There are potential issues with an unplanned role swap. Execution steps are easily missed. Steps can be done more than once. The witness can miss executions. And batch record signatures can be forgotten.

In order to enhance positive control, where what happens is what is intended to happen, there can be no unplanned swapping of performer and witness roles during unit operation. The performer and witness must stay in role for the natural duration of the unit operation, unless there is a discussion and both agree to swap at a specific point. This is a very simple human performance tool that is very powerful to ensure that steps are not missed and data integrity is maintained.

Touch-Say-Do

Multiple industries use a practice where a person performing a step in a task uses hand gestures while verbalizing information related to the object. Some believe this approach improves mindfulness, and fewer mistakes are made when a person is mindful. Mindfulness, in simple terms, is moment-to-moment awareness. Thich Nhat Hanh[86] describes mindfulness as "The energy of being aware and awake to the present moment." Hanh believes that mindfulness is possible during everyday activities. "If, while washing dishes," he says, "we think only of the cup of tea that awaits us, thus hurrying to get the dishes out of the way as if they were a nuisance, then we are not washing the dishes to wash the dishes."

How often are humans not mindful, where their minds are wandering? One study found that people's minds wander 46.9 percent of the time, and the nature of people's activities had only a modest impact on whether their minds wandered. Considering the many unfavorable workplace local factors present in biopharmaceutical manufacturing, there is a need for practices that keep people mindful during high-risk operations.

In the commercial nuclear power industry, the practice used to improve mindfulness is known as *self-checking* or STAR (*Stop*, *Think*, *Act*, and *Review*). Many biopharmaceutical organizations have attempted to adopt self-checking, with poor results. Part of the problem is that self-checking has been generalized

---

86   Thich Nhat Hanh was a Vietnamese Zen Buddhist monk, peace activist, and leading voice in opposition of the Vietnam War. He helped pioneer the concept of mindfulness in the West and socially engaged Buddhism in the East.

and its structure does not easily allow an observer to see what is happening at every step. If you can't see something happening, it's impossible to provide feedback. What does *stop* look like, exactly? How does one know what a person is thinking about at the *think* step? Also, the use of self-checking in the nuclear industry infrequently includes verbalizing the step to be performed, the *act*, when working alone, which detracts from the effectiveness of the practice.

The aviation industry uses a practice known as *call out*. A call out is a spoken data read-out by a crew member in the cockpit. For example, the pilot might call out the air speed by stating the parameter name and value aloud. Call outs are used to maximize crew awareness of conditions. In some applications of call out, the crew member may also point to or touch the instrument of interest on the control panel or point to an object in view outside the cockpit windshield.

In the Japanese railways industry, they call their practice of gesturing and verbalizing *shisa kanko*, or pointing and calling. A study by Japan's Railway Technical Research Institute showed that when asked to perform a simple task people typically make 2.38 mistakes per 100 actions. When using shisa kanko, this number reduced to just 0.38—an impressive 85 percent improvement. The practice of pointing and calling has been adopted by other railway organizations around the world.

In the biopharmaceutical industry, a practice that can be used during work execution to improve positive control is called *touch-say-do*. Just as the name states, there are three steps to this practice:

1. Touch: Place your hand on the object that will be operated.

2. Say: With your hand on the object, state aloud the action to be performed and the name of the object.

3. Do: Perform the action.

For work where you are unable to touch an object due to the potential triggering of the operation or causing other problems, you can substitute pointing for touching. Touch-say-do can be used when working alone to improve mindfulness or when working as part of a team to enhance team awareness. Touch-say-do is beneficial when changing the status of a device, entering data, selecting a recipe, or responding to a prompt though an HMI.

Flagging

The practice of *flagging* helps to avoid mix-ups similar to that in the case study in this chapter. The plant designs in biopharmaceutical facilities often do not adequately consider the possibility of people operating the wrong device as a result of similar devices being located in close proximity. Labeling and marking is often not distinct enough to help prevent mix-ups. In these situations, flagging can be used to create distinctions before and during the execution of the work. One way to do flagging is to use flagging tape, which can be found online.

Here is an example of the flagging process:

1. The performer and witness identify a potential mix-up during their risk-ready review or pre-job brief.

2. The performer and witness go to the work location where the mix-up could occur.

3. The performer and witness identify the device that will be operated and attach a piece of flagging tape on or near the device.

4. The performer and witness perform the work.

5. The performer and witness remove the flagging tape to closeout the work.

It is common for biopharmaceutical organizations to feel anxious about implementing flagging based on speculations and what-ifs. What if workers forget to remove the flagging tape? What if the company is viewed as doing something against GMP? A reasonable way to deal with what-ifs is to add flagging to a policy that provides recognition of the practice and sets general expectations of performance while avoiding deviation traps if performance is not as imagined. The benefits of flagging outweigh the consequences associated with the uncounted what-ifs.

LEARN

Post-Job Review

A *post-job review* creates the opportunity for workers at the sharp end to learn and share what is and is not working well. This typically includes manufacturing associates, lab analysts, and warehouse associates.

A post-job review is a five to ten-minute reflective conversation performed by the people who have just completed a unit operation or work task. The post-job review takes place as soon as the work concludes, at or near the place where the work happened, and includes all the workers who had a hand in executing that work. The post-job review is not the same as a *shift handover*[87].

---

87 A shift handover, also known as a shift changeover or shift turnover, is the process of transferring responsibility and authority for a shift from one worker or team to another. It is common in manufacturing plants and other operations where workers work on an assigned shift.

Here are three questions and follow-up prompts to conduct a post-job review:

1. Did the work happen the way we expected? If not, where was the team surprised?

2. Did we have to make do, improvise, or adapt? If yes, where?

3. What learning should we share with others in the organization?

Organizations that do post-job reviews have a means to easily capture and share information. One way to improve learning from post-job reviews is by providing a user-friendly digital solution for workers conducting post-job reviews. An example of such a solution could be created as a workflow in DevonWay[88]. A homegrown, less elegant solution would be Microsoft Forms for data submission and Microsoft Power BI for data visualization. Submitted post-job reviews are then shared with the entire organization through an open-access repository or a targeted audience based on location, work task, or the preference to share with key stakeholders who have an interest or ability to improve the work situation. Since management does not attend post-job reviews, it is advised to have a method to ensure learning gets from the floor to management.

After Action Review

The purpose of an *after action review* (AAR) is to understand how things went right, as well as how things went wrong. When learning how a process goes right, more is learned regarding how things could go wrong. This knowledge

---

88 DevonWay is a software solutions company that provides a no-code SaaS platform for quickly configuring web-based, mobile-capable enterprise software applications.

helps the team and the organization improve things that make it difficult to achieve the intended goal. An AAR is longer and involves more stakeholders than a post-job review.

An AAR is a guided reflection and review process, typically executed at the group level, intended to create learning used for improvement. The U.S. Army is an example of an organization that has institutionalized the process. AARs were introduced in the mid-1970s and were originally designed to capture lessons from simulated battles of the National Training Centers. The AAR technique diffused slowly, and in a decade, the process was fully accepted by line officers and embedded in the culture. By the late 1990s, AARs became common practice. AARs sprang up during the Gulf War as small groups of soldiers gathered in foxholes or around vehicles in the middle of the desert to review their most recent missions and identify possible improvements. The U.S. Army's Field Manual 7-0 states "An after action review is a guided analysis of an organization's performance, conducted at appropriate times during and at the conclusion of a training event or operation with the objective of improving future performance." The World Health Organization also has AAR resources describing different ways to learn following an event or activity[89].

Conducting an AAR is as simple as facilitating dialogue with a team by asking specific questions. The AAR process may be formal or informal, involve large or small groups, and take less than an hour or multiple hours. The team typically includes all stakeholders who participated in some way in creating and executing a work activity or project. For example, at the end of a product campaign, the participants would include scientists, engineers,

---

89 The World Health Organization (WHO) AAR materials can be found here: https://www.euro.who.int/en/health-topics/health-emergencies/international-health-regulations/monitoring-and-evaluation/after-action-review. They describe multiple levels and types of AARs. We recommend keeping your AAR process simple and have not found it necessary to implement the multi-tier AAR system they describe.

schedulers, and manufacturing floor staff. Facilitation of an AAR can become difficult for groups that exceed fifteen participants.

Here are questions and desired learning outcomes for effective AAR learning:

1. What did we set out to do? Describe in detail the overall objective of the activity, as well as the specific measures that define success.

2. What actually occurred? List the actual results achieved for the overall objective and success measures.

3. How did it happen? Follow a path of exploration by reconstructing a timeline of events. Identify the conditions, actions, and context that influenced performance along the timeline.

4. What are we going to do next time? Brainstorm and agree on changes that will improve performance for next time. Document the changes, make them actionable, and assign them to owners.

Note: Roughly 25 percent of the time should be devoted to the first two questions, 25 percent to the third question, and 50 percent to the fourth question.

The *Etsy Debriefing Guide* provides helpful guidance on event learning focus that translates well to an AAR. The AAR facilitator should ask questions that help reveal the following:

- The context for assessments or judgments
- The rationale for choices or decisions

- Things that people know (and might assume are common knowledge)
- People's states of mind at the time
- Mental models for how things *should* work
- Factors that led people to take a specific action

Key steps to a successful AAR include the following:

1. Kick off the meeting by explaining the AAR's purpose and process.

2. Set the ground rules, such as only one person talking at a time, avoid using words that imply blame to people and groups, and provide candid and respectful descriptions of performance.

3. Strive to create an inclusive environment.

4. Demonstrate empathy for attendees who may be embarrassed or blaming themselves for the performance being reviewed.

5. Set the stage for psychological safety by reminding the team that they work in a complex work environment that includes constraints, goal conflicts, trade-offs, and interdependencies within systems.

6. Focus on the *how* of what happened, not the *why*.

The scribe for the AAR meeting should write exactly what the participants say as they speak, using their words. The words scribed should be displayed for all participants to see in real time. Ask attendees to check the written notes for accuracy. Read the scribed notes aloud before moving to the next AAR question.

The AAR facilitator will need to counter the urge to find a single explanation and single fix aimed at improvement. There will be multiple conditions that drive performance in most cases. The people participating in the AAR will need to be reminded of that fact.

Chapter Summary

Non-technical risk management practices, or human performance tools, are not the stand-alone solution to improved operational performance. Human performance tools complement a strong human and organizational performance integration by providing structure to work execution while the organization addresses system gaps. Be wary of shifting blame from operator error to "The operator did not use human performance tools well." Both perspectives are a dead end. That also means that assigning a single CAPA following an investigation that requires the use of human performance tools for a specific step is not an effective way to improve a system, so don't do that. However, there is value in learning activities that help people practice human performance tools, as well as teaching leaders what work looks like when human performance tools are used well. Examples of such learning activities can be found in the appendices of this book.

Maturity Assessment

Consider using the following statements to assess the maturity of your organization regarding non-technical risk management practices. Each statement has three possible choices. A higher total score indicates a higher maturity.

[Chapter 12]

1. There are few exceptions in our organization where the Performer does not put their eyes on the written guidance for a step immediately before the action is executed.

   Agree 20, Sometimes 10, Disagree 0

2. Our performers and witnesses stay in their roles for the duration of a unit operation.

   Agree 20, Sometimes 10, Disagree 0

3. Our organization provides time and space for post-event operational learning to occur at the conclusion of a work activity.

   Agree 20, Sometimes 10, Disagree 0

4. Workers prepare for a unit operation by discussing risks and how they will be managed.

   Agree 20, Sometimes 10, Disagree 0

5. Our investigations do not lead to CAPAs for coaching on how to better use human performance tools.

   Agree 20, Sometimes 10, Disagree 0

Creating Sustainable Success

Imagine you are a business partner guest invitee to a meeting with a global functional leadership team, there to provide an update. During the roundtable part of the agenda, one of the team members informs the others of a batch loss that occurred at one of your sites. A human action triggered the event, explained as human error at the time.

Hearing this update, the team leader turns to you and says, "I thought we were doing human performance. If this can happen, it must not be working."

What do you say?

How do you create sustainable success despite challenges, obstacles, and setbacks? How do you prepare and address situations that will arise—most often when you do not feel ready? How do you handle hiccups in a way that does not derail or negatively impact human and organizational performance integration?

This chapter is about helping you (and your organization) navigate the overall integration of human and organizational performance for the long term. As you implement new practices and mental models, you will need to navigate the following:

- The dynamics of your organization, its context and environment
- Individuals, their biases, and existing mental models
- Situations and circumstances that have the potential to change the course of or undermine your efforts

You will have ups, you will have downs, you will have successes, and you will face choice and compromise. We offer our collective experience and insights here in hopes that you have many more ups and successes and that you will be well positioned to hold steadfast through the downs—recognizing they are not indications of failure but rather opportunities to learn and shift your approach.

Organizational Dynamics

Imagine your organization as a house with many rooms, each powered with lighting in some form or fashion. Though your organization today has all of these rooms powered in some way, based on human and organizational performance principles and practices, some rooms do not have enough lights, some lights need to be rewired, and some need to be completely disconnected and removed. How do you determine your desired lighting plan? We recommended in chapter four that you identify your overall integration plan based on human and organizational performance principles and your assessment of practices that need to be changed or newly integrated. In order to do this, you need to have a good awareness and understanding of your organization's practices and dynamics—or, in our analogy, a good understanding of the electrical wiring and lighting setup.

You will have based your initial integration plan on knowing what the desired results need to be. You'll have taken things one step at a time in the order your organization demonstrates it is ready. Organizational readiness will shift over time given changes in leadership, changes in overall strategic focus, and changes in performance. How do you anticipate and respond to these challenges? By doing the following:

1. Constantly assess your environment and look for openings to drive and expand your integration plan.

2. Adapt and align with what the organization sees as important.

3. Watch for integrations gone wrong, and learn from the experience.

How do you find openings to drive and expand your integration plan? Keeping with the house lighting analogy, when you see a room being worked on, consider it an opportunity to get in and do the rewiring or relighting to integrate human and organizational performance. As an example, one of our organizations was undertaking a large change project associated with how deviations were classified and deviation investigations were performed. This became an opening to add specific changes related to human and organizational performance at the same time.

As you attend huddle meetings, operational meetings, quality management review meetings, etc., keep a constant lookout for human and organizational performance integration opportunities. These will often present as problems you recognize would benefit from human and organizational performance, though the organization will not necessarily recognize this as a whole.

Perhaps you are experiencing impactful issues triggered by human action in production. This is a great opportunity to try out new investigation methods and human performance tools. In one of our companies, the organization experienced a large number of batch losses in one year, catching leadership by surprise. In a cursory analysis, more than half were triggered by human action. This provided a great opportunity to learn from these instances in a new way, and the organization was ready because they truly did not know how they got there or how to fix it. The organization recognized that prior ways of learning were likely not sufficient.

Another example of an opening is having a lingering problem that technical or engineering solutions may be insufficient to address. This provided an opening in one of our organizations to try *Learning Teams*[90]. We experienced over-pressurization events at an unacceptable rate, and though multiple technical changes were implemented, the changes did not have the impact desired. So, we took the opportunity to try Learning Teams. It was not difficult to get buy-in to do this because it was not a commitment beyond trying it out. After doing one that exceeded expectations due to the multiple enhanced controls that were implemented as a result, we now had a pathway to continue the practice and demonstrate its value.

Trends also provide great openings for rewiring. We had an example at one site where Quality observed what they identified as negative trends in performance that posed risks and needed to be addressed. We raised our hands to facilitate the process of bringing the various operational groups together to discuss a path forward. We could then guide that path towards doing more work observation in these areas to drive an increased understanding of what was going on in the field to lead to recurring events. It required consistent and persistent follow-up to support leaders in doing this, but ultimately it helped support and increase awareness of the value of observing and learning directly from how work is performed.

---

90 According to Andrea Baker, a human and organizational performance consultant, a Learning Team is a facilitated conversation between those who do the work and those who design the work to share operational intelligence between the two groups and improve system design.

The simplest opportunities often arise with respect to organizational learning. An issue will be discussed at a meeting, and someone might say, "We should figure out what happened here, so it doesn't happen again."

This is a fabulous opportunity for you to say, "That's a great idea. I would be happy to facilitate an after-action review so we can do that." And now you have your opening to role model this practice and demonstrate that it's not hard, it does not take too much time, and it adds value to the organization—another light on.

How do you adapt and align to what your organization sees as important? This is a multi-year effort, which means that the plan you develop at the outset will need to be regularly adjusted. Your initial sponsor may leave your organization, and it is extremely likely you will have turnover in impactful leader positions. You will always need continued sponsor support, so any sponsor departure means you must find another partner to drive and support efforts. When new leaders come into influential roles, ensure you create the opportunity to meet with them individually to discuss human and organizational performance.

Before meeting with these leaders, listen to the words they use and how they describe what is important to them. Then, tailor your conversation to demonstrate your awareness of their focus areas and how human and organizational performance supports improvement in those areas. For example, in one of our organizations, we had a new operations head join the team. This individual talked about worker safety being a number one priority and wanted to enable the organization to improve its focus on risks. The human and organizational performance conversation with this leader was then centered around safety and the risks to workers, which mirrored solutions around safety and the risks to product.

Over the years you work on integrating human and organizational performance, your organization will implement multiple programs and initiatives.

Though many will not have a relationship or impact on your plan, be mindful of those that will. If your organization decides to implement a new production system based on lean thinking, become a part of that team and ensure human and organizational performance is integrated with that plan. If your organization enlists a large consulting firm to lower costs and improve efficiency, monitor and engage in that effort to the extent possible. Watch for and get ahead of increased risks as a potential result of redundancies and slack[91] being removed. Regardless of the initiative, consider possible impacts to human and organizational performance integration and position yourself to influence others in a positive direction.

Another organizational dynamic to pay close attention to, which you will be doing anyway, is overall performance. Though you will be working towards addressing the problem statement you defined with your sponsor at the outset, your integration and progress towards human and organizational performance maturity will take steps in all directions—forwards, sideways, and backwards. While working through that, your organization will also be navigating through new and different challenges from internal and external sources.

In chapter six, we introduced a Cost-Effort-Controls System Model, simplifying Rasmussen's performance model that describes various boundaries and pressures that can drive a system past the threshold of acceptable performance. Since human error can be a symptom of any number of such pressures, and those pressures can combine in unique ways to create overall performance failures, you may be faced with a story similar to the conversation described at the beginning of this chapter, the one suggesting human and

---

91 Slack may sound like waste or inefficiency to some people, but there are counterintuitive benefits. Slack is essential for operational resilience as a hedge against unexpected demands and a buffer against external or internal shocks.

organizational performance was supposed to fix every performance challenge. When this occurs, position yourself to continue to be a part of the solution. Help the organization understand its true level of human and organizational performance maturity. Shift your focus to support those areas where you know you can make the biggest difference.

What do you do when human performance implementation goes wrong? As you expand training and leverage communications about these new ideas and practices within the organization, you will have individuals and groups on board who drive changes within their teams and areas. Though this is generally what you want, it is important to maintain a good view of what is being done in the name of human and organizational performance. Some people will get it and do an amazing job driving change in their area. Others will misinterpret the plan or focus on aspects that are not helpful.

When this happens, talk about human and organizational performance as a process of integration, not a program. An example of misguided implementation is when someone focuses their efforts on creating a marketing campaign. You will see resources applied to fancy posters, gimmicky games with prizes, or songs and poems about human performance. These things, in and of themselves, may not hurt, especially if you want to raise awareness, but these shouldn't be the only actions taken. The caution is when this is all you see. If you see the marketing, but no real action or implementation, this is an opportunity for you to course correct and redirect focus to the fundamental practices that will actually make a difference.

If you receive negative feedback about how human and organizational performance practices are being integrated, there is a potential that one of the causes lies in misguided or poor implementation. For example, an initial pre-job brief implementation in one of our factories was not going well. We were hearing feedback about the complexity and inflexibility of the process.

This was a key indicator of an implementation gone wrong. Pre-job briefs, though they follow a structure and have a purpose, should not be inflexible. They certainly should not feel complex. So, we stepped in and reset the process, reengaging the people who did the work (and who led and participated in the pre-job briefs) to recreate them in a format and level of detail they found worked best to achieve their purpose.

Individual Biases

An organization itself is a collective of individuals. The cases we outlined above are focused on broad, organizational openings or challenges with functions or groups. Other situations you will encounter are with individuals. These are situations in which an individual or leader with some degree of influence has a bias or mental model that negatively impacts human and organizational performance integration. These individuals' bias or mental model may not reflect that of the overall organization, but they still have an impact. Based on our collective experience, and stories we have heard from others, there are scenarios you have a high probability of encountering. We've compiled these scenarios, and our learnings from them, in order to help you prepare for the possibility of facing something similar.

Here are three to consider:

1. Someone being action-oriented. "I need an immediate fix."

2. Someone protective. "This is my shop. Please stay out."

3. Someone who misinterprets cause and effect. "Something is off track, and since you take a different approach than what I'm used to, your approach must be the cause."

Sometimes, you encounter a team member who is action-oriented. Especially in operations, it is our experience that leaders tend to be action-oriented. They want problems fixed fast, and fixed permanently. The idea of taking a step back to learn and better understand system issue contributors is foreign to them. Some won't want to take the time. The notion that systems are dynamic and fixes in one area may lead to new issues in another will sound like crazy talk and an excuse for not solving a problem. How do you manage the expectations of these individuals? By choosing language that mirrors the action they expect, like "Yes, that will be addressed." Or, "We will not only address the current issue but will also ensure related issues are identified and taken care of."

We encountered a situation that truthfully was not managed well in the moment, but created the learning we are sharing with you here. Within operations, we were experiencing what was generically grouped as *mix-up* problems. These were similar but different situations in which unintended tanks, valves, solutions, and components were being used during processing. The operations leader organized a meeting, including those focusing on human and organizational performance, and they discussed how to fix the problem. The mistake made in the moment was explaining how work would need to be done to identify how each type of mix-up was occurring since each would likely have a unique solution based on the work context. This did not sit well with this leader. He simply wanted the problem fixed immediately.

The problems you will be brought in to address will require analysis and specific types of approaches to address them effectively. Instead of meeting this leader where he was—frustrated and needing the problem addressed quickly—we tried to explain the approach and methodology that would help. Doing so led to additional frustration. Though we ultimately did what needed to be done to help, we made this leader feel irritated instead of reassured.

You might encounter a team member who isn't open to others within his or her area of responsibility. "This is my shop, and I want you to stay out." We piloted an approach to investigations similar to what the National Transportation Safety Board (NTSB) does for significant events—by sending a *Go Team*[92]. In situations with high consequences and high impact, we would deploy an objective, external team of cross-functional subject matter experts (SME) to perform the investigation. The intent was a quick response in determining possible causes. We taught Go Team members problem-solving and cause analysis techniques to prepare them in advance.

The first deployment came when we had a mix-up that ended in a significant batch loss. We had senior leadership support to bring in this team, and communication was done in advance to let the involved parties know what to expect. Despite these efforts, the manager of the area where the mix-up occurred would not allow us to speak to the team.

A similar instance occurred during an early *Learning Team* deployment as well. Since Learning Teams were new, when we set out to hold one, we deliberately made an effort to explain, especially to area management, what to expect, and the reasons we did not want management present[93]. Despite these preparations, in one situation, when we arrived at the scheduled session, we found the supervisor present. Despite our requests for the supervisor to leave, they refused and instead decided to be the spokesperson for the entire group.

What do you do in these situations?

In the first situation, we talked to the team anyway. We had a mission to fulfill and we needed to talk to the team to do it. This obviously was upsetting

---

92 You can read more about the NTSB Go Team concept here: https://www.ntsb.gov/investigations/process/Pages/goteam.aspx

93 Even where psychological safety is high, management being present during a Learning Team may lead to participants deferring to their manager's perspectives or not being candid.

to the manager, but because we had leadership support, we ensured the people who performed the work and were involved in the event had a voice. Since the manager retained authority over recommendation decisions and report content, some of what we might have considered priority improvements were characterized as *long-term enhancements*. As you can imagine, it was a challenging dynamic to manage. Still, had we not completed the data collection and analysis appropriately, the systems changes required would not have even been identified at all.

In the second situation, we halted the Learning Team. Our obligation was to the psychological safety of this supervisor's team and the sanctity of the Learning Team process. Though in this case the Learning Team would have been the best approach, we ended up conducting traditional interviews the supervisor did not object to.

When you are faced with such individuals, those who simply do not welcome you or your help, you will need to assess the context. Proceed if you have the backing to do so, and stop or switch gears if you don't.

Sometimes, you'll face someone who misinterprets cause and effect. "Something is off-track," they'll say, "and since you take a different approach than what I'm used to, your approach must be the cause."

In some ways, this is similar to the story opening this chapter, the leader who said, "I thought we were doing human performance. If this can happen, it must not be working."

Another might say, "We are struggling with the investigation metric on time performance, so it must be the human and organizational performance approaches causing the problems." Or, "People are not meeting performance expectations or being held accountable, and so this must be due to human and organizational performance."

In any of these situations, it is imperative to meet people where they are.

It is in the face of this real concern, and real doubt, that you have your greatest opportunity to partner. Respond with clarity. Explain how incremental steps move the company in the right direction, even when failures occasionally occur. Establish realistic expectations.

Try responses like, "I certainly appreciate your questions and concerns, and I understand that, given our focus on human performance, we expect less errors that trigger a significant consequence to happen. We will take what we learn from this case and apply it to our efforts to ensure we better anticipate this type of *error-likely situation*[94] in the future." This type of response accomplishes a lot. It meets a leader where they are and takes ownership of the issue. It indicates your intent to be part of the solution—without making empty or impossible promises.

Your human and organizational performance journey will be unique. Stay true to the principles while meeting others where they are. Sometimes this means letting the organization learn the hard way. The point is, people are ready to listen or they are not. If they are not, it is best to wait. Your human and organizational performance efforts will be better off in the long run if you do.

Notable Situations

You will be a part of investigations into occurrences with significant negative impact, including batch losses that cost the organization millions of dollars. In situations where the triggering event was a human action, reactions may result in contractors or employees getting terminated. These are especially

---

94 The Center for Chemical Process Safety defines an error-likely situation as a work situation in which the performance-shaping factors are not compatible with the capabilities, limitations, or needs of the worker. In such situations, workers are much more likely to make errors, particularly under stressful conditions. https://www.aiche.org/ccps/resources/glossary/process-safety-glossary/error-likely-situation

challenging situations to face as a human and organizational performance practitioner.

We have been a part of several conversations with leaders who have taken or expressed that they want to take action against individuals. These conversations have been helpful only when they occur following thorough learning, and before any action is taken. Once learning is complete or at least at a sufficient point in the process, you can share contributing factors that need to be considered before decisions are made on punitive action.

In these types of conversations, we have asked questions like, "If the worker is getting suspended or fired, why isn't the supervisor? What about the area manager?" Remember, everyone is part of the system. We've suggested, "If this employee did the exact same action, but the outcome was different, would you sanction the employee in the same manner?" These questions may or may not be appropriate for your situation, but consider how you'll deal with these situations before they occur. Be ready to engage in a helpful and constructive way.

In situations where a leader or investigator insists that human error (or similar terms that blame) is documented as the root cause in an investigation, consider asking some of the following questions to help the leader or investigator think differently. Their thinking may not shift this time, but the discussion cannot be undone and they will remember for next time when the same or similar event occurs.

- This person has historically been one of your best employees. What happened to change them so suddenly?
- You say that this person has a history of past performance issues. How has the performance management by you and your leadership team not successfully mitigated this occurrence?

- How will taking action against this employee fix the system so that others will not make the same mistake in the future?
- How will a recurrence of this event involving another employee be explained to senior leadership?

Remote Work

When considering human and organizational performance practices, don't forget the changing dynamics of remote work. During the COVID-19 pandemic, businesses discovered which work can be done successfully outside an office or work environment. Many senior leaders may not be on-site as often as in the past. This change has impacted human and organizational performance regarding work observation expectations. People may not be present to see Work As Done at the same frequency as in the past. In this situation, we would encourage you to ensure you have measures to monitor how much work observation is being done. This will allow you to work with your organization to determine what targets make sense and support those who aim to achieve them.

The human and organizational performance resources you started with may get absorbed, removed, or downsized. This is where having an eye toward integrating new practices makes a difference. If you had success from the start, anchoring your changes to organizational practices that are not easily changed with shifts in resources, then more of what you put in place will be sustained. Also, the more you have done to educate and bring along as many people as possible, the less dependent the sustainability of your overall human and organizational performance efforts on the specific number or types of resources assigned will be.

Take Care of Yourself

As a human and organizational performance practitioner, you are an agent of change. You are working on practices, concepts, and ideas that are not standard practice, are not well understood, and are often completely misunderstood, especially in the biopharma industry. You are a coach, advisor, role model, and facilitator, and will continue to develop your expertise in human and organizational performance.

Recognize that you will be learning as you lead change. Keep your learning at least one step ahead of your organization, and connect to various networks that can help, some of which are listed at www.doqualitydifferently.com. Your greatest learnings will come from what you try, even when something does not work like you thought it would.

We have learned all of the lessons shared with you. We've done some things well, and some things, in hindsight, we would have done differently.

We ground our work on a mantra from Edgar Schein's book, *Humble Consulting*. Schein says humble consulting *"presumes that you are committed to being helpful, bring a great deal of honest curiosity, and have the right caring attitude, a willingness to find out what is really on the client's mind."* We are all of these things: committed, curious, and caring. We are committed to making a difference in our organizations. We want to help our fellow colleagues. And we are curious about ways to make things better. Helping frontline workers, managers, leaders, and designers enjoy a better work experience is one of the uplifting and energizing parts of being a human and organizational performance practitioner. We recognize and embrace joint accountability for positive results.

You will have ups, downs, successes, and failures. They are all part of the learning process. Link with a support group so you have a sounding board for the challenges—and a community that will celebrate your successes with you.

[Chapter 13]

We are a part of that community. We understand how to *do quality differently,* and are as committed to your success as you are.

Afterword

Personal Reflection
Amy Wilson, Ph.D.

I was first exposed to human performance in the mid-2000s. At the time, I was relatively early in my career, having many years of education as an Industrial Engineer and having gained several years of experience driving efficiency, effectiveness, and process improvements. At the core, I was good at organizing processes and information so they would produce good results. I was good at engaging with and facilitating teams to drive good results. I knew that worker engagement was critical and always went to where work was done before I took any steps to think differently about how that work might be done or improved. I was trained and experienced in the Lean and Six Sigma ways of driving improvement (which I always believed were basically different names for what Industrial Engineers learn already by education), and felt pretty good about how I identified and approached operational challenges and problems.

I did not see human performance as different from what I already knew. When I was provided explanations and reading materials, primarily from the nuclear industry, I drew connections to what I had already been taught. I tended to think that all of it was pretty much covered. Within the company I worked for at the time, a human performance initiative was in place. It drove new practices, the introduction of a new language, and suggested improvements in investigations and documentation. All of this was good work, but in my mind, did not require changes in culture or ways of thinking. I would later learn that I was wrong.

I started a job at a different company in early 2011. I saw a lot of opportunities to enhance the same processes and practices we were working on at my prior company, but not wanting to be the *at my prior company we did this* person, I just observed and learned. *What was this organization focused on? What were they willing to change? What were they not willing to change?*

Fast forward to 2013, one of the manufacturing sites in the company was introduced to human performance. This was an exciting turn of events from my perspective because I knew it would open the door to improvement opportunities, such as learning from where work is performed and improving documentation. The company, at that time, had no Operational Excellence program or approach, so human performance was implemented to help fill that void.

I happened to be in a new, global role supporting manufacturing operations across our network when, in late 2013, we set goals for 2014 and I had the opportunity to lobby for human performance to be integrated globally. I raised my hand to lead because I believed in it—I felt it would help our people and operations.

Once approved, I needed to learn—a lot. We engaged Tony Muschara to do a site assessment, evaluating how we managed risk in our operations. This assessment and the resulting recommendations formed the initial *roadmap* for what would become human performance for this company. I give full credit to Tony for helping me learn where I was wrong in my prior perspectives. I vividly recall my initial reaction to a statement he made in an Advanced Human Performance course he was teaching for us. He said, "Managers control worker decisions."

I thought, *no one controls the decisions of others.* So I asked, "What do you mean when you say 'Managers control worker decisions'?"

His response was, "No one in an organizational setting makes decisions in a vacuum." By the end of that training week, I got it. I saw how human and organizational performance was different. I saw what was really going on in organizations. I also saw what needed to change: how we understood how workers worked and the interconnections with systems and processes, and how that all worked together to get the results we experienced. I had been transformed from the Industrial Engineer who believed that a well-designed process would work for itself to a person now eager to learn more about true systems thinking and its application.

Tony was a huge, huge help to me in so many ways. He helped me define an approach for human performance integration and ensured I did not make it a program. He expanded my network and provided resources and references for me to read. He did all of this with an approach I will forever be grateful for—ensuring I could be an independent leader for human performance. Tony was different from other consultants. He wanted to work himself out of needing to work for us.

There was a lot to do—an overall strategy and action plan needed to be developed and executed. Not every site leader was fully aligned and on board with this new *thing* called human performance. Many felt this was not transformational or different, as I had for many years. Some thought it was not even needed.

Once I talked with the site leadership teams and developed a strategy, vision, and initial implementation plan, I wanted to start executing and not look back. While that's pretty much what I did, I had lessons to learn. I did not consider how leadership was constantly changing. Though the human performance journey is an organizational one, it is also a personal journey for company leaders. Individual leaders need to be engaged, have the opportunity to ask questions, and learn. And when new leaders come into the organization, the process starts over.

This book describes the different strategic and tactical steps taken to integrate human performance into operations. It provides a lot of references and resources that were instrumental in my learning. Various organizations and conferences were useful for guidance. This notably includes the Resilience Engineering Association and their periodic symposiums. There were no college degrees or accepted certifications in human and organizational performance—there still aren't. Yet, the more I learned, the better prepared I was. I faced whatever questions and challenges arose. I found confidants and like-minded people with whom I could engage openly, share, and grow. Cliff was one of those people. I was and still am grateful for the many, many people who were inspirational along the way.

Today, I am in a different role within my organization. While I am no longer directly responsible for human and organizational performance integration, I'm in a good position to reflect on accomplishments and lessons learned. I can see where we were able to positively influence leaders, sustain human performance changes, and how areas could drift back to prior ways of working. These changes, over time, were a primary inspiration for this book. I realized human performance concepts, ideas, and practices must become the standard rather than something new.

Cliff and I hope to play a role in changing industry expectations. We aim to open the minds of regulators, leaders, and everyone who works within complex systems. We know this book can provide organizations with new approaches to make human and organizational performance integration successful. Together, we can make a difference.

Bibliography

CHAPTER ONE

Agarwal, Ipsita. "Interview with Dr. David D. Woods" *Increment* (February 2021) https://increment.com/reliability/resilience-engineering-david-woods/ (accessed June 30th, 2022)

"Backgrounder on the Three Mile Island Accident" *United States Nuclear Regulatory Commission* https://www.nrc.gov/reading-rm/doc-collections/fact-sheets/3mile-isle.html (accessed June 5th, 2022)

Christophe, Jean. "The 'new view' of human error. Origins, ambiguities, successes and critiques" *Le Coze, Saf Sci*, 154:105853. doi: 10.1016/j.ssci.2022.105853 (2022)

Department of Defense for the United States of America, *Department of Defense Standard Practice for System Safety*. MIL-STD-882E, May 11th, 2012

Fox, Jeremy C. "Seabrook Nuclear Power Station false alarm last month caused by human error" *The Boston Globe* (August 11th, 2022) https://www.bostonglobe.com/2022/08/11/metro/seabrook-nuclear-power-station-false-alarm-last-month-cause-by-human-error/ (accessed August 11th, 2022)

Hollnagel, Erik. *Safety-II in Practice: Developing the Resilience Potentials*. First edition Routledge, June 21st, 2017

Hollnagel, Erik. "Ideas: Resilience Engineering" https://erikhollnagel.com/ideas/resilience-engineering.html (accessed June 30th, 2022)

Leveson, Nancy. *Engineering a Safer World*. The MIT Press, 2012

McNab, Duncan, John McKay, Steven Shorrock, Sarah Luty, and Paul Bowie. "Development and application of 'systems thinking' principles for quality improvement". *BMJ Open Qual.* 2020 Mar;9(1):e000714. doi: 10.1136/bmjoq-2019-000714. PMID: 32209593; PMCID: PMC7103793

Read, Gemma, Steven Shorrock, Guy H. Walker, and Paul M. Salmon. "State of science: evolving perspectives on 'human error'". *Ergonomics.* 2021 Sep;64(9):1091-1114. doi: 10.1080/00140139.2021.1953615. Epub 2021 Aug 6. PMID: 34243698

Wears, Robert L. and Kathleen M. Sutcliffe. *Still Not Safe: Patient Safety and the Middle-Managing of American Medicine*. First edition, Oxford University Press (December 3rd, 2019)

Wilson, John R. "Fundamentals of systems ergonomics/human factors" *Applied Ergonomics*, Volume 45, Issue 1 (January 2014) https://doi.org/10.1016/j.apergo.2013.03.021

2019 FDA report, *Drug Shortages: Root Causes and Potential Solutions*. https://www.fda.gov/media/131130/download (accessed May 13th, 2022)

Bibliography

CHAPTER TWO

Conklin, Todd. *Pre-Accident Investigations: An Introduction to Organizational Safety.* First edition CRC Press, September 5th, 2012

Dekker, Sidney W. A. *The Field Guide to Human Error Investigations.* First edition Routledge, September 14th, 2017

Dekker, Sidney W. A. *Human Factors and Aerospace Safety, The re-invention of human error,* 1(3), 247-266, Ashgate Publishing, 2001

Hollnagel, Erik. "Can We Ever Imagine How Work Is Done?" *Hindsight25* (2017) https://skybrary.aero/sites/default/files/bookshelf/3934.pdf

Woods, David D., Sidney W. A. Dekker, Richard Cook, Leila Johannesen, and Nadine Sarter. *Behind Human Error.* Second edition CRC Press, August 28th, 2010

CHAPTER THREE

Carse, James P. *Finite and Infinite Games.* 1987 edition Ballantine Books

Crosby, Gilmore. *Planned Change: Why Kurt Lewin's Social Science is Still Best Practice for Business Results, Change Management, and Human Progress.* First edition Routledge, August 28th, 2020

Dekker, Sidney and Shawn Pruchnicki. "Drifting into failure: theorizing the dynamics of disaster incubation" *Theoretical Issues in Ergonomics Science,* 15:6, 534, DOI: 10.1080/1463922X.2013.856495 (2014)

Hollnagel, Erik. "Human Error, Position Paper For NATO Conference On Human Error" (August 1983)

Kotter, John P. *Leading Change.* Illustrated edition Harvard Business Review Press, November 6th, 2012

Lanir, Zvi. *Fundamental Surprises.* Decision Research and Center for Strategic Studies, 1983

Rogers, Everett M. *Diffusion of Innovations.* Fifth edition Free Press, August 16th, 2003

Rumelt, Richard. *Good Strategy Bad Strategy: The Difference and Why It Matters.* Illustrated edition Currency, July 19th, 2011

Schein, Edgar. *Humble Consulting: How to Provide Real Help Faster.* Illustrated edition Berrett-Koehler Publishers, April 4th, 2016

Sinek, Simon. *The Infinite Game.* Portfolio, October 15th, 2019

Wears, Robert L. and L. Kendall Webb. *Fundamental On Situational Surprise: A Case Study With Implications For Resilience,* DOI:10.4000/BOOKS.PRESSESMINES.1122 Corpus ID: 143265721. Presses des Mines, licensed by OpenEdition Books, 2011

Weick, Karl E., Kathleen M. Sutcliffe, and David Obstfeld. "Organizing and the Process of Sensemaking" *Organization Science,* 16(4):409-421, DOI:10.1287/orsc.1050.0133 (July 2005)

Bibliography

Woods, David D. "Four concepts for resilience and the implications for the future of resilience engineering" *Reliability Engineering & System Safety*, Volume 141 (September 2015)

CHAPTER FOUR

Conklin, Todd. *The 5 Principles of Human Performance*. Independently published January 23rd, 2019

Dekker, Sidney W. A. "Illusions of explanation: A critical essay on error classification" *International Journal of Aviation Psychology*, Volume 13, Issue 2, 13(2), 95-106 (2003)

Gilbert, Thomas F. *Human Competence: Engineering Worthy Performance*. McGraw-Hill, 1978

Schein, Edgar. *Organizational Culture and Leadership*. Fifth edition Wiley, December 27th, 2016

CHAPTER FIVE

Cook, Richard I. and David D. Woods. "Operating at the Sharp End: The Complexity of Human Error" *Human Error in Medicine* (1994)

Hollnagel, Erik, David D. Woods, and Nancy Leveson. *Resilience Engineering: Concepts and Precepts*. First edition CRC Press, 2006

Hollnagel, Erik. *Safety-II in Practice: Developing the Resilience Potentials*. First edition Routledge, June 21st, 2017

Kalantari, Behrooz. "Herbert A. Simon on making decisions: enduring insights and bounded rationality" *Journal of Management History*, Vol. 16, No. 4 (2010)

Meadows, Donella H. *Thinking in Systems*. Illustrated edition Chelsea Green Publishing, December 3rd, 2008

Muschara, Tony. *Risk-Based Thinking: Managing the Uncertainty of Human Error in Operations*. First edition Routledge, November 9th, 2017

Snook, Scott. *Friendly Fire: The Accidental Shootdown of U.S. Black Hawks Over Northern Iraq*. Revised edition Princeton University Press, January 27th, 2002

Woods, David D., Sidney W. A. Dekker, Richard Cook, Leila Johannesen, and Nadine Sarter. *Behind Human Error*. Second edition CRC Press, August 28th, 2010

Woods, David D. and Erik Hollnagel. *Joint Cognitive Systems: Patterns in Cognitive Systems Engineering*. First edition CRC Press, March 27th, 2006

Woods, David D. *Conflicts Between Learning and Accountability in Patient Safety*. 54 DePaul L. Rev. 485, 2005 https://via.library.depaul.edu/law-review/vol54/iss2/13

Woods, David D. "Resilience as Graceful Extensibility to Overcome Brittleness" *IRGC Resource Guide on Resilience*, Lausanne: EPFL International Risk Governance Center, v29-07 (2016) https://www.irgc.org/riskgovernance/resilience/

Bibliography

CHAPTER SIX

Allspaw, John, Morgan Evans, and Daniel Schauenberg. *Debriefing Facilitation Guide: Leading Groups at Etsy to Learn From Accidents*, 2016

Chua, Melissa. "What is Psychological Safety at Work, and Why It Matters" *Pigeonhole Live* https://blog.pigeonholelive.com/what-is-psychological-safety-at-work-and-why-it-matters (May 28th, 2020)

Clark, Timothy R. *The 4 Stages of Psychological Safety: Defining the Path to Inclusion and Innovation.* Berrett-Koehler Publishers, March 3rd, 2020

Conklin, Todd. *Pre-Accident Investigations: An Introduction to Organizational Safety.* First edition CRC Press, September 5th, 2012

Cook, Richard and Jens Rasmussen "Going solid: a model of system dynamics and consequences for patient safety" *Quality and Safety in Health Care* (April 14th, 2005)

DePree, Max. *Leadership Is an Art.* Reprint edition Currency, May 18th, 2004

Edmondson, Amy C. *The Fearless Organization: Creating Psychological Safety in the Workplace for Learning, Innovation, and Growth.* First edition Wiley, November 20th, 2018

Edmondson, Amy. "The Role of Psychological Safety in Diversity and Inclusion" *Psychology Today* (June 22, 2020) https://www.psychologytoday.com/us/blog/the-fearless-organization/202006/the-role-psychological-safety-in-diversity-and-inclusion (accessed July 17th, 2022)

Hollnagel, Erik. "Cognitive Reliability and Error Analysis Method (CREAM)" *Elsevier Science* (January 23rd, 1998)

Kassem, Rasha and Andrew Higson. "The New Fraud Triangle Model" *Journal of Emerging Trends in Economics and Management Sciences* (JETEMS), Volume 3, Number 3, https://papers.ssrn.com/sol3/papers.cfm?abstract_id=2121206 (2012)

Paul, Marilyn. "Moving From Blame to Accountability" *The Systems Thinker* https://thesystemsthinker.com/moving-from-blame-to-accountability (accessed August 13th, 2022)

Rasmussen, Jens. "Risk management in a dynamic society: a modeling problem" *Safety Science*, Volume 27, Issues 2 and 3 (1997)

Rasmussen, Jens. "The role of error in organizing behavior" *Quality and Safety in Health Care*, DOI:10.1136/qhc.12.5.377, Corpus ID: 9546781 (1990)

Reason, James. *Managing the Risks of Organizational Accidents.* First edition Routledge, December 1st, 1997

Reason, James. *Human Error.* Cambridge University Press, October 26th, 1990

Schein, Edgar. *Organizational Culture and Leadership.* Fifth edition Wiley, December 27th, 2016

Schein, Edgar H. *Humble Inquiry: The Gentle Art of Asking Instead of Telling.* Expanded edition Berrett-Koehler Publishers, February 23rd, 2021

Slack Team. "Psychological safety first: building trust among teams" *Slack* https://slack.com/blog/collaboration/psychological-safety-building-trust-teams (February 19th, 2019)

Willink, Jocko and Leif Babin. *Extreme Ownership: How U.S. Navy SEALs Lead and Win.* St. Martin's Press, November 21st, 2017

Woods, David D. "Rasmussen's S-R-K 30 Years Later: Is Human Factors Best in 3's?" *Human Factors and Ergonomics Society from the Proceedings of the Human Factors and Ergonomics Society Annual Meeting, 53*(4), 217–221 https://doi.org/10.1177/154193120905300412, (2009)

CHAPTER SEVEN

Ansoff, Igor H. "Managing Strategic Surprise by Response to Weak Signals" *California Management Review* 18 21-33 (1975)

Blumberg, Melvin and Charles D. Pringle. "The Missing Opportunity in Organizational Research: Some Implications for a Theory of Work Performance" *The Academy of Management*, Review 7, Number 4 https://doi.org/10.2307/257222 (1982)

Boutout, Ali and Rachid Wahabi. "Weak Signals Interpretation to prevent strategic surprises: a literature review" (2020)

Dolev, Jacqueline, Linda Friedlaender, and Irwin Braverman. "Use of fine art to enhance visual diagnostic skills" *JAMA*, 286(9):1020-1. doi: 10.1001/jama.286.9.1020. PMID: 11559280, (September 5th, 2001)

Edmondson, Amy. "How to turn a group of strangers into a team" *TED Salon: Brightline Initiative* https://www.ted.com/talks/amy_edmondson_how_to_turn_a_group_of_strangers_into_a_team

Edwards, Bob and Andrea Baker. *Bob's Guide to Operational Learning: How to Think Like a Human and Organizational Performance (HOP) Coach.* Independently published, December 16th, 2020

Elahi, Bijan. *Safety Risk Management for Medical Devices.* Second edition Academic Press, January 20th, 2022

Hackworth, David H. and Eilhys England. *Steel My Soldiers' Hearts.* First edition Rugged Land, May 1st, 2002

Herman, Amy E. *Visual Intelligence: Sharpen Your Perception, Change Your Life.* First edition Eamon Dolan/Houghton Mifflin Harcourt, May 3rd, 2016

Hollnagal, Erik. "Can We Ever Imagine How Work Is Done?" *Hindsight25* (2017) https://skybrary.aero/sites/default/files/bookshelf/3934.pdf

Hollnagel, Erik, Robert Wears, and Jeffrey Braithwaite. "From Safety-I to Safety-II: A White Paper" *Resilient Health Care Net* (January 2015)

Holopainen, Mari and Marja Toivonen. "Weak Signals: Ansoff Today" *Science Direct*, Volume 44, Issue 3 (April 2012)

Hopkins, Andrew P. "The Problem of Defining High Reliability Organisations" *Semantic Scholar*, Corpus ID: 40041787 (2007)

Bibliography

"How looking at paintings became a required course in medical school" *Yale Medicine Magazine*, Yale School of Medicine (2014) https://medicine.yale.edu/news/yale-medicine-magazine/article/how-looking-at-paintings-became-a-required-course/ (accessed July 5th, 2022)

Lewin, Kurt. *Field Theory in Social Science*. Harper, 1951

Nemeth, Christopher P. and Erik Hollnagel. *Becoming Resilient: Resilience Engineering in Practice, Volume 2*. CRC Press, November 30th, 2016

Price, Erika D., Victor Ottati, Chase Wilson, and Soyeon Kim. "Open-Minded Cognition" *Society for Personality and Social Psychology*, Volume 41, Issue 11 https://doi.org/10.1177/0146167215600528 (2015)

Sandoval, Vicente. "The Origins of the Word Risk (Etymology)" (February 23rd, 2016) https://vicentesandoval.wordpress.com/2016/02/23/the-origins-of-the-word-risk-etymology/ (accessed July 5th, 2022)

Schein, Edgar H. *Humble Inquiry: The Gentle Art of Asking Instead of Telling*. Expanded edition Berrett-Koehler Publishers, February 23rd, 2021

Suzuki, Shunryu. *Zen Mind, Beginner's Mind*. 50th Anniversary edition Shambhala, June 2nd, 2020

The Shingo Model Booklet, The Shingo Institute, a program in the Jon M. Huntsman School of Business at Utah State University, 2020

CHAPTER EIGHT

Barnett, Robert. "Redesigning Centrelink Forms: A Case Study of Government Forms" *UX User Experience* https://uxpamagazine.org/redesigning_centrelink_forms/ (2009)

Dekker, Sidney. *Patient Safety: A Human Factors Approach*. CRC Press, May 20th, 2011

Deming, W. Edwards. *Out of the Crisis*. The MIT Press, 1986

Muschara, Tony. *Critical Steps: How to Identify and Manage the Most Important Human Performance Risks in Operations*, August 22nd, 2014

Muschara, Tony. *Risk-Based Thinking: Managing the Uncertainty of Human Error in Operations*. First edition Routledge, November 9th, 2017

Procedure Use and Adherence. Pacific Gas and Electric Company, Nuclear Power Generation, Revision 5, Interdepartmental Administrative Procedure, AD2.ID1, 1996

Procedure Writer's Guide. Wisconsin Public Service Corporation, Kewaunee Nuclear Power Plant, September 14th, 1993

Reason, James. *Managing the Risks of Organizational Accidents*. First edition Routledge, December 1st, 1997

Wogalter, Michael S., N. Clayton Silver, S. David Leonard, and Helen Zaikina. *Warning Symbols*. Chapter twelve of *Handbook of Warnings* by Michael S. Wogalter, Lawrence Erlbaum Associates, 2006

Bibliography

Wreathall, J., W.S. Brown, L. Militello, S.E. Cooper, C. Lopez, and C. Franklin. *A Risk-Informed Approach to Understanding Human Error in Radiation Therapy (NUREG-2170)* United States Nuclear Regulatory Commission, Office of Nuclear Regulatory Research, June 2017

Writer's Guide for Technical Procedures. Department of Energy, December 1992

CHAPTER NINE

Allspaw, John, Morgan Evans, and Daniel Schauenberg. *Debriefing Facilitation Guide: Leading Groups at Etsy to Learn From Accidents,* 2016

Ammerman, Max. *The Root Cause Analysis Handbook.* First edition Productivity Press, January 1st, 1998

Dekker, Sidney, Paul Cilliers, and Jan-Hendrik Hofmeyr. "The complexity of failure: Implications of complexity theory for safety investigations" *Safety Science,* Volume 49 (2011)

Dekker, Sidney and Todd Conklin. *Do Safety Differently.* Independently published February 6th, 2022

Events and Causal Factor Charting. Department of Energy, DOE 76-45/14, SSDC-14, 1978

Guidelines for Investigating Chemical Process Incidents. Center for Chemical Process Safety. Second edition Wiley-AIChE, March 15th, 2003

Kepner, Charles H. and Benjamin Tregoe. *The Rational Manager: A Systematic Approach to Problem Solving and Decision Making.* First edition McGraw-Hill Book Company, January 1st, 1965

Lundberg, Jonas, Carl Rollenhagen, and Erik Hollnagel. "What-You-Look-For-Is-What-You-Find – The consequences of underlying accident models in eight accident investigation manuals" *Safety Science,* (47), 10, 1297-1311. http://dx.doi.org/10.1016/j.ssci.2009.01.004 Copyright: Elsevier http://www.elsevier.com/ (2009)

Robbins, Tim, Stephen Tipper, Justin King, Satya Krishna Ramachandran, Jaideep J. Pandit, and Meghana Pandit. "Evaluation of Learning Teams Versus Root Cause Analysis for Incident Investigation in a Large United Kingdom National Health Service Hospital" *The Journal of Patient Safety* (March 24th, 2020)

Smalley, Art. *Four Types of Problems.* Lean Enterprise Institute, September 2018

Woods, David D., Sidney W. A. Dekker, Richard Cook, Leila Johannesen, and Nadine Sarter. *Behind Human Error.* Second edition CRC Press, August 28th, 2010

CHAPTER TEN

Dorst, Kees. *Frame Innovation: Create New Thinking by Design.* Illustrated edition The MIT Press, March 27th, 2015

Dorst, Kees. *Notes on Design: How Creative Practice Works.* Laurence King Publishing, January 30th, 2018

Bibliography

Fitts, Paul M., M.S. Viteles, N.L. Barr, D.R. Brimhall, Glen Finch, Eric Gardner, W.F. Grether, and W.E. Kellum. *Human Engineering for an Effective Air-Navigation and Traffic-Control System*. Defense Technical Information Center, 1951

Guidelines for Investigating Chemical Process Incidents. Center for Chemical Process Safety. Second edition Wiley-AlChE, March 15th, 2003

Haddon, William. "Energy Damage and the Ten Countermeasure Strategies" *Human Factors and Ergonomics Society* (August 1st, 1973)

Haddon, William. "On the escape of tigers: an ecologic note" *American Journal of Public Health and the Nation's Health* (December 1st, 1970)

Lee, John D., Christopher D. Wickens, Yili Liu, and Linda Ng Boyle. *Designing For People: An Introduction to Human Factors Engineering*. Third edition independently published August 31st, 2017

Lewin, Kurt. *Field Theory in Social Science*. Harper, 1951

Muschara, Tony. *Risk-Based Thinking: Managing the Uncertainty of Human Error in Operations*. First edition Routledge, November 9th, 2017

Ohno, Taichi. *Toyota Production System: Beyond Large-Scale Production*. CRC Press, March 1st, 1988

Papanel, Victor. *Design for the Real World*. First edition Thames & Hudson Ltd., January 1st, 1972

Sanders, Mark S., and Ernest James McCormick. *Human Factors in Engineering and Design*. Illustrated edition McGraw-Hill, 1993

Schein, Edgar. *The Corporate Culture Survival Guide*. First edition Jossey-Bass, September 1st, 1999

Shingo, Shigeo. *A Study of the Toyota Production System*. First edition Routledge, October 1st, 1989

Sklet, Snorre. "Safety barriers: Definition, classification, and performance" *Science Direct*, *Journal of Loss Prevention in the Process Industries*, Volume 19, Issue, 5 (September, 2006)

Smith, David J. *Reliability, Maintainability and Risk*. Elsevier, 2000

Wedell-Wedellsborg, Thomas. *What's Your Problem: To Solve Your Toughest Problems, Change the Problems You Solve*. Harvard Business Review Press, March 17th, 2020

Yuan, Shuaiqi, Ming Yang, Genserik Reniers, Chao Chen, and Jiansong Wu. "Safety barriers in the chemical process industries: A state-of-the-art review on their classification, assessment, and management" *Safety Science*, Volume 148 (January 4th, 2022)

CHAPTER ELEVEN

Decius, Julian, Andreas Seifert, and Niclas Schaper. "Informal workplace learning: Development and validation of a measure" (August 1st, 2019)

Dekker, Sidney. *Patient Safety: A Human Factors Approach*. CRC Press, May 20th, 2011

Bibliography

Hollnagel, Erik. *Safety-II in Practice: Developing the Resilience Potentials*. First edition Routledge, June 21st, 2017

Kahneman, Daniel. *Thinking, Fast and Slow*. Anchor Canada, April 2nd, 2013

Weick, Karl. "Enacted Sensemaking in Crisis Situations" *Journal of Management Studies* (July 1st, 1988)

CHAPTER TWELVE

Allspaw, John, Morgan Evans, and Daniel Schauenberg. "Debriefing Facilitation Guide: Leading Groups at Etsy to Learn From Accidents" (2016)

Clarke, Gen. Bruce C. *Guidelines for the Leader and the Commander*. Stackpole Books, April 15th, 2021

Field Manual 7-0. Department of the U.S. Army (2021) https://armypubs.army.mil/

Hackworth, David. *The Vietnam Primer: Lessons Learned*. Twin Eagles Ink, March 1st, 2003

Hanh, Thich Nhat. *The Miracle of Mindfulness: An Introduction to the Practice of Meditation*. First edition Beacon Press, May 1st, 1999

Human Performance Improvement Handbook, Volume 2, Human Performance Tools for Individuals, Work Teams, and Management. U.S. Department of Energy, DOE-HDBK-1028 (2009) https://www.standards.doe.gov/standards-documents/1000/1028-BHdbk-2009-v1/@@ images/file

Iwasaki, Masahiro and Kaori Fujinami. "Recognition of Pointing and Calling for Industrial Safety Management" *Computer Science* (2012)

Killingsworth, Matthew A., and Daniel T. Gilbert. *"A Wandering Mind Is an Unhappy Mind"* *Science*, 330, 932 (2010) DOI: 10.1126/science.1192439, (November 12th, 2010)

Reason, James. "Understanding adverse events: human factors" *Quality in Health Care*, DOI: 10.1136/qshc.4.2.80. PMID: 10151618; PMCID: PMC1055294 (June 4th, 1995)

Reason, James. *The Human Contribution: Unsafe Acts, Accidents and Heroic Recoveries*. First edition CRC Press, December 19th, 2008

Reason, James. "Human error: models and management" *BMJ*, DOI: 10.1136/bmj.320.7237.7868 (2000)

Safety Culture. Australian Radiation Protection and Nuclear Safety Agency, 2021 https://www.arpansa.gov.au/regulation-and-licensing/safety-security-transport/holistic-safety/safety-culture

Schein, Edgar. *Organizational Culture and Leadership*. Fifth edition Wiley, December 27th, 2016

Schein, Edgar. "National and Occupational Culture Factors in Safety Culture" Revised draft for IAEA Meeting (April 9th, 2014)

Bibliography

Schein, Edgar. "National and Occupational Culture Factors in Safety Culture" Revised draft for IAEA Meeting (April 9th, 2014)

Schwartz, Maria E. "How a Questioning Attitude Encourages Safety". *U.S. Nuclear Regulatory Commission* (2013) https://public-blog.nrc-gateway.gov/2013/05/21/how-a-questioning-attitude-encourages-safety/

Shinohara, Kazumitsu, Hiroshi Naito, Yuko Matsui, and Masaru Hikono. "The effects of 'finger pointing and calling' on cognitive control processes in the task-switching paradigm" *International Journal of Industrial Ergonomics* (March 1st, 2003)

Lego Activity For Humble Inquiry

Here is a simple and fun learning activity where the concept of Work As Imagined and Work As Done is used as a means to practice humble inquiry. The learning activity can be included as part of a lesson on watching work, or it could stand on its own as part of a short session with leaders to reinforce previous learning on humble inquiry.

1. Gather Supplies

You will need to purchase four to six Lego baseplates. The 10" x 10" baseplate works well. You will also need to purchase a large amount of Lego bricks in a variety of colors and sizes. Buy more Lego pieces than will be used for the activity. The most useful pieces for this activity are the 2 x 2, 2 x 4, 2 x 6, and 2 x 8 bricks. Mix them in a bag or box. You will also need Post-It Notes and pens.

2. Organize Teams

Divide the group into teams of two. A manageable number of teams is eight to twelve. Half of the teams will be builders, and the other half will be observers assigned to watch the work of a builder team.

3. Brief The Builders

Move the observers into a hallway or another room as you brief the builders. You do not want the observers to hear the builders' briefing. Provide each builder team with a handout including the following information:

Caution: Do not show this guide to the observers.

Objective

*   Build a Lego brick pipeline using the procedure at the bottom of this scenario guide.

Work Context

*   Use of white Legos are known to result in air leaking into the pipeline due to a poor sealing surface. Avoid using white Lego bricks or the work activity that follows later that contains a critical step will fail due to the Lego pump tripping.
*   Use a red Lego near the middle of the Lego brick pipeline. This is known to improve the yield of Lego drug product.
*   Build toward the bottom of the Lego baseplate. Your coworkers will appreciate more room at the top of the baseplate for their work to be executed quickly and with less chance of ergonomic injuries.
*   Work quickly! The execution of the SOP must be completed in less than three minutes in order to move to another work assignment that is behind schedule.

Procedure

*   Obtain a Lego baseplate.
*   Lay the Lego baseplate on a sturdy, level surface.
*   Construct a Lego brick pipeline from left to right on the Lego baseplate.

4. Brief The Observers

Leave the builders to brief the observers. Provide each observer team with a handout with the following information:

Objective

* Observe the work activity, and then use humble inquiry to learn the story of how the Work As Imagined differs from the Work As Done.
* Write one humble inquiry question on a Post-It Note provided by the instructor.
* If the builders agree the question is humble inquiry in nature, they will be allowed to answer the question.
* The instructor should explain how each question does or does not meet the humble inquiry criteria to ensure understanding.

Work Setting

Builders will be building a Lego brick pipeline. Observers are observing. The activity is a risk-important step for a later activity that contains critical steps. Your Work As Imagined looks like the illustration below. The context of the work to be performed (based on your experience) is located below the illustration.

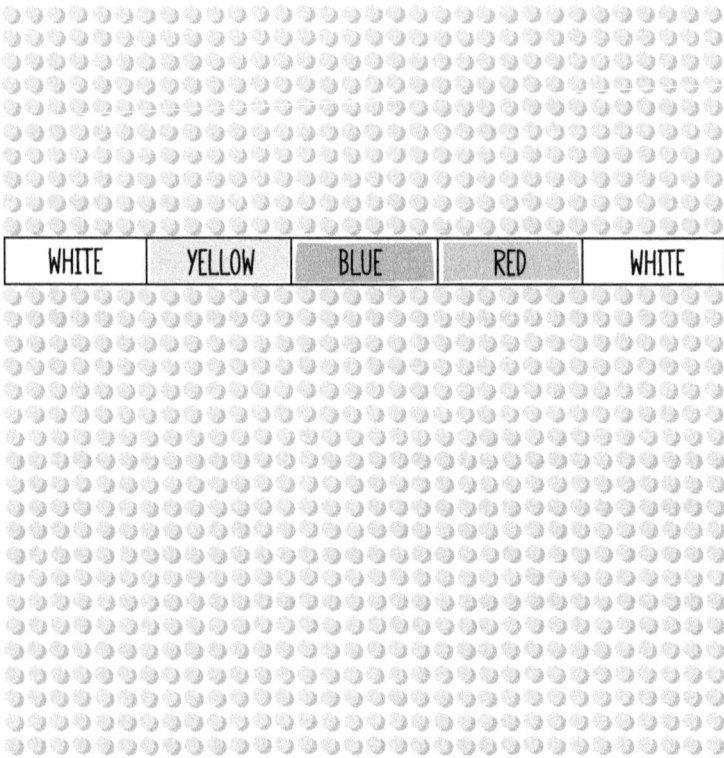

WHITE	YELLOW	BLUE	RED	WHITE

Work Context

- The Lego baseplate may be any color.
- The line of Lego must be built from left to right. This is necessary to keep air out of the Lego brick pipeline, resulting in the Lego pump tripping during a later activity that contains the critical step.
- The line of Lego must begin with white and end with white. This is necessary as it is specified in the method designed by the Lego sciences group.
- A blue Lego should be installed near the center of the pipeline. This saves money because the blue Lego costs 50 percent less than the other colors while providing equal performance.

- The Lego brick pipeline must be positioned with ten baseplate studs visible between the top of the baseplate and the top edge of the Lego brick pipleline. This is important to address known work environment ergonomic issues that occur later in the work process. Workers have recently experienced back strains when there are not enough studs.

Procedure
- Obtain a Lego baseplate.
- Lay the Lego baseplate on a sturdy, level surface.
- Construct a Lego brick pipeline from left to right on the Lego baseplate.

5. Conduct The Activity

Bring the observers back into the room with the builders. Match and position each observer team with a builder team. Inform the participants that you will set a timer for three minutes, and the builders will build their pipeline during that time. There will be no questions asked by the observers during the building. After three minutes have elapsed and all the pipelines have been built, the observer teams will write a humble inquiry question on a Post-It Note and hand it to the facilitator. The facilitator will read each submitted question, and only allow the builder team to answer the question if there is consensus that the question is a humble inquiry. The question should meet the following parameters:
- Open-ended in nature.
- A question based on non-judgmental curiosity.
- Does not begin with the word why.
- Does not begin with the word you.

Learn From People Who Do The Work

Continue with the questions until the observers determine the *how* behind the difference between Work As Imagined and Work As Done.

Jenga Activity For Risk-Ready Review And Post-Job Review

This learning activity uses a Jenga tower for a classroom-based work activity where people are presented with a situation that requires a risk-ready review before work begins and a post-job review when the work is completed. The learning activity is also suitable for practicing a pre-job brief in place of the risk-ready review, though a pre-job brief guide would need to be created. The Jenga Activity works best for an even-numbered group of six to eight trainees. You may also run the activity in parallel for more than one group at a time if you have more Jenga towers.

1. Gather Supplies
You will need a Jenga tower game and disposable gloves.

2. Organize Teams
Participants are organized into pairs. One participant is assigned the role of block puller, and the other is the block placer. The paired participants will work as a team. Introduce the work situation and define success.

3. Brief The Players

- The success criteria for the Jenga activity are as follows:
- Ten blocks moved to the top of the tower within three minutes or less.
- Jenga tower stays upright.
- No skin contact with the Jenga blocks—no contamination.
- Only block pullers pull, and only block placers place.
- When one paired group moves a block, another group moves the next block, and so on, until each group has taken a turn and the order begins again.
- When the Jenga tower falls over all blocks remain on the table tap and do not touch the floor.

4. Conduct The Activity

- Ask the team to perform a risk-ready review.
- Provide feedback on the effectiveness of the risk-ready review through open-ended questions, ideally in a humble inquiry format.
- Place a timer near the Jenga tower, start the timer, and have the team begin the game.
- Allow the learning activity to proceed until the Jenga tower falls or ten blocks are removed.

5. Learning from Success and Failure

- Ask the team to perform a post-job review.
- Provide feedback on the effectiveness of their post-job review with open-ended questions in a humble inquiry format.

Soma Cube Activity For
After Action Review

A Soma cube is a solid dissection puzzle made up of seven pieces of unit cubes that must be assembled into a 3x3x3 cube. There are 240 solutions to the Soma cube puzzle, excluding rotations and reflections. When purchasing Soma cubes for this activity, it is recommended that the cube pieces be one color. This learning activity is a classroom-based work activity where people are presented with a situation that requires a team to design end user guidance on how to assemble a Soma cube. The end user watches but cannot touch the Soma cube or communicate with the team. When the guidance is complete, the end user has ninety seconds to assemble the Soma cube.

1. Gather Supplies
You'll need Soma cubes, one for each team and one additional cube shared by all the teams to study the pieces. You'll also need a dry-erase board or flip chart, enough for each team.

2. Organize Teams
The Soma cube learning activity works best with teams of four to seven participants. You may also run the activity in parallel for more than one team

if you have additional Soma cubes. Ask the attendees to raise their hands if they are good at puzzles. Identify one person on each team who did not identify as good at puzzles as the Soma cube end user. Designate the other members as Soma cube work designers.

3. Brief The Players

Explain the goal of the activity as follows:

- The Soma cube work designers will create guidance for an inexperienced end user to assemble a Soma cube.
- Guidance can be anything the group chooses.
- Groups are not allowed to access the internet to find Soma cube solutions.
- An unassembled Soma cube is located in the room as an aid.
- No members of the team can touch the unassembled Soma cube.
- The Soma cube end user cannot touch the Soma cube during design time or communicate with the Soma cube work designers.
- If the Soma cube work designers want to dry run their guidance, they may if they have enough time.
- The Soma cube end user will use the guidance provided to assemble the Soma cube in ninety seconds without prior practice.

4. Conduct The Activity

- Place an assembled Soma cube on a table in front of each team, rotated differently for each team. Do not let the participants see how you built the Soma cube.
- Place one unassembled Soma cube on a table somewhere in the room so participants can see the puzzle pieces.
- Direct the teams to create guidance on how to assemble a Soma cube.
- Set the timer for ten minutes.

- When the timer dings, the Soma cube work designers give the guidance they created to the end user.
- Set the timer for ninety seconds.
- Using the guidance provided, the end user must assemble the Soma cube.

5. Learning from Success and Failure

- When the ninety seconds are up, ask the group to perform an after-action review.
- Provide feedback on the effectiveness of the after-action review with open-ended questions, ideally in a humble inquiry format.

APPENDIX D

Behavior Engineering Model (BEM) Analysis Worksheet

Actual Performance:

Desired Performance:

Instructions: Use the following chart to assess the current strengths and weaknesses necessary to achieve the desired performance:

EXPECTATIONS AND FEEDBACK (35%)	TOOLS AND RESOURCES (29%)	INCENTIVES AND CONSEQUENCES (11%)
1. Are expectations clearly communicated? 2. Are there any conflicting expectations? 3. Are there adequate role models of acceptable performance? 4. Are there performance standards? 5. Do workers receive feedback?	1. Are required equipment and tools readily available? 2. Are materials and supplies available? 3. Is there time to perform correctly? 4. Are there adequate job aids, performance support tools, and reference materials? 5. Is the work environment supportive of the desired performance? 6. Is there adequate worker support to monitor and encourage desired performance? 7. Is written guidance supportive of desired performance?	1. Is compensation adequate for desired performance? 2. Are there appropriate financial rewards for the desired performance? 3. Are there meaningful non-pay incentives for recognition of desired performance? 4. Do workers see a relationship between superior performance and career advancement? 5. Are incentives and rewards scheduled appropriately? 6. Are workers rewarded for performing incorrectly?

SKILLS AND KNOWLEDGE (11%)	SELECTION AND ASSIGNMENT - CAPACITY (8%)	MOTIVES AND PREFERENCES - ATTITUDE (6%)
1. Do workers possess the essential skills and knowledge to perform adequately? 2. Are workers able to discern between good and poor behavior? 3. Are workers smooth and fluent in their performance? 4. Do workers have sufficient opportunities to apply their skills and knowledge to maintain proficiency?	1. Do workers have the required physical, emotional, etc. capacity to perform correctly? 2. Do workers possess the required education and experience perquisites to perform correctly? 3. Do workers possess the appropriate linguistic capacity to perform correctly? 4. Do workers have personal limitations that prevent them from performing as desired?	1. Do workers value the required performance? 2. Are workers confident that they can perform as desired? 3. Do workers feel threatened in their work? 4. Do workers perceive they are treated fairly?

Instructions: Use the table below to expand and clarify the next steps from the analysis on page one:

BOX AND QUESTION #	ACTION DESCRIPTION	OWNER	DUE DATE

Application of Force Field Analysis and Behavior Engineering Model Worksheet

Actual Performance:

Desired Performance:

Instructions: Use this chart to assess the current strengths and weaknesses necessary to achieve the desired performance:

ENVIRONMENTAL FACTORS	DRIVING FORCES +4 +3 +2 +1	0	RESISTING FORCES -1 -2 -3 -4
Expectations & Feedback 1. Are expectations clearly communicated? 2. Are there any conflicting expectations? 3. Are there adequate role models of acceptable performance? 4. Are there performance standards? 5. Do workers receive feedback?			
Tools & Resources 6. Are required equipment and tools readily available? 7. Are materials and supplies available? 8. Is there time to perform correctly? 9. Are there adequate job aids, performance support tools, and/or reference materials? 10. Is the work environment supportive of desired performance? 11. Is there adequate human support to monitor and encourage desired performance? 12. Is written guidance supportive of desired performance?			

ENVIRONMENTAL FACTORS	DRIVING FORCES +4 +3 +2 +1	0	RESISTING FORCES -1 -2 -3 -4
Incentives & Consequences			
13. Is compensation adequate for desired performance?			
14. Appropriate financial rewards for desired performance?			
15. Are there meaningful non-pay incentives for recognition of desired performance?			
16. Do workers see a relationship between superior performance and career advancement?			
17. Are incentives and rewards scheduled appropriately? Are workers rewarded for performing incorrectly?			

INTERNAL FACTORS	DRIVING FORCES +4 +3 +2 +1	0	RESISTING FORCES -1 -2 -3 -4
Skills And Knowledge			
18. Do workers possess the essential skills and knowledge to perform adequately?			
19. Are workers able to discern between good and poor behavior?			
20. Are workers smooth and fluent in their performance?			
21. Do workers have sufficient opportunities to apply skills and knowledge to maintain proficiency?			
Selection And Assignment			
22. Do workers have the required physical, emotional, etc. capacity to perform correctly?			
23. Do workers possess the required education and experience perquisites to perform correctly?			
24. Do workers possess the appropriate linguistic capacity to perform correctly?			
25. Do workers have personal limitations that prevent them from performing as desired?			

INTERNAL FACTORS	DRIVING FORCES +4 +3 +2 +1	0	RESISTING FORCES -1 -2 -3 -4
Motives And Preferences			
26. Do workers value the required performance?			
27. Are workers confident they can perform as desired?			
28. Do workers feel threatened in their work?			
29. Do workers perceive they are treated fairly?			

Acknowledgments

We are indebted to the following thought leaders. These people provided inspiration and insight: Sidney Dekker, David Woods, Erik Hollnagel, Tony Muschara, Robert Wears, and Shawn Pruchnicki. A special thanks also to Todd Conklin, who uniquely brought this information to life. We are grateful to Todd for including us in groups of experts in this space and continuing to be a strong partner, advisor, and mentor.

We are extremely grateful for the following sponsors and key biopharma manufacturing influencers who had the courage to try something different. These people created space for practitioners, provided resources, and supported human and organizational performance through strong leadership: Bob Kenyon, Sophia Koutoulas, John Jewett, Jay Benson, and Matt Payne.

We appreciate the practitioners and stakeholders who reviewed an early draft of this book and provided critical comments and encouragement: Jim Ball, Ashley Waddey, Emily Carney, Jad Sakr, and Tony Muschara.

We salute the following practitioners for their dedication, perseverance, and willingness to collaborate as exceptional partners in progressing human and organizational performance in biopharma manufacturing: Daan Purbrick, Ashley Waddey, Jim Ball, Luisa Antonopoulos, Kristen Pham, and Emily Carney.

We acknowledge the people not individually named who challenged our thinking, brought these practices to life in their work areas, championed our ideas, and continue to make human and organizational performance a vital element of the biopharmaceutical industry.

Clifford Berry and Amy D. Wilson, Ph.D.

About the Authors

Clifford Berry has over twenty years of experience in human and organizational performance. He has worked in the commercial nuclear electric generation industry, electric transmission and distribution, gas distribution, nuclear plant systems controls hardware and software integration, and biopharmaceutical manufacturing. With a successful record of diagnosing operational problems using a systems thinking, risk-based approach that reveals solutions for long-lasting improvement, Clifford has helped multiple companies in various industries build this vital capacity within their organizations.

Clifford's passion for solving operational problems began in the U.S. Navy in the 1980s as an enlisted leader in the nuclear power engineering program. That passion was combined with a fundamental understanding of human and organizational performance while working in the U.S. commercial nuclear power industry. Thirsting for knowledge and different perspectives to improve systems performance, Clifford attended the University of Massachusetts Lowell and received his M.S. in Work Environment (Ergonomics & Safety) in 2004.

In 2015, Clifford joined the biopharmaceutical manufacturing sector, where he applied human factors and system safety principles and practices to operations. Since then, Clifford has shared his knowledge with multiple biopharmaceutical manufacturing organizations and maneuvered the industry's unique challenges in improving performance with patients in mind. To Cliff, *Do Quality Differently* can shift how the industry thinks about improving quality.

Amy Wilson, Ph.D.

"Simple to describe, yet amazingly complex to address" is how Amy Wilson describes production system challenges and why she has always been drawn to tackle them.

Amy has over twenty years of experience improving performance in manufacturing operations across multiple industry sectors. She began her career in the biopharmaceutical industry in 2001 after completing her Ph.D. in Industrial Engineering. Though she learned the importance of engaging workers in process improvements in her first co-op job as an Industrial Engineer in 1993, she did not fully appreciate how to bring together and implement multi-disciplinary concepts to drive holistic performance gains until her introduction to human and organizational performance.

Amy has implemented operational excellence efforts at single sites and across global sites—projects and programs. She discovered human and organizational performance was the missing piece in driving real and sustained improvement, especially in biopharmaceutical manufacturing, where robustness and resiliency are often significant financial drivers. She earned a reputation for communicating with clarity, leading change efforts effectively, and asking good questions.

Amy is currently a biopharmaceutical manufacturing professional leading strategic operations for a global business unit. She would love to support you in your performance improvement efforts. You can reach her at www.doqualitydifferently.com.

Index

[Index]

[Index]